DEPOLARIZING FOOD
AND AGRICULTURE

Many issues in food and agriculture are portrayed as increasingly polarized. These include industrial vs. sustainable agriculture, conventional vs. organic production methods, and global vs. local food sourcing, to name only three. This book addresses the origins, validity, consequences, and potential resolution of these and other divergences.

Political and legal actions have resulted in significant monetary and psycho-social costs for groups on both sides of these divides. Rhetoric on many issues has caused misinformation and confusion among consumers, who are unsure about the impact of their food choices on nutrition, health, the environment, animal welfare, and hunger. In some cases distrust has intensified to embitterment on both sides of many issues, and even to violence. The book uses economic principles to help readers better understand the divisiveness that prevails in the agricultural production, food processing, and food retailing industries.

The authors propose solutions to promote resolution and depolarization between advocates with seemingly irreconcilable differences. A multifaceted, diverse, but targeted approach to food production and consumption is suggested to promote social well-being, and reduce or eliminate misinformation, anxiety, transaction costs, and hunger.

Andrew Barkley is Professor and University Distinguished Teaching Scholar in the Department of Agricultural Economics at Kansas State University, USA. Andrew teaches courses in the economics of agriculture and public policy. His research includes assessment of teaching and learning methods and the economic evaluation of the wheat industry.

Paul W. Barkley is Professor Emeritus, Department of Agricultural Economics, Washington State University and Adjunct Professor, Applied Economics Department at Oregon State University, USA. Paul has made major contributions to the fields of rural (community) development and environmental economics. He is a Fellow of the Agricultural and Applied Economics Association.

Other books in the Earthscan Food and Agriculture Series

The Sociology of Food and Agriculture
Michael Carolan

Competition and Efficiency in International Food Supply Chains
Improving food security
John Williams

Organic Agriculture for Sustainable Livelihoods
Edited by Niels Halberg and Adrian Muller

The Politics of Land and Food Scarcity
Paolo De Castro, Felice Adinolfi, Fabian Capitanio, Salvatore Di Falco and Angelo Di Mambro

Principles of Sustainable Aquaculture
Promoting social, economic and environmental resilience
Stuart Bunting

Reclaiming Food Security
Michael S. Carolan

Food Policy in the United States
An introduction
Parke Wilde

Precision Agriculture for Sustainability and Environmental Protection
Edited by Margaret A. Oliver, Thomas F. A. Bishop and Ben P. Marchant

Agricultural Supply Chains and the Management of Price Risk
John Williams

The Neoliberal Regime in the Agri-Food Sector
Crisis, resilience and restructuring
Edited by Steven Wolf and Alessandro Bonanno

Sustainable Food Systems
Building a new paradigm
Edited by Terry Marsden and Adrian Morley

Seasonal Workers in Mediterranean Agriculture
The social costs of eating fresh
Edited by Jörg Gertel and Sarah Ruth Sippel

Food Security, Food Prices and Climate Variability
Molly E. Brown

Depolarizing Food and Agriculture
An economic approach
Andrew Barkley and Paul W. Barkley

For further details please visit the series page on the Routledge website: http://www.routledge.com/books/series/ECEFA/

DEPOLARIZING FOOD AND AGRICULTURE

An economic approach

Andrew Barkley and Paul W. Barkley

Routledge
Taylor & Francis Group

LONDON AND NEW YORK

earthscan
from Routledge

First published 2015
by Routledge
2 Park Square, Milton Park, Abingdon, Oxon OX14 4RN

And by Routledge
711 Third Avenue, New York, NY 10017

Routledge is an imprint of the Taylor & Francis Group, an informa business

British Library Cataloguing in Publication Data
A catalogue record for this book is available from the British Library

Library of Congress Cataloging in Publication Data
Barkley, Andrew, 1962-
Depolarizing food and agriculture : an economic approach / Andrew
Barkley and Paul W. Barkley.
pages cm. -- (Earthscan food and agriculture series)
Includes bibliographical references and index.
1. Agriculture--Economic aspects. 2. Agriculture and politics. 3. Food
industry and trade--Political aspects. 4. Agriculture and state. I. Barkley,
Paul W. II. Title.
HD1415.B286 2015
338.1--dc23
2014020167

ISBN: 978-0-415-71422-8 (hbk)
ISBN: 978-0-415-71423-5 (pbk)
ISBN: 978-1-315-88282-6 (ebk)

Typeset in Bembo
by Saxon Graphics Ltd, Derby

CONTENTS

FIGURES

TABLES

BOXES

ACKNOWLEDGMENTS

We would like to share our hearty and sincere appreciation to Tim Hardwick and Ashley Wright of Earthscan from Routledge. It has been a true pleasure to work with them. The manuscript was read by reviewers including Gary Burke, John Crespi, Bailey Norwood, Glynn Tonsor, and Parke Wilde. It was greatly improved by this group's close attention, critical reading, and willingness to share ideas. They saved us from a great number of embarrassing errors, hyperbole, poor judgment, weak logic, and excessive enthusiasm. The revision process was an easy pleasure, given the high quality suggestions, ideas, and critiques provided by the editor and reviewers. We would also like to thank our students at Kansas State University and Oregon State University. These knowledgeable, interested, and intelligent students provided excellent feedback to the ideas contained in this book.

ACRONYMS AND ABBREVIATIONS

AAA	Agricultural Adjustment Act
AFO	animal feeding operation
AMA	American Medical Association
BCI	Better Cotton Initiative
BSE	Bovine spongiform encephalopathy (mad cow disease)
bST	Bovine somatotropin
CAFO	concentrated animal feeding operation
CR	concentration ratio
CR4	four-firm concentration ratio
CR8	eight-firm concentration ratio
CUESA	Center for Urban Education about Sustainable Agriculture
DDT	dichloro-diphenyl-trichloroethane
DNA	deoxyribonucleic acid
DOJ	Department of Justice
EB	economic benefits
EKC	Environmental Kuznets Curve
EPA	Environmental Protection Agency
EU	European Union
FAO	Food and Agriculture Organization
FDA	Food and Drug Administration
FTA	Free trade area
FTC	Federal Trade Commission
GATT	General Agreement on Tariffs and Trade
GDP	gross domestic product
GE	genetically engineered
GIPSA	Grain Inspection and Packers and Stockyards Administration
GM	genetically modified

GMOs	genetically modified organisms
GPS	global positioning systems
HFCS	high-fructose corn syrup
HRW	Hard Red Wheat
JBS USA	American food processing company, subsidiary of JBS SA
LFTB	lean, fine-textured beef
NAFTA	North American Free Trade Agreement
NCBA	National Cattlemen's Beef Association
NOSB	National Organic Standards Board
OCA	Organic Consumers Association
PTA	preferential trade agreement
SC	social costs
SPS	sanitary and phytosanitary
USDA	United States Department of Agriculture
WBCSD	World Business Council for Sustainable Development
WTO	World Trade Organization
WTP	willingness to pay
WWF	World Wildlife Federation

With gratitude, to Mary Ellen and Lela.

1

INTRODUCTION

The industrialization and de-industrialization of agriculture

Farming: The practice of agriculture.
Agriculture: The science or art of cultivating the soil, harvesting crops, and raising livestock.
Polarization: A sharp division, as of a population or group, into opposing factions.
Webster's Third New International Dictionary, unabridged (Gove, 2002)

There are no gains without pains.
Benjamin Franklin, *The Way to Wealth* (1758)

Introduction

The growth of agriculture – in many ways, one of the greatest success stories in all of human history – has resulted in criticism, opposition, and increasing divisiveness in many issues in the food and agricultural sectors. Farming is not only the most important, but also the oldest continuously operating industry on Earth. For uncounted millennia, early *homo sapiens* depended on hunting and gathering for their food and for the materials needed for protection against adverse weather and other aspects of the environment. During this time, early peoples undoubtedly noticed the cycles of plant and animal growth and perhaps noted that, within limits, rearranging the growth characteristics of plants and animals could yield more uniform and more satisfying products. This was the beginning of agriculture. Little additional knowledge about those beginnings survives. Informed study suggests, however, that approximately 10,000 years ago – the exact year or era is not certain – humans began to exert some control over the production of their food and the manufacture of their clothing. Gaining this control, or even partial control, was not an easy task. It required knowledge of the plants and animals, their growing habits, the environment, and the means of preparing edible food and protective clothing from unprocessed plant and animal materials. Each step in the path from raw material to finished product may have taken years or even decades to perfect. These endeavors allowed important changes in human societies and behaviors. Relieved of the constant need to hunt and gather, and assured of at least a minimally adequate supply of food and clothing, humans could spend time in pursuits that made life fuller and helped expand their knowledge of the world.

It is not clear where farming began. Quite likely, the control of animals and crops began in several places at about the same time. Climate undoubtedly played a part, as did the traditions and superstitions of the people themselves. There may have been some random attempts at selective breeding of plants and animals, but most systematic progress in plant and animal development did not begin until agriculture embraced the methods of science during and after the Enlightenment of the seventeenth and eighteenth centuries. From that time to the present, science, coupled with experience, imagination, and inventiveness, took over and generated a constant stream of changes that improved the ability of humans to produce food and fiber that was superior in production and superior in use. Producing food became more efficient, fiber became stronger and more durable, and animals converted fewer and fewer quantities of feedstuffs into greater quantities of useful products: meat, eggs, milk, hides, and the like. After the beginning of scientific, or well-disciplined farming, populations of humans the world over began to enjoy a constant stream of progress and improvement in the world's agricultural systems.

BOX 1.1: THE BEGINNING OF AGRICULTURE

Agriculture likely began about 10,000 years ago. Surely, before that time, some primitive farming activities were taking place in Africa, the Middle East, and in Asia. By that time, potato cultivation had begun in the South American Andes, and maize production stemming from its ancestor, *teosinte*, began soon after in mid-America. Even with these scattered hints regarding the development of agriculture, the major continuous development of human involvement with the production of food and fiber appears to have occurred in the Middle East's Fertile Crescent. This crescent is a vast area that runs from the mouth of the Nile River to the eastern edge of the Mediterranean Sea then continues north and east before turning south to follow the valleys of the Tigris and Euphrates Rivers to the Persian Gulf. In earlier centuries, the region had fertile soil and sufficient moisture to grow edible plants that eventually became cultivated crops.

The area was home to seven crops important to the development of early agriculture: emmer wheat, einkorn, barley, flax, chickpeas, peas, and lentils. Additionally, four important species of domesticated farm animals – cows, goats, sheep, and pigs – lived in or near the crescent. The area was highly productive and, although many crops grown there also grew in other places, the Fertile Crescent is the region in which agriculture, or farming, likely acquired a measure of discipline, and farmers began to flourish.

Global agriculture

Agricultural growth and increased food production allowed early societies to expand their activities into nonfarm pursuits, leading to a decrease in agriculture's share in the total economy. This trend continued, unabated, as economies grew and incomes rose. This universal trend is illustrated in Table 1.1, where the 2010 share of agricultural employment for eight diverse nations is shown, together with per capita Gross Domestic Product (GDP, a measure of output per person), and cereal yield, a measure of agricultural productivity.

A clear and striking relationship is evident: wealthier nations have smaller agricultural labor forces relative to the rest of their economies. The transition from agricultural to nonfarm economies receives detailed treatment in Chapter 4. Table 1.1 also demonstrates that nations with higher levels of agricultural productivity (as measured by cereal yields) also have higher levels of output per capita. While the trend is strong and obvious, it is less clear whether agricultural productivity causes economic growth, or vice versa. Interestingly, economic growth requires the movement of workers out of agriculture: if every individual were a farmer, society would produce only food. As agricultural productivity increases, an economy becomes capable of producing consumer goods including houses, automobiles, more comfortable clothes, and a host of electronic devices that make living easier, more efficient, and more entertaining. The availability of these goods requires workers to migrate out of agriculture and into nonfarm pursuits.

The fundamental relationship between income growth and agricultural change is an underlying characteristic of many, if not most, of the polarizing issues in food and agriculture: progress and growth require change. The book's primary thesis can be summarized as follows:

- Progress requires change.
- Change can be disruptive, difficult, and it produces winners and losers.
- Therefore, progress can be polarizing.

TABLE 1.1 Global agriculture summary statistics for eight representative nations, 2010

	Agricultural employment (% of total employment)	Fertilizer consumption (kg/ha)	GDP per capita (current US$)	Cereal yield (kg/ha)	Trade to GDP ratio (percent)
India	51	179	1,489	2,954	50.9
Ghana	42	18	1,605	1,768	82.7
Thailand	38	162	5,480	3,092	144.8
China	37	548	6,091	5,837	53.2
Romania	30	53	9,036	2,364	82.3
Brazil	16	143	10,978	4,041	24.0
Japan	4	261	46,720	5,020	31.6
USA	2	121	51,749	5,922	30.5

Sources: World Bank Data data.worldbank.org, 2014 (columns 1–4); World Trade Organization. Statistics Database, stat.wto.org, 2014 (column 5).

The remaining chapters of this book evaluate the causes, consequences, and possible solutions of polarized issues in food and agriculture. Progress in agricultural productivity is often a cause of polarization. Scientific discoveries and practical enhancements in agricultural production methods can be controversial. Some groups such as the Amish in the United States (US) do not use electricity or mechanical power, relying instead on horses to provide the power needed for agricultural fieldwork. There are numerous ways to produce food and fiber. Table 1.1 shows a great disparity in fertilizer use across the eight representative nations in 2010. Fertilizer and chemicals used to enhance food and fiber production have both benefits and costs: increased yields (benefits) can come at the expense of environmental quality (costs). Tradeoffs that occur with each production technique will have proponents, opponents, advocates, and detractors. This is true for countless agricultural techniques, whether they be pesticides sprayed on crops to eliminate weeds, insects, or fungi, growth hormones and antibiotics used in meat production, or genetic modification of crop seeds to capture productivity-enhancing attributes and traits. Advocacy for or against these techniques is often determined by self-interest, or the economic impact of the technique or method on an individual or group. The book highlights the economic motivation behind advocates and activists on both sides of each issue.

Some economic motivations are straightforward, such as the desire of many producers to adopt and use cost-saving or output-enhancing technologies such as Genetically Modified Organisms (GMOs), chemicals, fertilizers, pharmaceuticals, or large-scale animal production facilities. In other situations, motivations are more complex. In interactions between affected parties, the actions of one group may affect the well-being of other groups. For example, if local food becomes popular, it could reduce the returns to conventional and organic food produced at some distance from consumers. Game theory, or the analysis of strategic interactions, is described in Chapter 10, and used to derive potential solutions to polarized issues.

International trade of agricultural products has become more important over the past several decades, as technological advances in transportation and communication have reduced the costs of moving food across national borders. The ratio of trade to a nation's GDP indicates the importance of trade to a nation (Table 1.1). The share of trade is large for all of the eight selected nations, indicating the universal significance of trade. This theme is further investigated in Chapter 9. Disputes in agriculture have occurred since the advent of progress, because technological advance is the foundation of disruption and change.

Polarization and agriculture

The extent and diversity of early agriculture in human society caused the industry and its supporting industries to influence all except the most reclusive of the world's residents. This interconnectedness brought with it typical human behaviors: it caused factions and animosities as well as alignments and realignments of trust and opinion relating to how farmers in all their diversity, and consumers in all of theirs, should react to each other. For example, should nations in Sub-Saharan Africa seek self-sufficiency in food by producing all of their caloric and nutrient needs, or would it be better for them to specialize in high-value exportable crops, and rely on less expensively produced food imports from other nations? Should European nations subsidize food production to become self-sufficient food exporters, or purchase food at lower cost from other nations?

How should ranchers who want to graze cattle on the vast acreages of the US Northern Plains react to farmers who want the same land divided into small "family" farms? How should bankers relate to farmers who have only a vague hope of being able to pay off the loans needed to purchase land? How should the US railroad magnates decide whether to lay rails through a northern pass (and instantly bring wealth to the towns along this route) or through a southern pass and thus condemn the northern towns to poverty or oblivion? Should farmers use agricultural chemicals to eliminate pests such as insects, crop diseases, and weeds? Should meat producers enhance productivity with growth hormones, antibiotics, growth promoters, and other pharmaceutical products? Should highly productive nations send their food surpluses to food-short nations, or will this result in dependencies and reduce incentives for domestic food production? Should farmers in the European Union (EU) adopt and grow genetically modified seeds to enhance food production, or avoid genetically engineered foods due to a host of uncertain and untested risks to the environment and long-term human health? The coming chapters discuss some of the complexities, and possible consequences of disputes and differences among farmers and between farmers and other groups. The narrative also describes some of the effects that these situations have had on farms, farm people, the broader industry, and food.

The Green Revolution, a term used to describe intensive research and development of food production during the 1940s to 1960s, provides an example of a major application of science to reducing human misery and hunger. It is also controversial because of a number of unintended consequences, highlighted below. Similarly, genetic modification of seeds used to produce food has provided what is perhaps the single most important contribution to increasing food production in the history of agriculture. Even so, many nations – rich and poor – ban genetically modified food because of the real or imagined risks that surround their use.

Neither agriculture nor economics has a word that suitably describes the problems engendered by the disputes and "uncomfortable situations" that develop when people interested in the same (or similar) goals choose to take incompatible paths toward reaching them. For that reason, the discussions here borrow from contemporary sociologists and political scientists who use the word "polarization" to describe the division of opinion. Two examples help convey this use of the word. Both examples have intelligent, reasonable, and caring individuals on each side of the issue.

Example 1: polarization in the beef industry

In the early years of the twenty-first century, nutritionists and other research scientists reported that eating beef could be harmful to human health. At approximately the same time, groups in many parts of the world questioned beef production because of the environmental damage done by beef animals trampling native pastures as well as discharging large volumes of intestinal gas and other body wastes that eventually contributed to global warming and other environmental problems. During the same time, animal rights advocates opposed the use of confined feeding facilities as an inhumane way to fatten beef animals. As if this were not enough, groups worrying about the adequacy of the world's food supply made strong arguments that beef animals are inefficient producers of calories – the same resources used to support the animals could produce significantly more calories (and other nutrients) if used to produce food grains, fruits, and vegetables – especially beans, peas, lentils, and other legumes.

Beef producers, processors, and beef industry organizations felt obligated to respond. These groups mounted their own research efforts and used print, radio, and electronic media to assure the beef-eating public that beef is nutritious and has a worthwhile place in human diets. Such strong disagreements between nutritionists, food producers, processors, and consumers are increasingly public and increasingly acrimonious. The arguments and the positions taken by the participants in these disputes have polarized conversations across the entire industry. These contrasting views require large amounts of societal resources from both sides of the issue; resources that could be used to produce goods and services.

The conflicts and confusion apparent in the above paragraphs go well beyond beef to include a more general category of meat or animal-based food supplies.[1] The existence of the conflicts begs a serious question: How did things get the way they are? One response says simply that food production (and consumption) has always brought contention, jealousy, envy, and enmity among those who are involved in the processes. Answering this question in a reasoned and complete way requires scrutiny of perhaps 10,000 years of human history – the time during which *homo sapiens* emerged from their millennia of hunting and gathering, domesticated plants and animals, and learned to exert some control over the production of foods and fibers (Mazoyer and Roudart, 2006).

It has not always been this way. A commonly held, nostalgic, and romantic view has the yeoman farmer "doing God's work" earning a livelihood by tilling the land and caring for the animals. Similarly, the idea of a family farm carries a strong emotional impact even today, when a small percentage of the population in high-income nations lives and works on farms (Table 1.1). The one feature of agriculture that has remained constant is continuous change: enormous productivity growth and changes in the production, processing, and consumption of food.

Example 2: the Green Revolution in India

Since the 1960s and 1970s, the "Green Revolution" has referred to the development and adoption of high-yielding seed varieties in agricultural nations. After World War II, international agricultural research centers were founded and funded primarily through private American institutions, including the Ford Foundation and the Rockefeller Foundation. The Green Revolution enhanced agricultural productivity enormously in many Asian and Latin American nations, but less so in Sub-Saharan Africa. The Green Revolution allowed India, food-short for decades, to become self-sufficient in food grains: wheat and rice. After a number of famines in the early 1960s, Green Revolution techniques helped rice yields in India increase from two tons per hectare to six tons per hectare. Rice became more affordable, with rice prices dropping from over $550 per ton in the 1970s to a low of less than $200 per ton in 2001 (Barta, 2007; Zwerdling, 2009).

The Green Revolution was based on the selection of high-yielding varieties of rice, wheat, maize, and soybeans. These new varieties required intensive applications of inputs, including fertilizer and purchased seeds, together with new cultivation methods. These specialized production systems and standardized cultivation methods were called "technology packages." Farmers desiring to take advantage of the new agricultural production systems were required to purchase the entire package of inputs and technical advice (Mazoyer and Roudart, 2006).

Norman Borlaug, an American agronomist named the "father" of the Green Revolution, is credited with saving over a billion people from starvation through the development of high-yielding, or modern, varieties of cereal grains. These new varieties required irrigation, and application of agricultural chemicals and pesticides. This resulted in industrial growth to produce these inputs, providing more jobs in the Indian economy.

The benefits of the Green Revolution in terms of human lives saved and improvement of the human condition are truly enormous. However, the Green Revolution has been criticized (Barta, 2007; Mazoyer and Roudart, 2006; Zwerdling, 2009) because the gains in yields were not universal. The high-yielding seeds were most effective in temperate, fertile regions. The marginal areas in tropical climates were unable to take advantage of the technological improvements. Similarly, the Green Revolution relied on standardized, homogeneous monocultures, rather than the diverse production systems characterized by ecological principles found in many parts of India. As India moves forward, it will continue to evolve and solve these issues, making agriculture more productive.

The Green Revolution provided large amounts of food that allowed India and other nations to feed a rapidly growing population. However, Indian agriculture faces future challenges even though the availability of food has increased. The modern varieties of rice and wheat require more water, and the water table is falling in some regions. As wells are dug deeper, salinity becomes a larger problem. The use of chemicals and fertilizer has resulted in an environmental challenge, and the purchase of modern inputs requires efficient sources of credit. Numerous additional issues in food and agricultural are increasingly polarized, including: (1) industrial vs. sustainable agriculture; (2) conventional vs. organic production methods; and (3) global vs. local food sources, to name only three. This book explores the causes, consequences, and potential resolution of these divergences, which have intensified from distrust, to embitterment on both sides of many issues, and to violence in some cases. Political and legal actions have resulted in significant monetary and psychic costs for groups on both sides of these divides. Rhetoric on both sides of each issue has caused misinformation and confusion among consumers, who are unsure about the impact of their food choices on nutrition, health, the environment, animal welfare, and hunger. This book provides a way forward toward understanding these divisions. The economic analysis in what follows provides greater understanding of the movement toward resolution of some of these polarized issues, and knowledge of why other issues are intractable.

Is polarization good or bad?

This appears to be a simple question, but in reality, it is complex, challenging, and dynamic. Examples throughout the book demonstrate controversies and disputes that have become bitter, divisive, and at times, irrational. In many cases, polarized issues in food and agriculture are costly: both sides believe that they must invest in public relations and marketing to share their message and negate the opposition's claims. As will be shown, in some cases the escalation of emotions can be enormously costly in terms of time, resources, and energy. Resources used to promote a cause or refute opponents could be used in productive and worthwhile causes. Given these large costs, a logical conclusion is "polarization is bad." Indeed, polarization can be disruptive, expensive, and counterproductive to both sides of an issue.

This conclusion is correct, but also simplistic and short-term in nature. Further consideration and deeper analysis leads to a second possible and equally logical conclusion: polarization can be beneficial, in spite of the costs. Polarization can be viewed as a type of "investment," characterized by costs in the present time period, and expectations of benefits in the future. Although divisive issues extract enormous costs, the resolution of controversial issues can provide benefits. The Latin phrase *per aspera ad astra* (to the stars through difficulties) captures the idea well: many rewards come at a cost or require an investment. For individuals, many rewards in professional life may be the result of costly investments in education, experience, and skill development. Similarly, societal benefits come from public investments in infrastructure, education, scientific research, the rule of law, and efficient political systems. Polarization in food and agriculture can also be considered an investment: it may appear bleak, costly, and hateful in the heat of the battle, but resolution often provides significant (at times, massive) benefits to producers and consumers. Science-based agriculture has extended human longevity, reduced hunger and famine, and allowed individuals and societies to devote time and energy to pursuits beyond hunting and gathering. However, the development of modern industrial food systems has also introduced issues, problems, and controversies, including a skewed distribution of the benefits, environmental damage, loss of family farms, nutritional issues, and animal welfare issues to name a few.

A nonagricultural example can illustrate the benefits and costs of economic growth and development. Industrialization brings large gains in productive efficiency, and increases in the quantity and quality of consumer goods. However, industrialization also brings compromised environmental quality, change in working conditions and a host of challenges that pre-industrial societies did not contend with. This is true of all societal advances: there are benefits and costs to all forms of progress. All worthwhile endeavors require resources, and many require disruption.

The economic approach to polarization

Economics is the study of choice. The economic approach to decision making focuses on the benefits and costs of each alternative. All options are considered to have both strengths and weaknesses, and economics provides a framework for making studied, well-informed choices. A major feature of the economic approach to decision making centers on purging all value judgments, opinions, and subjectivity from the choice itself, so it can be viewed in a neutral, unbiased fashion. Given human limitations, a complete lack of bias is not an achievable goal, but a laudable ideal to pursue.

This book uses the economic approach, and attempts to frame all sides of polarized issues in a fair, even-handed, and respectful fashion. Every attempt has been made to identify the most contentious emotional and strongly-held viewpoints of the covered issues. Experience suggests, however, that some readers will disagree with some statements, topics, ideas, and conclusions. These divergences of opinion about the polarized issues and their presentation will be unique to each individual. A book on polarized issues thus becomes ... for lack of a better term ... polarizing.

The economic approach comes with built-in biases. Economists value market-based solutions to disputes and controversies, whereas producers and consumers make voluntary, mutually beneficial trades. Under appropriate conditions, markets can lead to higher levels of freedom and efficiency than nonmarket solutions. However, there are numerous problems and consequences with market-based economies, including income inequality and lack of social programs, as further discussed in Chapter 3. Experts other than economists have different useful and popular concepts of society and polarized issues. For example, many political scientists and philosophers view society as a political community, or "polis," which makes shared decisions on issues. Lawyers and legal scholars analyze decision making in terms of what is allowed by the precedents of the Constitution, statutes, and common law. These alternative views do not emphasize markets, trades, or efficiency to the degree that the economic approach does.[2]

Major themes and book summary

The application of economic principles to better understand the divide between issues such as industrialized compared to sustainable agriculture, global compared to local food, and organic compared to conventional production is unique, timely, and important. Recent advances in economic theory are used to explain several aspects of current food dichotomies. The discussions include commentaries on DDT, sustainable agricultural production, genetically engineered crops, and concentrated animal feeding operations. These examples – as well as many others

– demonstrate that every agricultural production practice has strengths and weaknesses, benefits and costs, and that production practices and consumer choices continually advance.

Chapter 2 provides a brief historical background of polarization in modern agriculture, including how mechanization and industrialization have changed the way food is produced, processed, distributed, and consumed. This historical summary demonstrates that agricultural production has been subjected to perennial, pervasive, and disruptive change, often leading to social and economic displacement. History, or the documentation and interpretation of past events, is necessary for successful participation in a democratic political process. Good public policy decisions rely on accurate understanding of past events, and particularly the sources, effects, and resolution of previous polarized issues. History itself is divisive, as it offers different, often conflicting, interpretations of past events. Knowledge of these differences, why they exist, and how they affect policy decisions in the present, allow for improved understanding of current polarizations, and how they might be resolved.

Market-based economics is summarized in Chapter 3, to show how a free-enterprise economic system can result in large, efficient, but impersonal and unequal food production and processing firms. "Consumer sovereignty," the idea that in a market-based economy, consumers will purchase whatever they desire, and producers will meet these wants and needs, is a dominant theme throughout the study of economics and throughout this book. It helps explain such things as why an increase in income could be followed by an increase in consumer demand for food with attributes such as "local," "organic," or "fair trade." Producers who respond proactively and rapidly to the changing desires of consumers have an advantage in the marketplace.

Chapter 4 includes a brief description and analysis of increases in the demand for locally produced food, ecological economics, and sustainable agriculture. Today's food markets are enormously diverse. The huge number of food attributes available can be considered desirable, since it reflects consumer diversity in tastes, preferences, wants, and needs. Many polarized issues in food and agriculture arise from the common human desire to share one's own viewpoints (including food choices) with others. Some organic food producers and consumers, for example, make strong statements that condemn chemical use in agricultural production. Producers of conventional grains, fruit, and vegetables often oppose regulations or legislation that limit chemical use. There are well-reasoned arguments for both of these positions, yet many individuals view chemicals as either "all good" or "all bad." Economists identify and emphasize both the benefits and the costs of all production techniques, food attributes, and public policies. This neutral, unbiased approach leads to greater understanding of many highly divisive issues in food and agriculture, by identifying the most important sources of disagreement.

Chapter 5 provides an economic explanation and analysis of the causes and consequences of the polarization in the food and agricultural industries. Although a market-based economy provides huge benefits to society in terms of high incomes and economic growth, free markets can be a messy, capricious way of delivering progress. One prevailing characteristic of economic growth is that some individuals and groups will be made better off while others will be made worse off by economic changes and technological advance. Economists have described the market process as "creative destruction," since new ideas, innovations, and ways of doing things lead to the destruction of old techniques, methods, and industries. Technological advance in food and agriculture frequently requires changes in occupation, location, and security.

Chapter 5 shows that new technologies and innovations often result in economic gains to the adopter, with early adopters reaping the largest rewards. Interestingly and importantly, early adopters have a strong incentive to exclude others from adopting, since economic gains are dissipated when an innovation or new product becomes commonplace. Therefore, an unexpected result is that the early adopters of a new product or technology can be allied with nonadopters, or the "opposition." The discussion highlights the most likely successful solution to polarized issues in food and agriculture: rapid economic growth and innovation. In times of rapid change, polarized individuals and groups do not have time to dwell on rhetorical arguments, or remain stagnant in their views and opinions.

Chapters 6 through 10 complete the discussion by advancing several potential solutions to polarized issues inherent in the food industry. Economic principles are used to help readers better understand the divisiveness that prevails in the agricultural production and food processing industries. The proposed solutions are innovative, providing potential agreement (the rationalization of issue polarization) between the groups that have seemingly irreconcilable differences. A major outcome of the economic analysis of polarized issues in food and agriculture is that polarization sets in motion economic and political forces that automatically come into play to resolve disputes. The market process of meeting consumer needs can result in market structures, institutions, and policies that productively and efficiently resolve some polarized issues. "Green" food products that combine environmentally sustainable production practices with good taste and nutrition can bring producers and consumers together through "bundling" food attributes together.

Chapter 6 is concerned with big business: economies of scale. This economic concept is straightforward: many productive processes provide lower production costs at larger size. The concept explains the source of "industrialized agriculture," sometimes called "big food." Large-scale production of food has both benefits and costs: food is available at a lower cost to consumers, but large firms can become non-competitive, or large enough to charge prices higher than the cost of production. These benefits and costs are explored in Chapter 6, with an unexpected outcome: criticism of the food industry, while contentious and polarizing in the short term, can be good for the entire food system in the long run, including farmers, food processors, and consumers. When large food processors take the ideas and concerns of food activists into account, they are meeting the ever-evolving needs and desires of consumers. A case is made that openness to criticism, coupled with transparency of operations, activities, and policies are one of the key prerequisites to future success in the food and agricultural industries. A second fascinating outcome of the analysis is that the production of organic and local food is also subject to economies of scale: larger organic and/or local farms will have cost advantages over smaller farms. The result is the cause of polarization between some organic producers who advocate "organic lifestyles" and others who view organic food as primarily a profit-making opportunity.

A useful and powerful economic idea is that of "externality," as showcased in Chapter 7. An externality occurs if one individual's actions affect another, in either a positive or negative way, without consent of the affected party. Externalities occur when costs or benefits "spillover" onto third parties. The potential for damage to the environment from agricultural chemicals, fertilizer use, and soil erosion are examples: if a farmer uses a chemical that causes downstream water pollution, a "negative externality" is incurred by the downstream users of water. Economists have put forth a bargaining solution to issues of externality, when both sides of a polarized issue negotiate with each other to resolve the problem. When property rights are assigned and enforced properly, negotiated settlement provides a powerful solution to many agricultural and food issues, as will be discussed and evaluated in Chapter 7.

The economics of "bundling" is considered in Chapter 8. Bundling of products together is common: examples include hamburgers, fries, and beverages at fast food restaurants, cable television and internet services, and vacation packages that include airfare, hotel, and rental car. Bundling provides a unique method of dispute resolution in food and agriculture, through combining food characteristics such as "natural" or "sustainable" with a food product. It will be shown that Chipotle's "sustainable food" marketing campaign is one example of a strategy that could be a major contributor to resolving many polarized issues. This marketing strategy was adopted by McDonald's and Walmart in 2013.

Globalization and international trade is the subject of Chapter 9. Specialization and gains from trade provide large economic benefits to those nations, individuals, and industries that produce what they do best, and trade for other goods. This process allows resources to be used in their most productive, efficient use. International trade expands the productive capacity of all nations. Trade can be polarizing, however, because not everyone is made better off from trade. The producers of an imported food product will be made worse off if imports increase. Imported food can cause economic dislocation of farmers. Economists are nearly unanimous in their strong advocacy of free trade, in spite of these costs, as will be explored in Chapter 9.

Game theory, or the "science of strategy," is usefully applied to polarized issues in food and agriculture in Chapter 10. "Games," or strategic interactions, all share the common feature of interdependence: the outcome for each participant depends on the choices of all participants. Thus, game theory studies show how people interact and make decisions in an environment where there is potential for mutual gain, mutual loss, or conflict between participants, since each individual's behavior affects everyone else in the game. Game theory identifies the most important aspects of real-world decisions, and therefore emphasizes that each participant should consider other participants' motivations and likely responses before taking action. In repeated games, coordination is possible through the use of threats, commitments, and reputation. Polarized issues in food and agriculture are more fully understood and resolved through the study and application of game theory.

The possibility for common ground and resolution of polarized issues is explored, and potential benefits analyzed. The enduring theme is that there are benefits and strengths, as well as costs and weaknesses, to every agricultural production technique and system. The proposed resolution to polarization will combine the best attributes of both food production and distribution systems, leaving undesired or outdated production methods (e.g. unsustainable or inhumane practices) behind. A multifaceted, diverse, targeted approach to food production and consumption could promote social well-being, and reduce or eliminate misinformation, anxiety, transaction costs, and hunger.

The ultimate message of the book is that today's polarizations are likely to be resolved over time, as economic forces come automatically into play to reduce, resolve, and eliminate divisive issues. However, it should be emphasized that although today's polarized issues will be resolved over time, new issues will arise to take their place, since each solution begins the process of creative destruction anew. The process of continuous introduction and solution of polarized issues allows society to advance by enhancing longevity and incomes, and reducing hunger, poverty, and malnutrition over time.

Notes

1 A recent critique of the meat industry is *The Meat Racket: The Secret Takeover of America's Food Business* by Christopher Leonard (2014).
2 Parke Wilde (2013) contributed these alternative approaches. Wilde also points out that the use of economic analysis is polarizing, since it emphasizes the market approach, and the benefits and costs of alternatives. In economics, the unit of analysis is often the individual, rather than groups or societies. This individualistic approach provides insights, but is limited by not considering larger groups.

2

A CONCISE HISTORY
OF AGRICULTURE

The advent of polarization

> Every agricultural policy, just like every economic policy, is a major social contest. And consequently it is the object of all types of demands, pressures, negotiations, representations, and influence games, which express the interests of different groups: national producers of all types (grain growers, animal breeders, vine growers, well-off farmers or those in difficulty, farmers from the plains or those from the mountains, foreign producers, industrialists, consumers, ecologists, regionalists, etc.).
>
> Mazoyer and Roudart (2006), p. 438

Introduction

Agriculture is a widely understood word that stems from two Latin words, *ager* meaning field, and *cultural* meaning cultivation. The combined word, *agriculture*, retains its meaning relating to the cultivation of fields so humans can use, directly or indirectly, a purposefully grown crop to serve the needs of the cultivators and those around them. The question of when and where agriculture first started, that is, when and where people began to grow (cultivate and manage) their food supply rather than hunt and gather it, is more complicated.[1]

Once started, agriculture spread rapidly across the Earth. Wherever agriculture went, it carried with it a unique co-dependency. Growing crops and rearing animals for food or fiber required a well-organized labor supply, and the laborers needed the food they were producing for their own sustenance. Given that transportation was slow, the possibility of meeting these needs required the labor supply to live close to the farming area so the workforce could labor in a timely manner and the finished product could reach the workers in time to sustain them. This necessary proximity inevitably meant that farming begat villages, communities, towns, and cities.

Agriculture moved quickly from its origins in the Fertile Crescent. It moved north into what is now Europe, where, after many centuries of cultivation, the productive capacity of the cultivated land began to diminish. The farmers began what eventually became effective methods of restoring the productivity of the soil by rotating crops and fallow land among an ever-increasing number of fields. Even the early Egyptians apparently followed the practice of planting half of the arable land and leaving the other half idle (fallow).

The early efforts in Europe divided the land into three fields with one field planted to wheat or rye, a second field used for a leguminous crop like peas or lentils, and a third field left fallow. The following year, the crops rotated among the fields. By the early 1700s, the British agriculturist, Charles Townshend (1674–1738) introduced a four-field system that used four land parcels to rotate crops including wheat (or rye), barley, turnips, and clover. The nitrogen-fixing properties of the clover made the fallow year unnecessary.

The extension of agriculture into Asia came somewhat earlier than the European adaptations. Asia, with its huge population and geographic diversity, concentrated on improving the yields of crops – especially rice.

BOX 2.1: THE DEVELOPMENT OF GLOBAL AGRICULTURAL SYSTEMS

With global population growth, the demand for food increased. Originally, this led to slash and burn agriculture, also called forest agrarian systems, where a rotation occurred between temporary cultivation and long periods of forest growth. This system lasted for thousands of years worldwide, with people and forests existing together. Complications arose as the population continued to grow after all of the virgin resources were used. Not only were new resources unavailable for slash and burn agriculture, but deforestation led to fertility decline, erosion, and a worsening of climate, in some cases desertification. Slash and burn agriculture continues today in some regions of Asia, Africa, and South America (Mazoyer and Roudart, 2006, p. 102).

Agriculture in many forested regions began to use irrigated cultivation in the fourteenth century BCE. Original irrigation techniques in the Egyptian Nile Valley used floodwater basins to retain water from annual floods. Early hydraulic agricultural states included Mesopotamia, the Indus, China, and Vietnam. Later, machines such as the Archimedean screw and the bucket wheel were employed to move water for irrigated crop production. Hydraulic agriculture in Egypt has continued with a long history of improvements over thousands of years.

In South America, the Incas developed a highly evolved system of agriculture, composed of complementary subsystems and trade, based on diverse ecological conditions at different elevations in each region of the vast Inca Empire. The Empire extended into today's nations of Ecuador, Peru, Bolivia, and Chile. In the temperate regions of Europe, slash and burn agriculture was replaced by food systems based on fallowing and cultivation, using animals for traction. Yields were low, due to poor means available for cultivation and transport. Low productivity led to subsistence living conditions for thousands of years. Mazoyer and Roudart (2006) argue that the low level of food production was "inseparable from the development of war, the formation of militarized city-states, colonization and slavery" that characterized European societies for generations, until about 1000 CE. Agricultural systems based on fallow and cultivation continue to exist in several regions of northern Africa, the Near East, Asia, and South America (p. 219).

The development of the metal plow allowed for the replacement of fallow systems with rotations that included useful production each year. This new agricultural production method started in Flanders in the fifteenth century, and spread throughout Europe over the next several centuries. New technologies led to massive upheaval in social and economic systems, as societies were transformed from feudal arrangements to modern political systems.

The development of US agriculture

In agriculture's early stages, oxen, horses, and other draft animals came into the production cycle, but even then, the requirements for manual labor were vast. This requirement stimulated labor-saving innovation wherever agriculture was taking hold. As innovations multiplied and cropping practices became more sophisticated, agriculture moved into new areas and quickly adapted to or overcame the area's problems and limitations. Food supplies increased, followed soon after by increases in well-fed and productive populations. The increases demonstrated a form of "progress." This chapter will concentrate on developments in US agriculture, as an example of innovations and events that occurred in many nations throughout the world. Although the circumstances differ widely, many nations share similar developments and histories.

Early European settlers arriving in North America brought very little knowledge or experience of agriculture with them but they found a reasonably sophisticated agriculture developed and maintained by the indigenous population. Among other things, the Native Americans grew tobacco, beans, corn, and squashes in small fields or plots cleared without the use of metal tools. There was little animal agriculture because the large animals indigenous to North America (bison and elk, for example) were not easily domesticated and fencing was not practical given the available tools and the forested environment of the Atlantic coastal areas.

By 1611 – four years after their arrival in Jamestown – the European immigrants to that area used iron and steel tools and draft animals to clear lands for farming in the traditional European style: reasonably large fields devoted to monoculture, or a small number of crops divided among fields.[2] During the first century of settlement, European-style agriculture, sometimes described as "Eurocentric agriculture," expanded rapidly on land in the coastal areas then moved inland to cover much of the area defined by the original 13 colonies. Immediately after the

Revolutionary War (1775–1783), the original colonies ceded their vast Western land claims to the newly formed United States government. Similarly, at the Treaty of Paris in 1783, the English monarch, George III, abandoned the British land claims in North America to the new nation. These aggregated cessions gave the new nation claims to all lands westward to the Mississippi River.[3] This gave United States agriculture room to expand westward.

The new government began almost immediately to measure its land in an orderly fashion in anticipation of distributing it to arriving immigrants. The land was marked off in a rectangular fashion so that after surveying, a map of the new areas showed baselines (running east and west), principal meridians (running north and south), and six-mile-square "townships." Each township was further marked off into 36 mile-square "sections" that – then as now – formed the basis for legal descriptions and distribution patterns of nearly all real property in the United States.

The distribution of land brought on a contentious policy discussion related to the expansion of agriculture in the United States. Alexander Hamilton and Thomas Jefferson, both of whom were "founding fathers," had opposing views regarding the method of distributing the millions of acres of land held by the federal government. Jefferson, always in favor of a strong agriculture populated by many free-holding small farmers, favored giving the land at near zero prices to qualified people who would immediately bring it into agricultural production. Hamilton, Secretary of the Treasury at the time, was conscious of the huge debt load already held by the fledgling federal government. He favored selling large acreages to speculators who would: (1) pay in cash to provide money for the national treasury: and (2) immediately resell small "farmable" parcels of the land to individuals who wished to farm. Although some very large parcels found their way into the hands of speculators, by far the majority of the land went to individual settlers interested in farming.

While general agriculture and animal agriculture dominated the Northern colonies, the Southern colonies produced four major crops that were important because of the export surpluses they generated. The four – tobacco, rice, indigo, and cotton – thrived in the warm and humid South but each of the crops required large commitments of labor, often supplied by slaves.

BOX 2.2: LAND, PRODUCTION, AND LOW FARM INCOMES IN THE UNITED STATES

Many early immigrants came to the "New Country" in search of an opportunity to farm. For some, the task of finding land and making a farm was simple. For others, the opportunities were scarce and difficult to find. Nonetheless, the country filled rapidly with farmers. The 1790 Census, the first census conducted by the federal government, showed the nation's population to be 3,929,214 with 90 percent of the labor force working in agriculture. Settlement at that time extended westward an average of 255 miles from the Atlantic seaboard

(US Bureau of the Census, 1914; Ottoson, 1963). On the West Coast and in the Southwest, Spain and Mexico had a large impact on US agriculture. California had a system of Spanish missions with advanced European-style fruit and nut farms beginning in the mid-eighteenth century. By 1830, the population was 12.9 million and the Mississippi River marked the western edge of the frontier. In 1840, the population reached 17 million of whom 9 million were farmers, who made up 69 percent of the labor force.

The nation filled with farmers who expanded farming so rapidly that the supplies of produced farm commodities exceeded the local demand. Economic principles suggest that large supplies result in low commodity prices. This was the case, and for most years in the nineteenth century, farm household income was well below the income of non-farm households in the United States. The question was one of the nature of markets for farm commodities. The demand for these goods was such that the more of the commodity placed on the market, the less revenue it would yield, since prices were very responsive to increases in production. The size of the land base made this a serious problem. The vast open spaces of the upper mid-West, then the plains, and finally the irrigated West invited settlers – most with the intent to farm. They were generally successful. Their success helped maintain low commodity prices and low farm incomes as major characteristics of US agriculture from the early years of settlement through several early decades of the twentieth century.

Consumers benefitted enormously from the ample, inexpensive supply of food available in the US. Low food costs allowed for investment and income growth in industrial pursuits, and these brought rapid economic growth for most of US history. Farmers, however, were subject to challenging economic conditions and massive movements of farm workers out of production agriculture due to low returns.

Slavery

Between the sixteenth and nineteenth centuries, an estimated 12 million Africans were transported to the Americas as slaves, with an estimated 645,000 in the United States (Segal, 1995, p. 4). Slavery began in the colonies as early as 1619 when a Dutch ship put ashore 19 Africans at the port at Jamestown, Virginia. Although there is question regarding whether these 19 came ashore as slaves or as indentured servants, they and many others expanded the agricultural labor force through the ownership and use of slave labor. Slavery became a feature of the Southern colonies. The major crops of the region required large crews of laborers to clear and prepare the land for farming as well as for harvesting and processing the crops after harvest. Slave numbers grew rapidly from 19 in 1619 to nearly 4 million at the time of emancipation in 1865. A large majority of the slaves lived in the South and worked in the fields. The North, although originally viewing slavery as legal, did not use slaves extensively in agriculture, in part due to the small size of Northern farms and the types of crops grown there. Partially because of differences in agriculture, people who lived north of the Mason–Dixon Line began a movement that divided the country and eventually led to the Civil War.[4]

The search for efficiency

In the 1790s, the search for a more efficient method of picking cotton and separating the fibers from the seeds continued to baffle cotton producers, inventors, and tinkerers. In 1793, and after several difficult attempts to develop a reliable "gin," Eli Whitney (1765–1825), a Yale graduate who chose to move south and make a living as a private tutor, developed a successful gin.[5] The machine gave increased impetus to the growth of the cotton industry. Huge labor requirements were no longer needed for ginning, so cotton profits increased demonstrably and cotton acreage soared. Land formerly used for other crops suddenly turned the southeastern states into a cotton kingdom that fed the textile mills of Great Britain for many decades. In 1796, three years after the invention of the gin, the entire Cotton South produced 21,000 bales of cleaned cotton.[6] Half a century later, production was at 1.6 million bales, and on the eve of the American Civil War (1861), cotton growers produced 4.8 million bales of the crop. The Civil War interrupted international sales of cotton so in 1864, only 299,000 bales reached market. While cotton was the South's dominant crop, tobacco, rice, and indigo also made significant contributions to the Southern economy. The four provided major export revenues at a time when the nation desperately needed commercial economic activity.

Like cotton, each of the other three crops required significant amounts of labor. These labor requirements kept people on the plantations and slowed the South's rural population from migrating to the nation's urban areas for employment in nonagricultural industries. In this sense, the crops were profitable for their producers but hindered the development and diversification of the South's economy.

The mechanization of American agriculture

Whitney's cotton gin seems to have put in motion a century of invention, innovation, and adaptation of machines for American agriculture. In very short order, farm-oriented inventors produced mechanical devices and improved tools to increase the productivity of agricultural labor and help make it possible for the workers to produce something other than food and fiber. Fewer workers using specialized equipment doing the same work allowed thousands of farmers and farm workers to join the industrial labor force and increase the output of industrial and consumer goods. The process of using machines or equipment to replace labor is called "the substitution of capital for labor." This substitution has been the source of intense and bitter contention and polarization since the process began centuries ago.

A brief list of the machines and tools that made this possible shows that the development of a mechanized agriculture, while enabling the nation's economy to grow, also created confusion and conflict as machines and tools took the place of laborers who had few skills other than working in or near the production of food and fiber. A short list of inventions and adaptations includes:

- 1600 to the late 1700s. Agricultural technology and farming methods did not make significant changes during this period. Oxen and horses were used for power and transport, plowing was done with crude wooden plows, seeds were sown by hand, hoes were used in cultivation, grain crops were cut with a sickle, and threshing was done using a flail or trampling by heavy animals.
- 1790. The scythe and cradle increased the speed of cutting (reaping) ripened grain crops. The scythe was a heavy implement, so its adoption excluded many individuals from the harvest season workforce, as it required great strength and endurance to operate.
- 1793. Eli Whitney invents and adapts the cotton gin allowing cotton acreage to expand and cotton exports to increase.
- 1794. Thomas Jefferson designs and tests, but does not patent or manufacture, a plow based on rigid scientific calculations. The objective was to develop a plow that required less effort to pull it through the earth. Not surprisingly, the Jefferson plow was called the "plow of least resistance."
- 1797. Charles Newbold, a New Jersey blacksmith, patented and manufactured a cast-iron plow based on Jefferson's design and cast as one piece. The plow was not a commercial success because farmers of the era held firm beliefs that the iron plow would "poison the soil."
- 1799–1840. Sowing seeds for small-grain crops (wheat, barley, buckwheat, rye, corn, etc.) puzzled inventors and experimenters for centuries. As early as 1701, Jethro Tull, a British agriculturist, built and patented a horse-drawn, one-row seed drill that dropped single seeds into trenches and covered them. The device worked and looked very much like modern multi-row drills. However, Tull's device was limited to a single row. Nearly a century later, in 1799, Eliakim Spooner, a Vermont mechanic, obtained the first US patent on a grain drill. Experimentation by Spooner and others continued until the 1840s when more reliable grain drills became available.[7]
- 1807. In New Jersey, David Peacock patented a cast-iron plow made in three replaceable parts making it possible to replace broken shares or moldboards rather than replacing the entire plow. The plow sold well – perhaps because the belief that metal plows "poisoned the soil" had proved false.
- 1819. Jethro Wood in New York, a friend of Jefferson, patented and successfully sold a plow with interchangeable parts and a steel plowshare. Although minor changes continued, his design became the standard for American plows for several decades.
- 1830s. The innovators and inventors – mostly grain growers looking for ways to reduce the need and cost of labor during harvest season – turned to developing machines to reap (cut) the ripened grain and thresh the seeds out of the heads. Crude machines for these farming operations came and went

without success in all parts of the grain-growing nations. The successes included the 1830 development of a mechanized, but stationary, thresher. In 1834, Cyrus McCormick developed and patented a practical reaper.

• 1836–1850s. For years, farmers had dreamed of combining the reaping and threshing functions into one machine. Success in this endeavor would drastically reduce the labor and time requirements of the harvest. Through the mid-1830s, Hiram Moore, a Michigan farmer, and several farm implement builders, built and tested such a machine. A Moore-built "combine" (patented in 1834) could harvest (cut, thresh, clean, and sack) 25 acres per day. A competing machine, the Marsh Monitor, harvested grain in the Great Lakes region and in the Central Valleys of California during the mid-1850s. Eventually and because they became a threat to farm laborers, one Marsh machine was burned in California, another in Michigan. Friction in a gearbox may have ignited the California fire, but the fire in Michigan was clearly arson perpetrated by laborers put out of work by the labor-saving characteristics of the modern combine. Mr. John Horner, Michigan, took two Moore machines to California and operated them successfully for 25 years, 1854–1879. The machines were reliable and could cut, thresh, clean, and sack about 20 acres per day (Higgins, 1958).

The long period 1840–1880 saw inventions and improvements in nearly all phases of agricultural fieldwork.[8] By this time, horses reached their maximum useful potential as a source of power in farming activities. Steam and internal combustion engines replaced the horses and ushered in a revolution in American agriculture.[9]

While indigo did not continue as a commercial crop in the United States, yields of the other three major crops, tobacco, rice, and cotton grew to higher and higher levels. Grain crops, mainly wheat and corn, became major export crops. With the huge expansion in agriculture and with opportunities to export the harvests that went unused at home, farmers and landowners should have been enjoying high incomes and new riches. This was not the case. Since the increased output caused farm prices to fall for nearly all agricultural products, the booming harvests and added acres did little or nothing to eradicate low farm incomes in the nation's rural areas.

Global diffusion of agricultural equipment

New equipment in agriculture, including animal-driven cultivation, provided massive productivity gains in industrialized temperate nations, reducing agricultural labor force requirements by half, thus doubling the cultivated area per worker. Mechanization first occurred in the US, due to large farms and labor scarcity. Vast amounts of available land in the US, Canada, Australia, and Argentina led to the rapid adoption of equipment and mechanized agricultural techniques during the nineteenth century (Mazoyer and Roudart, 2006, p. 364). Agricultural productivity growth due to mechanization in the Americas, Australia, New Zealand, and South Africa led to food surpluses that were made available to Europe through transcontinental railways and steamships.

The Civil War period: Abraham Lincoln signs five important laws affecting agriculture

The Civil War (1861–1865) brought changes to agriculture in the United States. Early in the war, President Abraham Lincoln took action with respect to five major issues related to agriculture. Although these issues and laws were uniquely American, most other nations used government policies to advance the development of agriculture through subsidies, education, research, and the elimination of slavery.

* The Homestead Act (1862) that eventually granted private ownership of over 270 million acres of generally unused public domain to 1.6 million settler families.
* The Morrill Land Grant College Act (1862) that provided the financial basis for an "agriculture and mechanic arts" college in every state.
* Lincoln created an independent Department of Agriculture (1862) headed by a "Commissioner." This executive action gave the nation's farmers a stand-alone federal agency.
* The Pacific Railway Act (1862) granted 175 million acres of unclaimed federal land to five railroad companies that promised to sell the land to farmers in order to raise money to offset some of the costs of constructing the transcontinental railroads.
* The Emancipation Proclamation (1863) which, coupled with the 13th Amendment to the US Constitution (1865), freed nearly 4 million slaves.

The Civil War brought serious changes to American agriculture. The changes were not limited to those brought by the new machines, inventions, and methods used to grow or process crops and animals. The North's industrial strength had grown rapidly during the war years – so rapidly that exports of food and industrial products from the North actually increased during the conflict.

The war, however, ravaged the agriculture of the South. The huge and bitterly fought battles, most of which took place in the South, destroyed farms, cities, and the infrastructure needed to grow crops and get them to market. More importantly, emancipation freed 4 million slaves who were now free, but who had to find employment in an economy essentially destroyed by war. The various cultural aspects of slavery as well as the Emancipation Act polarized nearly all activities – economic and social – in the South.

BOX 2.3: SOCIAL AND POLITICAL ORGANIZATIONS IN AGRICULTURE

Andrew Johnson, the post-Civil War President, appointed an investigating committee to go to the South and prepare an on-the-scene report of economic and social conditions in the South's agricultural areas. The 1867 report of the committee led Oliver Hudson Kelley, the committee chairman, and a group of seven others to form the Patrons of Husbandry, a nongovernmental fraternal organization dedicated to improving economic, social, and educational conditions in the South. The Patrons of Husbandry, now commonly called "the Grange," grew rapidly in its early years. Although prohibited by its own doctrines from engaging in political activity, it quickly moved to seek regulation of rail rates and warehousing activities, particularly in the mid-West and the Plains States. The Grange enjoyed brief and mainly local political success during the 1870s and 1880s. The organization soon, however, began to lose membership because of poor management, increased nonagricultural opportunities for potential members, and its own unwillingness to endorse candidates or political issues. The Patrons of Husbandry had nearly one million members in 1875, but membership dropped sharply in succeeding years. Today, the Grange has become primarily a social and public service organization with fewer than 200,000 members.

The Grange was only one of many organizations formed by farmers and other rural people during the second half of the nineteenth century. Prior to the Civil War and almost from the time Europeans settled on the North American continent, towns, neighborhoods, cities, and colonies had "agricultural clubs" that helped unify farmers and casual producers of farm products. The clubs differed widely in structure and purpose but all seemed to be interested in new crops, new methods of crop production, disease control, and marketing. Most such clubs merged with the larger farm-related organizations leaving few indications of their early existence.

Many farm-related organizations of this era had their own purposes or desires to serve a specific geographic area. Most included aspirations that they believed would enhance the economic position of agriculture, including paying off the national debt, preventing aliens from owning land, and ending futures trading of agricultural commodities.

The creation of these and other farm- and rural-oriented organizations is testimony to idea that the people living in the nation's rural areas had common concerns and could best discuss them by making specific arrangements for personal contacts in a club-like or organizational setting. Rural people took these steps because of their isolation, general poverty, and the constant feeling that the railroads, the banks, the warehouses, and the merchants were attempting to exploit the weaknesses that came with farming and rural living.[10]

The government and US agriculture: the development of agricultural protectionism

Perhaps the boldest attempt to help close the gap between rural and urban America came from President Theodore Roosevelt. Near the end of his second term, Roosevelt appointed a Commission on Country Life headed by Liberty Hyde Bailey, a highly regarded professor of horticulture at Cornell University. The

Commission's charge was to investigate ways to make life and work more appealing to the people who lived in the nation's rural areas. Its report, delivered to the President in January 1909, mentioned but did not provide solutions to the many problems faced by farmers and the nation's rural population. Roosevelt forwarded it to Congress for consideration.

Although no single activity, agency, or law came directly from the Commission's report, Congress and the general population gained much knowledge and understanding of rural America because of it.[11] A number of bills and political activities related to rural life and living followed. The major ones included:

- The Smith-Lever Act (1914) linked rural areas to research done at each state's Land Grant College. The Smith-Hughes Act of 1917 followed to provide monies to rural school districts to help fund teaching vocational subjects at the high school level.
- The Federal Farm Loan Act of 1916 led to a multi-layered credit system that provided or guaranteed credit to many agricultural enterprises.
- The formation of the "Farm Bloc" in Congress to unify actions related to agriculture. Senators and Representatives from all major farm states belonged to the bloc and usually voted as a group on farm-related legislation.
- Passage of the Packers and Stockyards Act in 1921 in an effort to reduce collusion among major livestock processing firms and packers.

Europe was preparing for war during this time and needed reliable sources of food. American farmers were quick to take advantage of the subsequent increases in commodity prices and by 1920 farm family incomes were nearly as high as the incomes of nonfarm families. It would not last forever. In the early 1920s, the war-torn farming areas of Europe came back into production, reducing the need for the European nations to import such large quantities of food from the United States. Prices of agricultural products dropped fast and far. Wheat prices reached a high of $2.19 per bushel in 1919, then fell to a low of 38 cents per bushel in 1932 (US Bureau of the Census, 1975). Corn that sold for $1.50 per bushel in 1919 went for 32 cents per bushel in 1931, and hogs that sold for $12.92 per hundredweight in 1919 brought $3.34 per hundredweight in 1932 (US Bureau of the Census, 1975). The prices of other crops and commodities followed similar paths. The annual net farm income per farm dropped from $1,196 in 1920 to $304 in 1932 (US Bureau of the Census, 1975). By 1929, US agriculture was in a depression of its own and the Great Depression of the 1930s was just beginning. One could guess neither how severe the economic climate would become nor how long it would last.

By the mid-1920s, conditions in agriculture and common-sense economics suggested that the low commodity prices and harsh poverty affecting American agriculture were a result of the rapid development of the industry that, in turn, caused supplies of agricultural products to outrun the demand for the goods – either domestically or internationally. This theme took time to develop and become a part of economists' understanding of farm policy. Secretary of Agriculture, Henry C. Wallace (1921–1924), was one of the few – possibly the first – public officials to warn that overproduction was a possible contributor to the agricultural dilemma.

By this time, the federal government had little undistributed or unassigned land to give to homesteaders, transportation routes were either in place or under construction, and international trade had settled into a steady pattern among several major trading nations. The federal government remained closely involved with the agricultural industry and with the people who depended on it. The isolation and poverty of farm and rural people made an impression on the federal government and policy makers.

In 1919, David Houston, President Wilson's Secretary of Agriculture, invited agricultural economist H. C. Taylor to move from the University of Wisconsin to Washington, DC, to become the leader of economics research in the US Department of Agriculture. Taylor's Bureau of Agricultural Economics actively watched the economic collapse of US farming and began to question the traditional approaches to poverty and instability in farming. The result was a new wave of policies that centered on the federal government's direct involvement in agriculture and farming. The Capper–Volstead Act of 1922 enhanced farmers' ability to coordinate marketing, which had been limited since 1890 by the Sherman Antitrust Act.

In the early to mid-1920s, Congress had considered dozens of bills and proposals aimed at revitalizing the US agricultural economy. Prominent among them was a bill authored by Senator Charles L. McNary and Congressman Gilbert N. Haugen. The bill proposed a complex plan to allow the sale of only a predetermined amount of a crop on the domestic market (enough to maintain the domestic price at a certain level) and sale of the remainder on the world market at whatever price it could command. The bill, known as "the McNary–Haugen Proposal," came before Congress five times between 1924 and 1928. It was defeated four times before passing both houses on May 14, 1928. The bill went to the White House where President Coolidge vetoed it. The Senate could not override the veto, so the farm state members of Congress had to begin again to find a way to help the agricultural industries climb out of the depressed conditions facing it.[12]

The Agricultural Marketing Act of 1929 created the Federal Farm Board, a committee of eight leading figures headed by Alexander Legge, president of the International Harvester Company. The Board had a $500 million budget to use in assisting the cooperative marketing associations that served agriculture and to form a long-term policy of stabilizing marketing activities. The Board may have been more successful in another time. Economic conditions were moving so rapidly and changing so drastically that an agency oriented to long-term problem solving had little chance of success. The outlook for the Federal Farm Board worsened with the general stock market crash in late 1929. After the crash, its operations seemed too little and too late. In 1933, after the Great Depression was underway, the agency was renamed the Farm Credit Administration, and its activities shifted to a more centralized credit agency for agriculture. It, however, did retain the power to lend to agricultural cooperatives and maintain efforts to use commercial storage facilities to help equalize supply and demand for several major crops.

Quite simply, the 1920s were a time for testing the waters of agricultural policy. The farming industry had fallen into a depression of its own in the early years of the decade. It asked for help from Congress and the federal government, but neither had experience with such large and expensive domestic efforts. Moreover, the specter of collectivization and anarchy were creeping over the globe, instilling a noticeable reluctance for the United States government to become involved with economic assistance for a particular industry. Poverty on the farms, bitter labor disputes in the processing industries, and depressed sales for farm machinery of all kinds made the puzzle more vexing. One of the few positive aspects of the decade was the introduction, discussion, and then failure of the McNary–Haugen plan. These frustrating failures of the era made it obvious to most observers that the federal government was the only force large enough and strong enough to bring order to the chaos facing the industry. The time for positive action came very soon.

Franklin Delano Roosevelt, a distant relative of Theodore Roosevelt, swept the presidency and the Congress into the hands of the Democratic Party in the election of 1932. Conditions in agriculture were so chaotic that the new president had an almost completely free hand to develop a policy or set of policies to help agriculture and to relieve the depressed economic conditions gripping the nation. Roosevelt was a pragmatic leader who recognized when individuals or agencies were not doing their intended job and changed them. This was apparent in agriculture.

The Agricultural Adjustment Act of 1933 (AAA) was the first part of Roosevelt's "New Deal" for farming and rural people. The AAA became law on May 12, 1933 – only 69 days after Roosevelt's inauguration. It established the Agricultural Adjustment Administration (later renamed the Agricultural Adjustment Agency) to subsidize farmers for reducing production of certain commodities. The objective was to reduce output as a means of driving prices up to levels with buying power equal to the buying power that the commodity enjoyed during the 1910–1914 "base period." The law also gave the Agency power to make loans to farmers who used their stored crops as collateral, and to stabilize prices using marketing agreements with growers and handlers of some commodities.[13] The law allowed the government to levy taxes on processors to help defray the costs of the adjustment efforts. By 1936, payments to growers of selected crops totaled more than $1.5 billion.[14] Although limited to farmers who grew specific crops, the farming community was generally in favor of the government's actions.

In 1936, the Supreme Court found certain parts of the AAA to be unconstitutional. Congress immediately crafted new legislation to replace the Agricultural Adjustment Act. The new law, the Soil Conservation and Domestic Allotment Act, passed in 1936. It had the same general objectives of the 1933 legislation, but instead of providing direct subsidies to farmers to make up for the low prices, the new law required farmers to reduce acreage of their crops and plant the diverted acres to soil-building or soil-conserving crops. In effect, the US government was "renting" land from US farmers and planting it to crops that held the soil in place but did not produce food. A slightly modified version of the law, the Agricultural Adjustment Act, appeared in 1938.

By 1938, Europe was once again preparing for war and needed food from the United States. Export demand increased and prices rose to levels that eliminated the need for special subsidies or land renting plans. The European war soon became a world war that brought high prices for commodities and new wealth to US farmers.

The 1930s and the New Deal brought huge changes to US farm policy. It tightened the way of handling farm credit, it found a way to limit production during times of surplus, it resettled farmers from sub-marginal lands, it moved toward international trade agreements and away from stifling tariffs, it introduced crop insurance, and generally made "life in the country" more appealing than it had been in earlier years. The major result of this New Deal activity was that government would forever after be directly involved with farming in the United States. In most respects, the farmers as individuals and as organizations would watch the policies and the changes with great care, but they would rather have the government involved than not involved. Interestingly, only some farmers are subsidized: mainly producers of grains such as wheat and corn. Fruit and vegetable producers are not subsidized, and meat producers do not receive subsidies. Farm subsidies have been resilient, and appear to be a permanent feature of the agricultural sector.

The increased use of chemical fertilizer

During the 200 years between Eli Whitney's game-changing invention of the cotton gin and the federal government's expanding the number of irrigated acres, hundreds of technological advances were introduced to farming. Horses replaced humans as a source of power, steam replaced horses, and petroleum fuels replaced steam. The increased understanding of the nutrient needs of plants and the possible addition of more than the plants' natural needs of these nutrients followed during the same general time. The inventions and discoveries were at first much less spectacular and perhaps less well understood. Chemists, horticulturists, and others knew of plant's nutrient needs as early as the nineteenth century or even before. Although plants, like other living things, need a wide variety of nutrients, plants respond well to applications of nitrogen, phosphorous, and potassium.[15] While these elements are available in nature, it is reasonably easy to increase their availability as a plant nutrient by applying additional amounts of them using "commercial fertilizer," either as a powder or in liquid form; sometimes alone and sometimes in combination. Careful application of the nutrients can result in increased plant growth and a larger harvest.

Justus von Liebig (1803–1873), a German chemist, is given credit for being the first modern scientist to devote his life's work to plant growth and plant nutrition. Working in the early nineteenth century, Liebig isolated the major elements needed for plant growth and found that nitrogen most often yielded the greatest response when applied to growing plants.

John Bennett Lawes, an English businessman/chemist contributed to the knowledge of artificial fertilizers as early as 1837 by treating phosphates with sulfuric acid before applying the mixture to experimental plots. He patented his discovery before going on to a half-century more of plant nutrition experiments (Russell, 1926). Two Norwegian industrialists began commercial production of nitrogen in 1903 using a method developed by Henry Cavendish in 1784. The Cavendish method depended on large amounts of electricity to produce nitric acid then used as the source of nitrates – the chemical product useable by plants. Phosphorus is as essential as the others are to plant growth, but it appears more often in nature and it requires less complicated processes to make the natural phosphate rock into material suitable for agricultural applications. Table 2.1 shows the quantities (in short tons) of these three major plant nutrients sold as commercial fertilizers in the US in selected years over the last half-century. Since 1960, nitrogen sales have soared while the sale of the other two nutrients have remained somewhat stable.

The use of commercial (chemical) fertilizers carries with it some dangers. Not only can the chemicals be unstable and subject to accident, but they instill in some consumers the idea that food crops that have been treated with these chemicals have been "altered" and are sometimes unfit – or at least dangerous – for human consumption. This possibility has helped increase the public's interest in organic foods and has resulted in some of the polarization between producers who want the increased output that comes from the use of chemical fertilizer and consumers who fear that the application of nitrogen, phosphorous, or potassium might make the plants or their fruit inedible or dangerous for human consumption. Put another way, it helps to pit conventional producers against organic producers of today's food crops.

This line of reasoning can be extended. During several decades of increased knowledge and increased use of fertilizers, crop and livestock producers have adopted other chemical-based products in their efforts to eradicate pests – insects, weeds, and crop diseases. This non-fertilizer form of agrochemical application goes by the generic term "pesticides," and while some pesticides have been used for decades, most are products of the last half-century. Consumers continue to be wary of pesticides and the increasing use of these agrochemicals has intensified the animosities among the food producers, the consumers, and the industrial manufacturers who supply the world's farmers with chemicals.

TABLE 2.1 US consumption of plant nutrients (1000 short tons)

Year	Nitrogen	Phosphate	Potash	Total
1960	2,738	2,572	2,513	7,464
1970	7,459	4,574	4,036	16,068
1980	11,407	5,432	6,245	23,083
1990	11,076	4,345	5,203	20,624
2000	12,334	4,314	4,972	21,616
2010	12,285	4,099	4,458	20,843

Source: US Department of Agriculture Economic Research Service (USDA/ERS) (2014) *Fertilizer Use and Price*, www.ers.usda.gov/data-products/fertilizer-use-and-price.aspx, accessed 5 May 2014.

Genetically modified plants and seeds

Even without fertilizers and pesticides, plants and animals change over time. For millions of years, nature has had a method of helping living things adapt to their surroundings. Examples include the giraffe, which grew to amazing heights, and the butterfly, which adopted the coloration of its environment as a means of protection from predators. In agriculture, selective breeding, which as a practical matter is little more than a way of helping nature speed the adaptation process of animals, yielded the Holstein–Friesian cow to produce huge quantities of milk while breeding the Jersey cow yielded an animal that produced smaller quantities of milk laced with large amounts of butterfat. The plant world is much the same. The domestication of wild plants has taken place for centuries. Selective breeding helped turn the descendants of the primitive corn *teosinte* into the full-eared sweet corn as well as the starchy field corn so prominent in today's agriculture.

These changes have been the product of nature, but humans, in their eagerness to speed changes and to improve most every part of the environment, have spent much time and effort working to make plants and animals fit with the needs and desires of people. This was traditionally done through careful selective breeding and the use of improved health and nutritional enhancements for a selected part of Earth's huge number of living things. At about the mid-point of the twentieth century, plant scientists who had been taken from their usual work by economic depression and world war, returned to their efforts to gain additional understanding of genes and the traits that pass from one generation to the next.

This study of genetics began as early as the late 1860s, yet it was not until the mid-1950s that the DNA chain was fully enough understood to allow experiments that changed the nature of the DNA chain as a means of altering some aspect of the chain's host.

An early agricultural application of this "transgene technique" focused on the tomato. Tomatoes are widely grown and appreciated for their flavor, texture, and color. Tomatoes grown on commercial tomato farms, however, are sometimes difficult to handle because they are fragile: they have a short shelf life because they lose their firmness and begin to break down a very few days after harvest.

In 1992, Calgene, a biotechnology research firm in Davis, California, made genetic changes on the tomato and produced what it called the Flavr-savr tomato. It was submitted to the US Food and Drug Administration (FDA) for testing and was approved for commercial sale in May 1994. It became the first genetically modified (often referred to as "GMOs" standing for Genetically Modified Organisms) food product approved for sale in the United States. The tomato was marked as "modified" and generated some resistance among potential buyers even though there was no evidence that the Flavr-savr harmed anyone. Calgene – quite apart from the tomato – did not survive as a research firm. Monsanto purchased it in 1996 and the Flavr-savr itself was taken off the market in 1997.

In spite of its short life, the Flavr-savr has the honor of being the first genetically modified agricultural commodity sold on the open market. Many others followed.

An increasing number of bioresearch firms began to concentrate on agricultural inputs and products such as the "Roundup Ready" seeds that became available for corn, soybeans, and cotton. While consumers in the United States were generally accepting of the new modified products, people in other parts of the world held skeptical views about the safety of the modified products. This skepticism led to several European nations refusing to purchase modified products from the US. In the spring of 2013, artificially modified wheat grown on an Oregon farm was found in a grain storage elevator just prior to shipment to Europe. FDA inspectors and experts could not identify the farm that produced the GMO crop, and no farmer or seed company ever stepped forward with information relating to the seed's origin. Since Europe is a major buyer of the Pacific Northwest's soft white wheat, the discovery of modified wheat ready for sale became an important international issue.

Skepticism of this kind has continued, but two themes remain: (1) genetic research and plant modification will continue to be present among seed and processing firms; and (2) given the extensive testing that has gone before, it seems unlikely that future modified agricultural products will pose a health threat for consumers. Recent developments in genetically modified food are further explored in Box 9.3 and Box 10.5.

Summary and conclusions

Agriculture began approximately 10,000 years ago, and until the past 100 to 150 years, change did not occur rapidly. Agriculture moved into new areas and quickly adapted to or overcame the area's problems and limitations. Beginning with the industrial revolution, agriculture became increasingly productive, through the innovation and application of labor-saving technological changes. These innovations, including mechanization and the use of modern inputs such as chemicals and fertilizer, allowed an increasing number of farmers to transition into nonfarming occupations. Indeed, when the US was formed, approximately 90 percent of all persons were employed in production agriculture. Today, less than one percent of the US population produces food, as is true in high-income nations throughout the world.

Two characteristics of technological change in agriculture are sources of dispute and potentially polarizing views: (1) productivity growth puts downward pressure on agricultural prices; and (2) labor-saving technological change requires occupational and societal changes as society becomes less rural and more urban. New innovations such as the plow, combine, and cotton gin provided more food and more fiber. This, coupled with increases in the amount of land cultivated during westward expansion of the US, resulted in an abundance of food relative to demand. Prices for agricultural products have been low during many of the past 150 years. As a result, farm family incomes were often lower than nonfarm family incomes. Necessary changes in occupation, while most often voluntary, have been disruptive as farmers sought gainful employment in nonfarm jobs. The lower rates of return, combined with the substitution of machines and chemicals for workers, resulted in opposing viewpoints, as major societal changes often do.

Change is disruptive, and agriculture, perhaps more than any other sector of the economy, has been characterized by rapid and persistent change. Horses replaced workers, and machines replaced horses and more workers. Plant nutrients were developed and included in the production practices of food and fiber. New ways of doing things are controversial: farmers believed that a plow could poison the soil. These controversies always accompany progress, and as the benefits of innovations become widely accepted, the controversy lessens, only to be replaced by new controversies surrounding a new set of innovations.

All new ideas, innovations, and ways of doing things have both benefits and costs. Progress occurs when technologies with larger benefits replace those with lower levels of benefits, or higher costs. Viewed in this way, polarization due to the disputes that surround change has a needed purpose as a prerequisite for growth, advancement, and progress. The history of agriculture in the US and throughout the world demonstrates that continual productivity gains have occurred due to the adoption, discussion, and use of polarizing ideas, farming practices, and food choices.

Notes

1 For a brief explanation of the beginning of agriculture, see the opening chapter of Wunderlich (2011).
2 By 1611, the immigrants had imported horses, oxen, cows, goats, and pigs. The Native Americans did not adopt these animals. Pigs were readily accepted by the colonists, and released to the forests to become available for anyone to capture.
3 Prior to the American Revolution, Spain claimed East Florida while Britain claimed the Western part. The Western (British) areas became part of the United States' claims during the Treaty of Paris (1783), and the Adams-Onis Treaty made the Spanish claims in Florida a part of the United States in 1819.
4 Although the legal description of this political boundary is complicated, a practical view of it shows it to follow the East–West border that separates Pennsylvania from West Virginia and Maryland and the North–South border between Delaware and Maryland. For decades, it was a shortcut method of dividing the nation into the "Free North" and the "Slave South."
5 The word "engine" describes many kinds of power-driven machines. "Gin," a shortened form of "engine," is often used in this context. The early cotton gins were small, hand-cranked devices with one worker turning the crank while a second worker fed in cotton bolls and swept away the cleaned cotton fibers.
6 In the marketplace, cotton is measured in "bales," large, tightly compressed, and burlap-wrapped bundles weighing approximately 500 pounds.
7 For a detailed discussion of development of the grain drill from antiquity until the 1930s, see Anderson (1936).
8 Picking cotton proved to be an exception. A mechanical cotton picker did not appear until 1926 when a moderately successful "cotton stripper" was used in the cotton fields of the Plains States. A truly successful machine did not appear until 1942.
9 This was frequently referred to as the second revolution for American agriculture, the first being the replacement of the workforce (handwork) by the horse in the first decade following the Civil War.
10 In addition to these general farm organizations and groups, individual commodity organizations and societies became popular during the twentieth century and later. At this time, nearly 200 such societies exist in the United States.

11 The Report of the Commission on Country Life was printed and made available to the public with a sub-title, "Special Message from the President of the United States Transmitting the Report of the Country Life Commission."

12 The McNary–Haugen proposal came from an idea advanced in 1922 by George N. Peek and Hugh H. Johnson, both high corporate officers in the Moline Plow Company of Moline, Illinois (Peek and Johnson, 1922).

13 The Agricultural Adjustment Act of 1933 had three titles. Title I was the popular and much analyzed Agricultural Adjustment Act, Title II was the Emergency Farm Mortgage Act of 1933, and Title III was a complex and broadly based effort to stabilize the value of money in the economy.

14 Some of the increase in farm prices and income was the result of low rainfall in important growing areas.

15 These three chemical elements are so important in the commercial fertilizer industry that the industry identifies them by their chemical abbreviations N, P, and K. Mixed fertilizers take their names or identities by the percentage of each element in the mix. A fertilizer identified as "16-8-4" contains materials that yield 16 percent available nitrogen, 8 percent available phosphorous and 4 percent available potassium, and likely some inert "filler" to make the chemicals easier to handle.

3

MARKETS AND POLARIZATION

> Consumption is the sole end and purpose of all production; and the interest of the producer ought to be attended to, only so far as it may be necessary for promoting that of the consumer.
>
> Adam Smith, *An Inquiry into the Nature and Causes of the Wealth of Nations* (1776)

Introduction

This chapter describes and explains the simple mechanics of a market-based economy, focusing on individual participants upgrading and improving production practices and responding to decisions made in the food and agricultural sectors. The market system of economic organization is a powerful human institution. Market-based economies are frequently characterized by high national incomes, a vast array of consumer choices, rapid economic growth, and innovation. In many countries, such economies have resulted in unprecedented levels of quality of life, together with increased longevity. These enormously favorable features of market-based economies go largely unnoticed and unappreciated. Nor is that all: market capitalism is subject to constant and forceful criticism from outside observers, as well as from citizens whose lives have been improved by the free markets. How can this apparent contradiction be reconciled? A move toward reconciliation invites people to "think like an economist." This phrase refers to recognizing that there are benefits and costs associated with everything, from the simplest decision to purchase a soda rather than a coffee to complex societal choices such as choosing the type of transportation system for a metropolitan area, and even to deciding the kind of economic system to use in guiding the performance of the overall economy. If a market economy is chosen, markets can bring long-term benefits, but often require short-term changes that may be undesired, disruptive, and polarizing.

BOX 3.1: THE ROLE OF POLARIZATION IN POLITICAL AND ECONOMIC SYSTEMS

The most important societal decisions are arguably the selection of a political system and an economic system. Therefore, the most highly polarized issues often surround these decisions. Millions of individuals and groups have lost their lives fighting about these decisions, and uncounted numbers of books have been written about the best and worst features of political and economic systems. Winston Churchill, the prime minister of Great Britain during the mid-twentieth century, concluded: "It has been said that democracy is the worst form of government except all the others that have been tried."[1] All real-world political systems have a large number of strengths and weaknesses, and democracy is no exception. Polarization in democracies can lead to dysfunctional outcomes, stalemates, and the inability to move forward on important issues.

Freedom of speech is an important component of an effective democratic nation. Quoting Churchill again: "Criticism may not be agreeable, but it is necessary. It fulfills the same function as pain in the human body. It calls attention to an unhealthy state of things."[2] A true democracy will have constant detractors, who strive to improve living conditions. At times, criticism, dissatisfaction, and demonstrations can give the impression that democracy, as a system, is at fault. Polarized policy debates, however, can lead to improved outcomes, through debate, sometimes rancorous, and at times impolite. Divided opinions and strife over divisive political issues are endemic to democracy, for it is through discussion, debate, and disagreement that continuous improvement occurs.

Citizens of nations with democratic political systems and market-based economies are in a continuous state of dissatisfaction: things could be better. A culture and ethos of constant improvement is bolstered by, and requires, ubiquitous and unending dissatisfaction with the status quo. When workers, firms, and leaders are satisfied, improvement comes to a halt. Change is replaced by stasis, innovation with inertia, and growth with the "tyranny of the status quo." To most individuals, this is unacceptable. The current state of affairs includes difficulties including hunger, environmental challenges, poverty, substance abuse, and war. To halt all criticism of the world would be accepting these issues as they are. Most citizens throughout the world are hopeful that the future will be better than the present, just as the present is an improvement over the past.

Individuals who live in a nation based on liberty are free to disagree with others, and be critical of their leaders, often making polarization and dissent the norm. Opposition to outcomes of democracy and capitalism lead to criticism of the institutions themselves. Dislike of economic inequality and poverty gave political thinkers such as Karl Marx, and leaders Mao Zedong, Fidel Castro, and others the desire to replace market-based economic systems with centralized economic systems, often called socialism or communism.[3]

Economists often warn critics of the market system that alternatives to markets are often worse than the system they seek to improve. Socialism and communism, like all political and economic systems, have benefits and costs, strengths and weaknesses. These alternatives to capitalism often have higher levels of equality, but at the expense of economic freedom and high levels of economic innovation and growth. To date, available evidence suggests that market-based economies result in outcomes that are likely to resolve a greater number of societal issues than other economic systems. It is often easier to resolve human wants and needs with higher levels of income than at lower levels. Leaders in China recognized this, and have moved their economy towards a market-based system in recent decades.

Polarized issues are important components to both democratic political systems and market-based economic systems. Debate, deliberation, and change are necessary components of a growing, improving, innovating economy. Paradoxically, the security and relative comfort of high national incomes are borne out of constant improvement in how we do things, often embodied by strife and disagreement. Polarization of economic issues in food and agriculture, while sometimes costly in the short term, is normal, healthy, and desirable in the long run. Over time, controversial issues will lead to superior outcomes, more desirable food products, less hunger, and healthier environments and ecosystems.

As big issues in agriculture and food are resolved, new issues appear. This is particularly true during periods of rapid change. When new things are discovered, innovations are adopted, and ideas are formed, the back and forth nature of human interaction is what leads to continuous improvement. In a diverse, growing, and well-functioning economy, citizens and workers often will be critical of many products, ways of doing things, and social outcomes of the market system.

BOX 3.2: CHINA'S HOUSEHOLD RESPONSIBILITY SYSTEM

Mao Zedong, the leader of the communist revolution in China, brought communism to China on October 1, 1949. Under Mao, the Chinese built a system that combined political ideology, economic production, and social control. The government maintained direct control over both agricultural and industrial production. In the 1950s and 1960s, the economic policies led to shortages, famine, and dislocation (Guthrie, 2012). Beginning in early 1981, China implemented its "household responsibility system," which allowed farmers to retain a part of their earnings from the sale of their agricultural products (Chung, 2000; Fewsmith, 1994). This policy departed from the long-standing communist policy of turning over all proceeds to the government.

By providing an economic incentive to produce food, the policy worked so well that China rose from a position of food dependency to one of near total self-sufficiency in food production. By 2000, China had become a low-cost producer of many vegetables. Continued investment in the sector resulted in products that were competitive in world markets (Shields and Tuan, 2001).

This was just the beginning. US food imports from China more than tripled in value between 2001 and 2008 (Gale and Buzby, 2009). The household responsibility system worked exceedingly well, and was subsequently adopted not only in agriculture, but also in many other sectors of the Chinese economy. The gains to farmers in China have been large, and China has gone from a subsistence-level economy to a middle-income economy in a relatively short time: approximately 30 years. Fruit and vegetable producers in other nations such as the US have faced competition from low production costs in Chinese agriculture.

For the past decade, the Chinese economy has been growing at the phenomenal rate of over 10 percent each year. Gross National Income per capita has increased from $220 in 1981 to $5,740 in 2012 (World Bank, 2013). This remarkable, unprecedented economic growth can be traced directly to the movement from a centralized economic system to a market-based system. In 2013, the Chinese Communist Party held the Third Plenum, a meeting of the governing "central committee," where it presented a 60-point document that provided a blueprint for future political and economic changes, continuing gains in individual freedom and economic rights (Browne, 2013).

Historical evolution of a circular flow economy

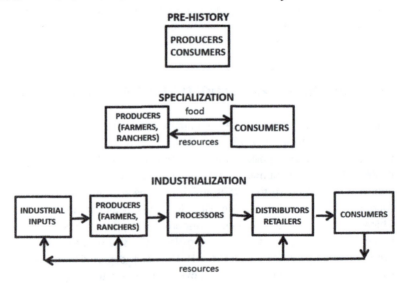

FIGURE 3.1 Historical evolution of a circular flow economy

The relationship between consumer desires and producer behavior is shown in Figure 3.1. During "pre-history," humans as individuals or families were largely self-sufficient. Consumption was determined by what the family, clan, or tribe produced through hunting, gathering, conquest, or later, agriculture. Specialization brought about a separation between production and consumption. In a primitive sense, consumers provided resources such as labor and trade goods to producers (farmers and ranchers), and the producers supplied food to the consumers. The circular flow of resources and food shows the interdependence of producers' well-being with consumers' desires. The connection is immediate and obvious: provision of highly desired goods (food) to consumers yields the greatest benefits.

Industrialization, the result of invention, discovery, and innovation, brought increasing levels of specialization to the food and agricultural sector and allowed the sector to produce more and different kinds of food as well as nonfood items – perhaps cloth or simple tools.

Today's industrial agriculture has followed a similar path by adding inputs such as chemicals, fertilizer, and machinery. These inputs to food production are generally produced by large corporations and sold to farmers and ranchers who, in turn, provide raw foods to processors, often large food corporations such as Kraft, ConAgra, or Beatrice. Retailers and distributors complete the circular flow through specialized and concentrated supermarket chains: Kroger, Safeway, and Walmart, who sell daily food needs to consumers. Different nations and different cultures organize their economy in different ways. We will explore these differences in the next section.

Market economies, command economies, and mixed economies

A "market economy" is an economy characterized by market interactions where resources and goods are allocated by prices. In contrast, a "command economy" is defined as an economy characterized by command and control, in which resources are allocated by whoever is in charge, whether it be a dictator, or a committee of appointed experts, or democratically elected officials. The characteristics of each of these two extreme cases of economic organization are explored below. In reality, the two polar cases are hypothetical, since market-based economies have high levels of government involvement, and command economies have many features of market systems. Thus, as a practical matter, all real-world economic systems are "mixed economies," that combine features of markets and government regulation and services. Large potential societal gains come from markets (high incomes and economic growth), as do costs of disruption, change, and income inequality (Piketty and Goldhammer, 2014). The benefits of markets come at a cost, and the costs lead to polarization of views and opinions on political and economic issues. The weaknesses and limitations of markets are presented and evaluated in later chapters of the book.

Market economies and consumer sovereignty

"Consumer sovereignty" is the foundation of market systems since consumer preferences determine the production of goods and services. The firms that do the best job of providing what consumers desire will be the most successful. Producers, firms, and distribution networks all respond to consumer wants and desires. Moreover, in a market economy, producers' activities must remain consistent with consumer demands (or desires), or firms will face going out of business. It is often argued that big firms such as Microsoft, Walmart, and McDonald's are bad for the economy and bad for consumers. In many ways, this is not the case in a competitive market economy with many choices of where to shop. The firms that earn the largest revenues from product sales provide evidence that consumers desire products from these large producers and sellers. While it is true that organizational and administrative problems may exist within each of these huge firms, just as they exist in firms of all sizes, it remains true that the firms must be doing something right, or they would not sell so much software, groceries and household goods, hamburgers, fries, and other products. In many cases, the most profitable firms are the ones that are most successful at dealing with market changes.

In a market-based economy, people earn a living by helping others (Gwartney *et al.*, 2005). Individuals and firms will be successful only if they provide others (customers) with goods and services that the customers value, at quality levels and at costs that they prefer. Gwartney *et al.* (2005) suggest that people in a market system will develop skills and acquire knowledge to help others, rather than exploit others. This is Adam Smith's greatest insight about market economies: through their own self-interest, citizens increase the welfare of others (Smith, 1776). The sum total of all market transactions provides for the highest level of society well-being.

Why do markets work?

Voluntary exchange is the cornerstone of markets. In a truly free market, no individual is coerced into buying or selling anything. Thus, all exchanges are mutually beneficial with buyer and seller benefitting from every transaction. Trade would not occur if this were not the case. An economy based on free markets is not coordinated by any central authority, but rather by the aggregation of independent decisions made by all individuals – buyers and sellers – in the market. The market price of a good contains all of the relevant information about how much it costs to produce the good (supply) and how much consumers are willing (and able) to pay for the good (demand). In this way, economic activity is coordinated. Some examples of this coordinating task may be helpful.

- Bad weather (sometimes too hot, sometimes too cold) in the Great Plains region of the US often results in a shortage of corn. If this occurs, the price of corn will increase as consumers (cattle feedlots, poultry producers, and pork producers) bid up the price. This increase in price causes grain producers to plant more acres of corn to capture the higher prices. To the extent possible, consumers will shift purchases out of corn-based products and into others: sorghum (also called milo), soybeans, and hay. Over time these changes (market forces) will bring the price of corn back down. This form of market coordination, based on the decentralized, impersonal actions of a large number of producers and consumers, is how markets work.

- Imagine the difficulty of a government attempting to plan and manage a large, interconnected economy that is subject to rapid changes in technology (or in weather). This is what the former Soviet Union (USSR) and Mao's People's Republic of China (PRC) tried to do, each with disastrous consequences.
- After the Cold War, West Germany was a successful, high-income, market-oriented nation. East Germany was subject to a centralized command economy. In 1961, an impregnable wall was built between these two nations to stop the flow of people and goods from East to West, due to the enormous differences in economic freedom, political freedom, and incomes.
- Following the Korean War, North Korea was subject to a communist system, while South Korea became a market-based economy. In the following decades, South Korea became a high-income nation, while North Korea has some of the worst hunger and poverty issues in the world. A large, complex modern economy will face difficulties if decisions are made by bureaucrats instead of consumers and producers.

Resource allocation and coordination in a market-based economy

One of the major difficulties of a centralized economy is coping with the changes that occur in a dynamic and rapidly-growing economy. All economic systems struggle to deal effectively with rapid change, since new ways of doing things require movement of workers, job displacement, and uncertainty. Francis Fukuyama in his 1992 book *The End of History and the Last Man* observed, "For capitalism flourishes best in a mobile and egalitarian society" (p. 120). In a market-based economy the market and price fluctuations act to coordinate new developments in a way that places high value on individual freedom. Workers in a declining industry can make their own decision about when to shift jobs. Change can be difficult, particularly for individuals and families who have a tradition of a certain job or profession. Unfortunately, such changes can lead to polarization. In a market economy, changing technologies and consumer desires require all firms to deal effectively with change. How does a decentralized, free market system coordinate economic activity?

Competitive firms must give consumers what they want, whether it is locally produced organic tofu or double cheeseburgers, or both.[4] Firms in a market economy must always and forever attempt to develop products that are closer to the moving target of consumer desires. Through these incentives, competition results in business structures and firm sizes that minimize production costs. Note that a market system does not necessarily favor the existence of either large or small firms. When consumers place high value on personalized service and individualized products, they are able to purchase high-quality goods provided by small firms such as hair styling in salons, locally produced foods, personal trainers and baristas. Giving customers what they want is central to understanding the current structure of food and agriculture in the market economy of the global food economy where a large number of small independent farms, agribusiness firms, and food retailers coexist and compete, often successfully, with a small number of large multinational corporations.

A market-based economy is flexible enough to accommodate any style of agricultural production, including communes, corporate farms, family farms, urban food, or however individuals choose to produce food. This is most often not the case in a command, or centralized, economic system. In a market-based economy, the structure of agriculture, and the type of production system, is a free choice among the producers and potential producers of food. Many people, both within and outside of the agricultural community, desire to set limits on the type and structure of food and agricultural businesses. Those who favor local and sustainable farm practices often oppose industrial agriculture, and large corporations often oppose movements toward small, local, and sustainable food production methods. A strength of a market-based economy is that consumers will have the ability to purchase food with the characteristics that they desire. Given the huge diversity of people, cultures, economic status, and tastes in a large economic system, this is a positive outcome of an economic system. In China, Mao's vision included small communes and self-sufficiency. The former Soviet Union (USSR) used large communes and attempts at large-scale efficiency. Both of these agricultural systems were based on centralized decision making, which proved very difficult to sustain in nations with large and diverse populations and regions. This difficulty becomes acute when rapid technological change occurs. This may have contributed to the dissolution of the USSR and the movement towards markets in China.

The profit motive is an often-maligned feature of market-based economic systems. However, higher profits are associated with products most desired by consumers, efficient ways of doing things, and continuous innovations. Firms that can find ways to produce goods at lower cost will earn more money, providing a strong incentive to lower production costs. Lower costs translate into lower prices for consumers, allowing individuals and families to purchase more goods with the same amount of money. This outcome transforms the lives of many people throughout the world from subsistence levels to higher income levels. Competition among firms, coupled with the profit motive, lead to ever-decreasing prices and ever-increasing quantities of many consumer goods over time. Automobiles continue to improve over time, with stronger tires, improved airbags, and other useful features. Air travel has become more affordable to travelers (US Department of Transportation, 2013), and food has become both cheaper and of higher quality (Gerrior *et al.*, 2004; Putnam and Allshouse, 1999). In pre-historic times, when *homo sapiens* emerged, a majority of time was spent hunting and gathering food. Even as recently as 1776, when the US was founded, over 90 percent of the population of the US was employed in production agriculture (Curley, 2005).

Today, farmers comprise less than 2 percent of the population of most high-income nations (World Bank, 2013), and less than 10 percent of the income is spent on food. The transformation from an economy based on agriculture, to industrialization, and later to a post-industrial economy based mainly on services, is primarily due to the profit motive: farmers and ranchers have become productive and efficient over time, due to their desire to increase profits.

Competition forces all business firms to keep up, innovate, improve, or get out of the industry. Therefore, competition requires constant change in a market economy. It is little wonder that market-based economic systems are criticized: at any given time, significant portions of the population are being forced to innovate, adopt, change careers, or otherwise adjust to new market situations, new products, and new ways of doing things. Polarization is endemic to a market-based economic system.

Price changes

The market system is characterized by change: new products, new inputs, and new ways of doing things. Not only are changes due to innovation and technological improvements, but market changes occur every second of every day. Prices are buffeted up and down based on changing market conditions. For example, a freeze in Florida causes the price of orange juice to increase; bad weather in Brazil results in high coffee prices; violence in the Middle East results in higher oil prices. Agriculture is particularly vulnerable to changes in oil prices, since modern, large-scale farming is a fuel-intensive process. Farmers use a great deal of diesel and gasoline to propel tractors, combines, planters, hay balers, and other farm equipment. But that is not all. Modern agriculture uses large quantities of fertilizer and agricultural chemicals. Fertilizer is produced using natural gas, and agricultural chemicals are derived from petroleum products. Therefore, as oil prices rise, production costs increase significantly in large-scale conventional food and fiber production.

In a market economy, all economic decisions are based on relative prices: how prices change relative to the prices of other goods. Intense polarization in food markets often results from the simple outcome characterized by price movements: every price change will benefit some, and result in economic harm to others. Producers (sellers) benefit from price increases, whereas consumers (buyers) are hurt by the same price increase. The simple idea that price changes are good for some and bad for others can explain a great deal of polarization … yet, this is how effective markets function. When price movements harm individuals and groups financially, there will often be criticism of the market, other stakeholders in the market, and the government.

Relative prices change when one price moves in relation to the prices of related goods. Related goods are ones that influence the purchase and sale of the good under investigation. Perhaps a description of the biofuel economy is the best way to demonstrate how price changes affect individuals and groups in food and agricultural markets.

BOX 3.3: THE IMPACT OF BIOFUELS ON FOOD AND AGRICULTURE

Biofuels are fuels derived from biological carbon fixation, such as ethanol made from fermented grain and biodiesel made from vegetable oils or animal fats. Biofuels have become more widespread in recent years, due to higher oil prices, the desire for energy independence, concern over climate change caused by emissions of greenhouse gases associated with fossil fuels, and support from government subsidies. In 2013, the production of ethanol fuel consumed 4.9 billion bushels of corn, or 42.6 percent of corn use in the US (Capehart, 2013). The huge and growing ethanol industry is recent. In 2000, only 8 percent of the US corn crop was used to produce ethanol.

The large increase in ethanol production resulted from a large number of ethanol plants built near corn-producing regions in the US, bolstering the local economy by hiring construction firms and their workers. The large increase in ethanol production led to a large increase in the demand for corn, and subsequently the price of corn increased. Corn has many "related" goods. High corn prices provide incentives for corn farmers to plant more acres of corn. Corn acreage has increased through adjustments to crop rotations between corn and soybeans, which has caused soybean acreage to decrease. Since soybeans are increasingly scarce, the price of soybeans has increased. The other major use of corn is livestock feeding. In 2013, 44.8 percent of the corn crop was used for feed (Capehart, 2013). As corn was diverted out of livestock feed to ethanol, the demand for alternative livestock feeds, including sorghum (milo), oats, and barley increased. The prices of these crops have increased dramatically since 2005, when ethanol production began its rapid increase. The situation with biodiesel is similar. Biodiesel is most often made from soybeans, placing greater demand pressure on soybeans. These changes in the crop market have resulted in historically high grain prices. The agricultural economy is booming as farmers attempt to keep up with the increased demands.

Not all sectors of the agricultural economy benefit from the large shift into biofuels. The livestock industry must now pay historically high prices for grain, the major ingredient to beef, pork, and poultry production. This increase in production costs has financially harmed the meat industry. The beverage and candy industries have also been adversely affected: corn usage has been shifted out of high fructose corn syrup (HFCS) production to meet the growing demand for ethanol. Agribusinesses that sell inputs to crop producers are also major beneficiaries of ethanol: higher grain prices result in greater sales of fertilizer, chemicals, seeds, machinery, and land. The shift to ethanol has also harmed overseas corn consumers. The crop is now used domestically and is not available for export.

Perhaps most interestingly, government programs and policies have been the main driver in all of these changes in corn and related markets (Capehart, 2013). Government policies have made HFCS an economic alternative to sugar through import fees, duties, and import quotas on sugar. Recent federal environmental laws have resulted in the boom in corn ethanol production. Many of the market impacts of biofuels will be further investigated in the following chapters.

Market changes in agriculture often lead to economic hardship, which can lead to controversy. Price changes have large impacts on nearly all firms in a market-based economy, and the mitigation of price risk is a large and growing industry. Risk management provides market-based tools such as futures market contracts, hedging, and forward pricing to alleviate unexpected price swings. Price changes are often due to market forces, or changes in the supply and demand of a product. A great deal of polarization in food and agriculture is based simply on the economic outcomes of market changes: producers and consumers favor innovations and price changes that favor them and oppose new conditions that cause economic hardship to them. The greater the magnitude of the technological or market change, the larger the reaction. When price movements are large, stakeholders who are adversely affected often seek government assistance. This is investigated further in Chapter 7.

Numerous policy groups working with agricultural problems provide evidence and research results to demonstrate that agricultural and food prices are either "too high" or "too low." Analysts and philanthropic organizations concerned with obesity often suggest that food prices are "too low," resulting in overconsumption (Pollan, 2007, 2008b; Popkin, 2009; Tillotson, 2004). Other individuals and groups worried about global hunger charge that food prices may be "too high," reducing access to food for hungry individuals and families (Angelo, 2012; Gale, 2014). Rickard *et al.* (2013) have shown that agricultural commodity prices have little effect on food consumption.

Corn producers earned record profits during the 2008–2013 crop years, but cattle producers suffered due to a large increase in the price of the major input to grain-fed beef: corn. This is one example of an ongoing, pervasive feature of life in a market-based economy: change. Economists typically recommend allowing the market to function, meaning no government intervention in response to market-based price changes. As the food and agricultural economies have become globalized, and subject to price risk from international sources, economists recommend risk management strategies to reduce the potential adverse impacts of price volatility.

What should be done about price volatility? Government interventions, in the form or price ceilings and/or price supports, often lead to unintended and undesirable consequences (Timmer, 1986). Specifically, price ceilings, or laws that mandate prices lower than market prices, lead to shortages, since the incentive to produce the product is diminished. Price supports, or laws that increase prices above market levels, typically lead to surpluses. An example is the European Union (EU) after World War II, where large agricultural price supports led to enormous surpluses of food and agricultural products that eventually went to other countries at subsidized rates (Johnson, 1991). Even though government action may produce price distortions that lead to surpluses or shortages, government continues to play an important and useful role in the food and agricultural sectors of any economy.

Limits to markets

Economists have identified five situations where competitive markets may not work well.

* Monopoly, also called, market power
* Externality
* Public goods
* Imperfect knowledge, and
* Income inequality.

Markets work in general, but are subject to limitations. A great deal of this book describes how limitations to market-based economies influence the causes, consequences, and potential solutions of polarized issues in food and agriculture.

The first four of these limitations are often referred to as "market failures," or situations where markets do not serve the public interest. The final limitation, income inequality, is an outcome of markets (Wilde, 2013). Monopoly power, also called market power, refers to a situation in which a single firm is large enough relative to a market to influence the market price. A true monopoly, or single firm in a market, has no rivals so competition does not exist. A firm with market power can charge a price higher than the cost of production, (analyzed extensively in Chapter 6). This situation occurs in agricultural and food markets when firms become so large that they dominate their industry.

An externality is defined as a situation in which one person affects another party through nonmarket actions. A positive externality occurs when one person's actions benefit others, such as a beekeeper's positive impact on fruit, nut, and some vegetable production. A negative externality occurs when one person's actions harm others, such as water pollution that occurs when agricultural chemicals and fertilizers used in one farmer's fields floods over into a neighbor's fields and damages the crops. Externalities are carefully evaluated in Chapter 7. Many of the major polarized issues in agriculture stem from externalities. Environmental issues associated with modern agricultural production techniques such as chemical and fertilizer use are examples.

The term "public good" has a specific definition in economics: a good that is nonexcludable (anyone can use it) and nonrivalous (one individual's consumption of the good does not affect the amount of the good available for another person's consumption). Examples of public goods are radio signals, roads (to a certain degree), lighthouses, and national defense. Public goods would not exist at the most useful quantities if they were not provided by the government or by group action. Thus, public goods are an exception to the well-functioning markets, thoroughly detailed in Chapter 7. Markets work well with abundant and inexpensive information. Imperfect knowledge is considered a market failure, and is highly important in food markets. Food consumers do not know many characteristics of their purchases, and have to rely on information provided by the producer or seller. Food qualities such as production and processing methods, and food safety attributes are subject to limited information being available to buyers (Chapter 10).

Poverty in a market-based economy

Poverty and income inequality are undesirable, unintended features of market-based economies (Chetty *et al.*, 2014). Inequality is an outcome of capitalism that receives an understandable degree of criticism. Piketty and Goldhammer (2014) have recently summarized and popularized an analysis of the causes and consequences of income inequality. In the United States, during 2011, there were 46.2 million people in poverty, and the official poverty rate was 15 percent (US Bureau of the Census, 2013b). Recent research demonstrates that social mobility has remained stable in the US since 1970 (Chetty *et al.*, 2014). Although poverty and inequality are not directly associated with the topic of this book, there are several important related issues. These include access to food and supermarkets, obesity, rural food security, and diet and nutrition.

Summary and conclusions

Market-based economic systems rely on the self-interest of citizens to produce and distribute products that consumers want to purchase. The government, or any other centralized decision maker, has a positive role to play in defining and enforcing property rights and contracts, regulating firms with market power, and resolving or mitigating other market failures, including externalities and public good issues. Market-based economic systems, rather than ignoring or denying the human desire for financial improvement, use self-interest as the driving force to get things done. While markets capture this enormous energy and use it to provide society with desirable outcomes, there are many limitations to a market-based economy.

Change, ever-present in a market economy, is most often reflected through changes in market price. Responses require flexibility, adaptation, and the ability to reallocate time, energy, and resources out of enterprises of low or declining value and into those of increasing profits. Polarization in food and agriculture is often caused by market changes: livestock producers are harmed by the production of corn-based ethanol, organic vegetable producers oppose GMOs, agricultural chemical manufacturers are opposed to organic production practices, but favor biofuels, and vegetable producers have strong opinions about the use of noncertified foreign workers, to name a few market problems that create controversy and animosity. When embroiled in a contentious situation, it often appears to participants and outside observers that polarized issues are a "bad" thing. However, when a broader perspective is taken, one can see the enormous benefits of discussion, debate, and divided opinions. Diverse viewpoints lead to improvement in society, as incomes grow, customs change, desires change, and economic growth occurs.

Political and economic systems with institutions that encourage change are likely to provide for better social and economic outcomes than those that do not. Rapid changes in food production methods, including mechanization, biotechnology, and industrialization of food processing required massive changes for both food consumers and producers. The process of working through the discovery, adoption, and acceptance or rejection of new food production practices has led to a future where practices deemed desirable are adopted and those that are found to be less desirable are rejected. These changes will occur through both economic and political systems: consumers will demand goods produced in ways that they approve of, and citizens will demand government oversight and regulation of new ideas, innovations, and ways of doing things.

Notes

1   Winston Churchill, speech, House of Commons, November 11, 1947, in Robert Rhodes James (ed.), *Winston S. Churchill: His Complete Speeches, 1897–1963*, vol. 7, p. 7566 (1974).
2   "Winston Churchill." BrainyQuote.com. XploreInc, 2014; www.brainyquote.com/quotes/quotes/w/winstonchu103863.html (accessed June 30, 2014).
3   Wolff (2013) explains: "Since the mid-19th century, socialism has mostly been differentiated from capitalism in two basic ways. Instead of capitalism's private ownership of means of production (land, factories, offices, stores, machinery, etcetera), socialism would transfer that ownership to the state as the administrator for public, social or collective ownership. Instead of capitalism's distribution of resources and products by means of market exchange, socialism would substitute state central planning to accomplish that distribution. Marxism was generally viewed as the basic theoretical criticism of capitalism that went on to define and justify a social transition from capitalism to socialism. Communism was generally viewed as a distant, rather utopian stage of social development beyond socialism wherein class differences would disappear, the state would wither away as a social institution, work activity would be transformed and distribution would be based purely on need." It should be noted that it is possible to have a socialist economy where resources are publicly owned, and market transactions are used to allocate resources and distribute goods and services.
4   Economists have a specific definition for firms in a competitive industry. Perfect competition is often defined as a market or industry with four characteristics: (1) numerous buyers and sellers; (2) a homogeneous product; (3) freedom of entry and exit; and (4) perfect information. This stringent definition is important in the study of economics, but for our purposes, competition simply refers to a market or industry that has many firms providing similar products.

4

FOOD MARKETS AND POLARIZATION

Farming looks mighty easy when your plow is a pencil and you're a thousand miles from the corn field.

US President Dwight D. Eisenhower

Right or wrong, the customer is always right.

Marshall Field, American retailer

Introduction

Food is important. Not merely important, but required for human existence. It is no wonder, then, that people have strong opinions and emotions about food, how it is produced, processed, distributed, consumed, and shared. People have an obvious need to eat and as the population grows, ever larger quantities of food must be produced. Food markets are unique in many ways. Food production is distinctively biological, depending on weather, soil, nature, and how humans interact with these biophysical conditions. The dependence on weather, climate, and soil creates risks and uncertainties unknown in most other industries. A great deal of food is perishable, making production, storage, and distribution challenging. Food security (having enough food) and food safety (assuring that foods are edible) are of primal importance. These features of food production and consumption cause food issues to be urgent, unique, and universal.

Food security has been at the top of the list of human needs for as long as *homo sapiens* have existed. The book of Genesis tells the Biblical creation story, where food wants and needs set the stage for the relationship between humans and food. According to the Biblical story, the first humans were placed in a garden with complete food security (eat as much as you want),[1] a unique food safety issue (the fruit on the tree of life is poisonous), and were challenged to behave appropriately (don't eat fruit from the tree of life).

The theory of evolution also includes elements regarding food needs: humans evolved from hunters and gatherers into agriculturalists approximately 10,000 years ago. Controversies about food are as commonplace as children protesting what is on their dinner plate, but they are as serious as poor food policies that frequently result in hunger, malnutrition, and starvation for millions of individuals. The desire for food security has led many political leaders to call for self-sufficiency in food, including Mohandas Gandhi (1869–1948) in India. Gandhi is credited with securing India's independence from the British Empire through civil disobedience. While it is difficult to find fault with a moral leader as effective and ethical as Gandhi, his economic policy of self-sufficiency is best viewed as a need based on local circumstances, rather than a universal program for all individuals, regions, or nations to pursue. Self-sufficiency removes the ability to specialize and trade for food produced at the most efficient location.

Many nations attempt to pursue Ghandi-like food security by producing enough food to feed an entire nation, instead of relying on imported food. Western European nations have done this since World War II, by heavily subsidizing food production, most likely as a result of experiences with food shortages during World War II, 1939–1945. Now, in 2014, Saudi Arabia subsidizes food production in the desert in an attempt to achieve food self-sufficiency.

A nation's desire to feed itself is a common and long-standing food policy objective. Many nations consider reliance on other nations for nutrients too risky to attempt. The desire for food self-sufficiency is strong and enduring. In England during the period 1815–1846, for example, the Corn Laws levied harsh taxes on imported grains to make domestic production of grain crops profitable and reduce England's reliance on imports. This allowed British landowners to produce the nation's food needs, but it resulted in higher domestic prices and higher food costs for consumers. Thomas Malthus (1766–1834), a leading English economist of the time, supported the barriers to trade as a method of keeping grain prices high. The Corn Laws were repealed in 1846, resulting in the importation of grain from other nations, primarily the US and Russia.

Even today, individuals, policy makers, and nations continue to make similar choices and are likely to continue to evaluate the decision to produce domestically or buy from others well into the future. Should a modern nation in today's global economy produce food to feed its citizens, or should it import food from other nations if imports are less expensive? Should a low-income nation in Africa produce staple crops such as grains, tuber crops, and cassava for food, or produce cash crops (sugar, bananas, cocoa, or flowers) for export, and use the earnings to purchase food? These controversial questions continue to be discussed, debated, and most importantly, answered by despots, democracies, and policy makers of all nations.

The outcomes of trade policies have massive effects on the livelihoods of billions of people. Regardless of who is making them, the decisions relating to food security are best made with informed decision making and evidence combined with common sense to achieve the best outcomes possible. These questions will be further explored in Chapter 9.

Food safety is another important, timely, and contentious societal objective. And, upon reflection, this will be the case, always and forever, as long as humans need to eat. Through much of modern history, humans have enjoyed ever-increasing levels of life expectancy (Fogel, 2003). However, continued criticism, objections, and strife over the safety of the food supply are a perennial feature of food and agricultural markets. This is as it should be. Continued criticism is not only productive, but it results in improved longevity and health. The industrialization of agriculture and food processing helps solve many food safety issues, but leads to many new food safety issues, as food production becomes increasingly mechanized and physically concentrated in specific locations. As food production methods evolve through the use of new machines, genetics, chemicals, farm structures, and other advances, consumers will need to adjust to food produced using these new production practices. Food issues such as these are as important today as they were at the beginning of human history.

Unlike the persons in the creation story, consumers today are enormously diverse and complex. Their needs are quite different, ranging from hungry people who need more calories to survive, to "foodies" who continue to elevate concern for food taste, appearance, and palatability, and consumer groups who care deeply about where food originates and how it is produced and processed. Claims about what is best for everyone are common in the information age, as the internet can magnify extreme views. Many media outlets and bloggers suggest, for example, that we should eat only organic food, we should not produce food using biotechnology (GMOs), we should not eat meat, we should reduce caloric intake, and we should exercise great discretion regarding what we choose to eat.[2] One of the main themes of this book is consumer sovereignty. If consumer sovereignty is present, people will have the right to eat what they want, unless their consumption decisions cause harm to others. The problem lies in the perception of what causes harm to others. Is an individual harmed if her neighbor eats meat, or conventional food, or too many calories? Or is the environment harmed more by conventional agriculture which uses chemicals and fertilizer, or organic farming, which requires more acres of land for the same level of output? These difficult questions will be investigated in what follows. Five questions will serve as the basis for investigating the controversies involved in food issues and the polarization that results from food markets.[3] The questions can be stated simply as follows:

- What food to produce?
- How much food to produce?
- How to produce food?
- When to produce food?
- For whom to produce food?

What food to produce?

On July 11, 2013, Stephen Dubner, an American author and journalist, publicized the claim that the McDonald's "McDouble" cheeseburger was "the cheapest, most nutritious, and bountiful food that has ever existed in history" (Smith, 2013). Dubner, a co-author of the best-selling book and blog *Freakonomics*, provided compelling evidence for the claim: the McDouble delivers to an eater 390 calories, 23 grams of protein (half of the recommended daily serving), 7 percent of daily fiber requirements, substantial portions of calcium and iron, typically costs approximately $1, and can be purchased at over 14,000 locations in the US. Dubner's intentionally provocative claim irritated those individuals and groups who find fault with fast food. In spite of fast food's popularity, its faults are detailed in Eric Schlosser's 2004 book, *Fast Food Nation: The Dark Side of the All-American Meal*, and Morgan Spurlock's 2004 film *Super Size Me*. Many food and nutrition groups find it difficult to say anything good about McDonald's, eating meat, or fast food in general. How could the most successful retail food chain in history be simultaneously considered bad for human nutrition, bad for the environment, and unethical? This super-sized debate in popular culture can be better understood through the lens of economic analysis. It is possible that the McDouble is simultaneously good and bad for consumers, health, and the environment: after all, economists assert that there are benefits and costs to everything. The keys to understanding this divergence of views include: (1) maintaining diversity among consumers and among available goods; and (2) framing all issues in a transparent fashion.

Consumer diversity

Humans are enormously, compellingly, and troublingly diverse. Language, culture, tradition, dress, appearance, race, ethnicity, political viewpoints, ability, intelligence, and income are just a few among many diverse human characteristics. Focus first on income. Approximately 40 percent of all humans live on less than $2 per day (World Bank, 2007). In the US in 2012, 46.5 million Americans, 15 percent of the population, lived in poverty (DeNavas-Walt *et al.*, 2013). Dubner's McDouble claim makes some sense for these individuals who are struggling to get by or others who find fast food to be convenient.[4] However, the McDouble's saturated fat and sodium levels could lead to health problems, and overconsumption of McDoubles could result in obesity and related health issues. As with most polarized issues, there is truth on both sides of the divide: fast food can provide an inexpensive, nutritious, and appetizing diet for many individuals. For these persons, a double cheeseburger provides many nutritional needs and greater health than other food choices of the same cost. However, if poor choices are made, fast food can be startlingly unhealthy. Some observers are calling for a ban on all fast food, or a tax on the fat content of many fast food items. Others are opposed to organic, local, and vegan food. Some believe that McDonald's advertising and marketing targets children, resulting in poor health for those who eat at fast food chains. Who is correct?

This question is similar to asking what type of clothing is best: Armani suits or Walmart tee shirts? Both types of clothing meet the differing needs and desires of different people at different times. Food is analogous: the diversity of available food is a great testament to the variety of consumers in the US economy, and a consequence of free markets. To restrict others' diets to conform to one's own views may be considered rude and result in unintended consequences. However, for persons who have strong views, it is certainly within their right to try to convince the public of the correctness of their opinions. Challenging views move society forward. Properly communicated and correct nutritional theories will be maintained and extended; incorrect health theories will be modified or replaced as evidence accumulates.

Nutritionists, food producers, philosophers, food industry leaders, and consumers debate the benefits and costs of eating fats (saturated, unsaturated, and trans), sweeteners (sucrose, fructose, and artificial), and sodium (refined, sea, and iodized). The evidence is mixed on each nutritional decision, and to claim that there is one, single, correct way of eating is likely to be erroneous. An economic approach to nutrition would lead to the "optimal" level of each nutrient. Human bodies need fat to function and prosper. The most beneficial level of fat is greater than zero, but less than people frequently consume. The optimal level of fat varies widely across individuals, cultures, ethnicities, body types, and locations. The optimal level is complicated, because it depends on a multitude of things. Marathon runners and people living in cold climates such as Alaska or near the southern tip of Argentina need more fat than those who do not exercise and live in Arizona or Mexico. The correct level of fat intake also depends on a highly complex and virtually unknowable list of other foods, lifestyles, and genetics. All of which recalls the need for consumer sovereignty and the freedom to choose.

To restrict others goes against the fundamental beliefs in political and economic freedom. Food consumption decisions are typically left up to the individual: as long as a person's choices don't adversely affect others, an individual can do whatever he or she wants to do.[5] McDouble consumption is noncoercive and voluntary, meaning that there are few, if any, situations in which one person's consumption of the burger will constrain another person in any meaningful way.

The story becomes more complicated when choices lead to outcomes that indirectly affect others. Risk takers such as mountain climbers and motorcyclists enjoy activities that carry a high risk of injury and/or death. From a point of view related to freedom, these individuals should certainly have the right to climb mountains and ride without helmets. However, when mountain climbers become stranded by avalanches or storms, providing rescue services is costly. Society also pays for motorcyclists who survive accidents involving massive head injuries and requiring prolonged efforts at life support. For individuals who make poor food and nutrition choices, society must pay for costly health care, missed work, lower productivity, and a battery of other consequences. These issues are difficult to resolve, because they are accompanied by a nearly infinite list of actions and behaviors that affect others.

Framing of issues

Opinions are often formed by the way issues are framed, questions are asked, thoughts are communicated, or how evidence is presented. Issues in food and agriculture can be organized, or presented, in ways that sound correct, intelligent, and agreeable. The logic and correctness of vegetarianism, for example, is often portrayed in terms of the food needs for a growing global population or in terms of the personal health of the practicing vegetarian. The counter arguments include the notion that eating meat must be appropriate fare for humans, since humans have eaten meat for thousands of years.

Many of the divergences of opinion in food and agriculture derive from the way factual evidence is framed. During the early years of research on genetic engineering, many consumers were led to believe that bioengineered food had a host of negative and potentially dangerous attributes. Similarly, many people became concerned that high fructose corn syrup (HFCS) results in obesity. McDonald's has been vilified by many, but is now glorified by Dubner, and certainly millions of consumers enjoy its products. Opinion formation often relies on how facts are presented.

As individuals and groups in society have become more interested and vocal about issues associated with food, many food producers have felt threatened by the manner in which many arguments are framed. The recent movement opposing "industrial agriculture" has been labeled "anti-agriculture" by many agricultural advocates, or "agvocates."[6] Most of the issues and complaints raised by consumer groups are not meant to oppose farmers, but instead focus on the highly industrial methods of farm production, food processing such as done in canneries, meat packing plants, food manufacturers, and food retailers, and fast food chains. All businesses involved in food and agriculture could benefit from the late-nineteenth-century advice of Marshall Field, the successful department store owner in Chicago, who famously stated, "Right or wrong, the customer is always right." If consumers perceive issues in industrialized agriculture, food industry advocates could address these complaints directly using factual information. If the critique is correct, food firms could correct the error.

The diversity of consumer tastes and preferences can be satisfied only through the availability of a huge variety of products that have been produced in a huge variety of ways. When food markets are globalized, the appropriate types of food and production methods become much more diverse. Business firms able to understand the magnitude of significant criticism can use polarized issues to their advantage. For example, some targeted consumers who desired healthy food and produced it using sustainable and organic methods, which led to profitable businesses such as Whole Foods. Other firms such as Walmart targeted consumers who preferred low-cost food. A third strategy, bundling food attributes, can be used to enhance profits, as discussed in Chapter 8.

What is the solution to the enormous perceived discrepancy between health food advocates and fast food junkies? Market research, education, time, and experience move forward through the revealed market preferences in order to provide consumers with what they want. McDonald's website states, "You told us you're trying harder to be more nutrition-minded for yourself and for your family. We listened. That's why we have been accelerating our efforts to serve food you feel better about eating, and to help you make informed nutrition choices" (McDonald's, 2014). Since 2011, McDonald's has lowered sodium and fat levels in many of its products, posted information related to nutrition on menus, lowered calories in bundled meals, and increased the number of menu items to meet specifications recommended by food groups (McDonald's, 2014). The company has a long history of giving customers what they want, and earning high profits as a result.

In 2014, McDonald's began to collaborate with the National Cattlemen's Beef Association (NCBA), the World Wildlife Federation (WWF), Cargill, JBS USA (a meat processing company), and others to advocate sustainable beef production in the US. The overall aim was to purchase only verified sustainable beef by 2016 (McDonald's, 2014). McDonald's leadership in improving nutrition, animal welfare, and sustainability is an example of how polarized issues lead to resolution. Changes in consumer wants and needs led to market forces providing change in how hamburgers are produced.

How can society know what food to produce? Markets answer this question. The price system reflects the willingness and ability of consumers to pay for a good, and the cost of resources required to produce the good. When given the freedom to do as they please, the actions of consumers and producers result in the optimal combination of goods for producers and consumers while answering the question of "what food to produce." This theme suggests that in many cases, widely divergent issues in food and agriculture are self-correcting, in the sense that market forces contribute to the resolution of disputes over time.

How much food to produce?

Many farmers, ranchers, and food industry stakeholders and participants are "productionists,"[7] meaning that their goal is to maximize food production. Farmers often have a strong desire to enhance crop yields using new varieties, new chemicals, fertilizers, machinery, and biotechnology. Many farmers have been successful in this quest. Global wheat production increased from 222 million tonnes in 1961 to 675 million tonnes in 2012. During the same period, corn production increased from 205 to 875 million tonnes, and rice production from 215 to 718 million tonnes (FAOSTAT, 2013). Similarly, cattle producers in the US have used improved nutrition and superior feedlot management to increase animal weight gains from 449 pounds per animal in 1960 to 632 pounds per animal in 2009 through nutrition, and feedlot management (National Cattlemen's Beef Association [NCBA], 2013).

Enhanced efficiencies have provided huge benefits to society in the form of lower food prices, improved nutrition, and increased food security. As a result of agriculture's impressive performance in productivity gains over the past several decades, the world is food secure with enough food to meet the dietary needs of today's global population (World Bank, 2007, p. 94). Increases in food production are certainly a good thing. Unfortunately, increased productivity can at times be carried too far, in the name of increased efficiency, feeding a hungry world, or in an effort to maintain farm incomes or food industry profits.

The argument for increased productivity to meet the food needs of a hungry world is often used to retain production practices that have been called into question, or to justify the adoption of a new technology. Throughout history, agriculturalists have occasionally adopted production practices that have emphasized the goal of productive efficiency over the goals of human health, ethics, and the environment. The most glaring example is the institution of slavery in the New World. African slaves were captured then transported against their will to many nations in North and South America and forced into agricultural labor. From today's perspective, slavery was a case of placing personal objectives and profits ahead of human rights, decency, and societal well-being.

The agrochemical DDT (dichloro-diphenyl-trichloroethane) was discovered in 1874. More than six decades later, in 1939, DDT began to provide enormous benefits in saving human lives by killing insects that carry diseases such as malaria, typhus, and sleeping sickness. In 1948, the Swiss chemist Paul Hermann Müller was awarded the Nobel Prize in Physiology and Medicine for the popularization of DDT as an insecticide. DDT's qualities as a carcinogen and a threat to wildlife as well as to the human population (Carson, 1962) resulted in the ban of the chemical in the US in 1972. Later, DDT was banned from agricultural use worldwide.[8] DDT brings both huge benefits and huge costs to society. These benefits and costs differ greatly in different nations. In high-income nations, malaria and other diseases are not prevalent, but cancer is a major source of health problems. In many low-income nations, cancer is not a serious problem (average longevity is short) but diseases carried by mosquitos are a problem. Also note that information changes as evidence accumulates over time, and the magnitude and measurement of the benefits and costs change. Sometimes, new information results in greater clarity and easier resolution of polarized issues. Other situations are sometimes complicated further by new information.

Bovine somatotropin (bST) is a naturally occurring hormone in cattle, used to enhance milk productivity in dairy cows. In the 1970s, pharmaceutical companies synthesized the hormone, and Monsanto began selling bST under the brand name Prosilac in 1994. The drug, approved by the US Food and Drug Administration (FDA), remained controversial. Dairy farmers enthusiastically adopted bST to increase milk output per cow. The downside was overuse. The hormone could provide increased milk production in the short run, but at the expense of animal health and animal welfare issues. Although bST has been shown to be safe for human consumption, the hormone can lead to shorter lives for dairy cows: increased production and profits in the short run result in loss of health and longevity in the long run.

Profit-seeking agriculturalists, like all people trying to do the best that they can, have occasionally used production practices considered unethical, or harmful to human health or to the ecosystem. To counter these practices, consumers in recent years have emphasized high-quality food, and developed an increased interest in how food is produced. Specifically, new markets have developed for organic, natural, ethical, environmentally safe, and fair production practices. In some cases, alternative production practices have been developed in response to conventional agricultural methods or industrial food processing techniques that are inconsistent with the values of consumer groups. Some of these consumer issues have resulted in contentious, highly publicized, and sometimes unresolved battles between those who defend conventional practices and those who desire to reduce or eliminate the practices.

Taking a long view, this form of polarization is a strong positive attribute of a free, democratic, market-based society in spite of the drama, emotion, and costly process of deliberation as suggested in earlier chapters. If society did not embrace this type of controversy, it would not move forward. In an era of rapid technological change in communication, transportation, and food production, this type of conflict is inevitable and desirable. To take advantage of technological and scientific advances, society must work through the adoption and transition to new ways of doing things. Society will also face new information, or evidence, that some practices are no longer desirable (e.g. abusive labor practices, bST, DDT, child labor). Society will need to deliberate and resolve issues that arise as new information becomes available.

The issue of how much food to produce hinges on which technologies and production practices are used. It is often claimed that the world needs new technologies (e.g. bioengineering; bST; lean, fine-textured beef; Zilmax) to "feed the world's rapidly growing population." These claims should be evaluated carefully, since there is presently enough food available to feed the world's population. The difficulty is that not all global citizens have acceptable levels of access to buy food. Therefore, production-enhancing technologies must be justified on a case-by-case basis, based on science, ethics, values, location of need, and the preferences of consumers, producers, and policy makers. Science is only one input into good public policy. After all, the most efficient production practices are not always desirable: slave labor, child labor, sweatshops, and some chemicals and pharmaceuticals are examples. Public policy related to agriculture must rely on scientific information, together with societal values. To rely on scientific information alone would cause the elimination or overlooking of many nonscience-based societal objectives that were not based on productive efficiency alone, such as ethical considerations, fairness, safety, security, and a clean environment.

How to produce food?

World history reflects nearly continuous population growth, interrupted by events such as the bubonic plague during the fourteenth century. Population growth results in an ever-increasing need for food. Curiously, as nations industrialized and experienced economic growth, the number of farms decreased dramatically. Currently, in North America, Western Europe, Japan, and Australia, small percentages of the population are farmers and ranchers. These relatively small groups produce enough food to feed their populations, and produce a surplus for export to other nations.

The history of agriculture in high-income nations is one of massive and continuous substitution of machines and chemicals for workers. Technological change and mechanization in agriculture have an impressive history of success (Chapter 2). Agricultural productivity gains allowed food to become more affordable over time, enhancing the welfare of the world. In market-based economies, food producers are free to choose how to provide food, and there is a wide variety of production practices, technologies and methods available and in use. How do farmers decide on the method they will use to produce food? Production decisions are based on personal preference, resource endowments, and profitability of each production practice. In high-income nations, most food is produced by commercial farmers seeking to maximize profits. In addition to large commercial farmers, there are many small, part-time farmers who make decisions based on lifestyle and other factors that may be unrelated to profitability alone (Peterson et al., 2012).

Commercial farmers have large farms, use large quantities of purchased inputs (e.g. seeds, fertilizer, chemicals, and machinery), and are often early adopters of new technology (see the following chapter). Over 50 percent of food production comes from approximately 2 percent of all farms (US Department of Agriculture, 2007). Food processing has become industrialized, creating major cost savings to consumers (see Chapter 6). The industrialization of food production has resulted in major criticism of "Big Food" by contemporary writers including Michael Pollan (2006a), Eric Schlosser (2004), film director Morgan Spurlock (*Super Size Me*, 2004), and Peter Pringle (2003).

In a market-based economy, producers are free to make choices about what to produce and how to produce it, as long as they are in compliance with laws and regulations intended to protect consumers, producers, and the environment. If agricultural and food production practices are opposed by consumers, then the consumers will demand and receive food produced in ways that are to their liking. As economic development occurs and incomes increase, diets change, and the new dietary choices influence the profitability of food products. For example, some consumers are willing to pay for fair trade products, which are imported goods that strive to compensate farmers in low-income nations fairly. In this case, some producers will supply enough fair trade products to meet the consumer willingness and desire to purchase them. Decentralized decision making in a market system gives consumers the opportunity to select from among large numbers of alternatives as long as they are able to pay the price.[9] If consumers desire a diversity of foods, they are able to purchase these desired items. Given the contentiousness and rancor of debates in food and agriculture, it is important to emphasize a few essential points.

- In general, a vast majority of consumers are pleased with the current selections of food and the ways that food is produced.

- Consumer preferences are changing, and the producers who pay careful attention to consumer purchasing trends will be the most successful businesses in the future food industry.
- The history of agriculture is one of constant change, with superior production practices replacing inferior methods, and producers who adopt new technology early are more likely to be successful.
- Arguments used to defend the status quo are unlikely to halt changes in consumer preferences or new technologies from replacing old ones. When new technologies or new consumer goods are desirable, they will be adopted rapidly in spite of complaint or opposition by some.

How do we know that most consumers are happy with available food products, and with the way food is produced? In a competitive, market-based economy, consumers get whatever they desire, whether it is opera or soap operas, kale or cheeseburgers, locally grown organic lettuce or conventionally produced potatoes. The food for sale in supermarkets is exactly what consumers most desire: a product that does not sell will be removed from the shelves and not reordered. This is as true at Whole Foods and health food stores as it is at Walmart. The quantity of vegan, health, organic, local, fair trade, and environmentally safe foods depends on how many consumers prefer these products. Farmers and ranchers will produce exactly the types of food in a manner that follows consumer desires. As these new food attributes became more popular, supermarkets have increasingly made them available.[10]

The huge number of choices available from food suppliers allow the conclusion that the goods produced and sold are what consumers desire. When consumer preferences change, producers will provide new products in line with these new consumer demands. This process occurs quickly and automatically, since the producers who provide the new products will earn larger returns than if they continued with the old way of doing things. Consumer sovereignty is a harsh taskmaster for producers: successful businesses in a market economy must constantly change to meet consumer wishes. At times, change can be difficult for producers. For example, if beef producers are using antibiotics and growth hormones in the production process, and prefer the productivity gains that accompany the use of these inputs, they may resist giving these up and producing "natural," "antibiotic-free," or "hormone-free" beef. As consumer preferences change, the producers who meet these new demands with new products will be the most successful. Of course, not all consumers desire to pay more for beef with these new attributes. Beef producers will need to discern which type of beef will provide the production choices, lifestyle, and income level that they most desire. This decision is similar for producers deciding whether or not to produce free-range pork or poultry, grass-fed beef, or any number of the huge diversity of meat products (attributes) desired by consumers. Farmers make similar decisions, also, about productive techniques, use of chemicals, fertilizer, machinery, migrant workers, and a growing list of food attributes requested by consumers.

Business firms, in general, and farmers and ranchers, in particular, will respond to changes based on fads, trends, and actual structural changes in consumer purchase decisions. If the latest consumer trend is temporary, transitory, or a fad, producers may wish to steer clear. On the other hand, producers can make mistakes by criticizing consumer demands as a "fad" when the changes become ongoing and/ or increasing. Producers who maintain a portfolio of different enterprises may do best in a rapidly changing food economy.

The yogurt industry has recently shown how a new product, Greek yogurt, can rapidly gain market share. Chobani entered the yogurt market in 2007, when 0.2 percent of the market was Greek yogurt. By 2012, over 50 percent of the yogurt market was Greek yogurt, and Chobani had approximately one-half of the yogurt market share (Durisin, 2013). As always, enormous success is not without issues: in September 2013, Chobani recalled a large volume of yogurt due to mold in the product (Laasby, 2013).

Not only do consumer preferences change, but production methods also change over time. Many, perhaps most, technological advances do not result in consumer reactions. A new wheat variety or new herbicide may not affect consumer tastes and preferences. However, if the new wheat variety is produced with biotechnology, or the new herbicide is shown to have a negative impact on human health or the environment, the new developments could become controversial and polarizing. Farmers, ranchers, and food industry stakeholders can have a broad range of reactions to changes in consumer preferences and technological advances. As discussed above, those who seek out change, adopt technology quickly, and adapt swiftly to new market realities will be the most successful in a market economy.

Consumer advocacy groups have caused many farmers and ranchers to feel threatened. As described above, the result has been an "agvocacy" (advocacy for agriculture) campaign, centered on educating nonfarmers on how their food is produced. This is certainly a productive activity, as more knowledge is better than less. An economist would, however, suggest that farm advocacy is a two-way street, with the information flow from consumers to producers being at least as important as the education about agriculture provided to city dwellers. Farmers and ranchers who seek out and learn the purchasing behavior and trends of diverse consumers of food products have a comparative advantage over those who do not. Rather than educating consumers about farming and ranching, firms that learn about urban lifestyles and preferences are likely to be most successful in adapting to future changes and trends in the food industry. Food consumers are different in many ways from those who produce food. Understanding these differences could lead to a more productive, less contentious future.

Defending the status quo may appear to be a strong argument with careful logic: "We have always used this production practice, so we have the right to continue." This argument has been used for many outdated practices, including bST, slavery, child labor, and DDT use. Agricultural production practices may be best viewed as temporary: chemicals and fertilizers, for example, were not widely used in farming until the 1950s. Given agriculture's 10,000-year history,

60 to 70 years of modern agriculture may or may not justify continued use of fertilizers and chemicals.

The resolution of many food and agricultural issues that involve how to produce food requires long-term thinking. Over time, any particular production practice appears fleeting. The loss of a specific production practice to societal demands is a rational, normal, and continuous process for enterprises in a democratic, free-market business environment. Certainly, bringing all of the relevant information to bear on an issue is an important ingredient of solid private and public decision making. If society decides against a long-used, effective, and productivity-enhancing input (DDT, GMOs, bST, etc.), then the food and agricultural industry must accept the decisions and move on. If all farmers cannot use certain practices, it will not affect the level of competition, since all firms are affected equally, at least within the same jurisdiction or nation.[11]

When to produce food?

Given the rapid and massive changes in science, transportation, communication, and globalization, how does society know when to make the transition to a new technology or out of an old technology? In a market economy, these decisions are made in a decentralized fashion by millions of consumers and producers. Producers will adopt and use new techniques based on the benefits and costs of each new method. Consumers always retain veto power over any new production practice. Some stakeholders in the food industry use five types of arguments for maintaining the current ways of doing things:

• Food is less expensive when produced using modern inputs such as chemicals, fertilizer, bioengineering (GMOs), Concentrated Animal Feeding Operations (CAFOs), feedlots, antibiotics, hormones, growth promotants such as Zilmax and Optaflexx … or virtually all production-enhancing, and thus cost-saving, technologies.
• We have "always used" a current technology, so we have the right to use it now.
• The use of "science" instead of "emotion" in food safety and food purchasing decisions will result in superior outcomes.
• If consumers were better educated about farmers, farming, rural lifestyles, food production, nutrition and food processing, they would change their views on many food issues.
• Food activists are considered "anti-agriculture."

Many of the issues that activists advocate for are against some aspects of industrialized agriculture, or the food processing industry. It may be difficult to find anyone who is truly "anti-agriculture." Many consumers could be characterized as "anti-chemical," or "anti-grain-fed meat," but not opposed to agriculture and food production in general. To generalize food issues as being against all farmers and ranchers may do more harm than good.

For example, the media suggested to consumers that lean, fine-textured beef (LFTB) was undesirable (Food Safety News, 2013). LFTB, also called, "pink slime," is a beef product used as a food additive to ground beef. LFTB is produced by heating and centrifuging beef trimmings to separate the fat from the meat. The resulting product is then exposed to ammonia gas or citric acid to kill bacteria. LFTB was used as an additive in approximately 70 percent of all ground beef sold in the US until it was discontinued in 2012. There are several features of LFTB that merit attention.

- LFTB is 100 percent safe, approved by the United States Department of Agriculture (USDA) and the US Food and Drug Administration (FDA), and was used in hamburgers for many years without any documentable negative effects on human health.
- LFTB had advantages to beef consumers, including lower hamburger prices and higher-quality burgers (LFTB is leaner than hamburger).
- When consumers were made aware of LFTB, their decision to reject it was not based on science, food safety, or price. Their decision was based on emotion, feelings, and consumer tastes and preferences.

Consumers thought that they were purchasing one thing (hamburger), but were getting hamburger with connective tissue and ammonia in it. Meat scraps and ammonia are safe, but they are not what consumers want. The product was safe, less expensive, and higher quality. Yet, consumers did not want it.

Many beef industry participants do not understand this. Upon reflection, the idea that consumers make choices based on what they like is intuitive. Science can be used to justify many positions, including the claim that the soyburger is safer, cheaper, and healthier than a hamburger. Yet, a majority of consumers prefer hamburgers to soyburgers. This outcome is reached in spite of nutrition, health, food safety, cost, and science. Many agriculturalists on both producer and consumer sides of an issue typically use "science" to defend and justify continuing their preferred practices. However, consumer desires are the driving force of business success in a market-based economy. Flexibility, adaptability, and a diverse portfolio allow food industry participants to remain productive and profitable during periods of rapid change. The interaction of technological change, science, human health, and consumer choices is dynamic, complex, and difficult to predict. Given this business climate, individuals and firms who develop flexible alternatives and strategies for change and adaptation will prosper. Nostalgia and preference for the "good old days" are often in conflict with progress and profitability in a globalized market economy. Society has numerous objectives, many of which are in conflict with one another. Consumers desire plentiful, affordable food, but also want food produced in specific ways that require more expense: chemical-free, no antibiotics or hormones, cage-free, free range, no industrial agriculture. Agriculturalists do well to maintain knowledge of the complex, dynamic, and at times paradoxical nature of consumer tastes and preferences.

For whom to produce food?

One of the greatest attributes of a market system is the impersonal nature of market transactions. Producing food is a noble profession and undertaking, but is subject to change. For centuries, apples were grown on trees in orchards. Modern-day apple production is characterized by high-density plantings, with trees planted close together on dwarfing (size-controlling) rootstocks. Tree densities have increased from 150 to 250 trees per acre to 500 to 1,000 (or more) trees per acre (Parker and Unrath, 1998). High-density apples provide earlier production, quicker return to investment, training, pruning, and harvesting done from the ground, potential for increased fruit quality, and greater pesticide application efficiency (Parker and Unrath, 1998).

In our times, issues surrounding food production can be controversial, contentious, and financially damaging. The most successful firms are also most heavily targeted by activists: McDonald's, Chipotle, and Walmart. Businesses with continued success over long time periods have developed strategies to deal with criticism and attack. The most important ingredients of public relations during such times include: (1) rapid response with factual information; and (2) transparency. Industrial agriculture and "Big Food" are likely to do better in the long run with policies of openness and transparency. For example, if a company desires to win over consumers, it should be open and accessible to any and all individuals and groups. For example, providing customer and watchdog groups access to the kill floor in a meat slaughterhouse may appear to be counter-productive, but in the long run it is an important ingredient to continued success. It also has a unique role in improving company behavior: when operations are public, there is no room for behaviors, actions, or policies that result in criticism and attack. In the information age, this is the only way forward. Openness, not secrecy (or worse, defensiveness), is a better strategy to prevent and resolve animal cruelty, labor abuse, and food safety issues when and where they occur.

Summary and conclusions

People have strong opinions about food, since it is crucial to human existence. Food production is unique, since it is biological and dependent on the weather. Once produced, food is often perishable. Both the quantity of food available (food security) and quality of food (food safety) are important and controversial. Polarized issues in food markets typically result from two things: consumer diversity, and how the issues are framed. The huge diversity of consumers results in vastly different wants and needs: dietary desires differ enormously across location, income, ethnicity, and personal preferences. What is good for some may not be good for all. There is a fundamental tradeoff between industrially produced, low-cost food and specialized, luxury food products that meet the needs of high-income consumers.

Food debates result in progress for society as controversial issues are debated, evaluated, and resolved. As knowledge is gained, solutions, whole or partial, can be found. However, new issues arise as new food production techniques and consumer desires develop. Opinions are often formed from the way that facts are presented. As food issues have become more prominent in high-income societies, many farmers have felt threatened and have promoted advocacy groups such as "agvocacy" to correct misconceptions and false statements about food and agriculture.

Markets provide business firms with information about what consumers desire. Farmers have been successful at increasing agricultural output to meet the needs of a growing population. Not all output-enhancing technologies are desirable, however. Agricultural inputs such as DDT and bST bring both large benefits and large costs to society. The use of contentious inputs in food production leads to polarization, and eventual resolution of issues. In this sense, polarization provides a catalyst to societal progress to higher levels of understanding, greater life expectancy, and higher qualities of life. Societal decisions on how to produce food are best met with both scientific information and societal values. Science alone cannot answer questions about ethics, values, and desires.

Food industry business firms that provide consumers with desired food products are the most likely to be profitable in the future. Consumer desires are a moving target, however: food and agriculture are continuously changing, and farmers and food processors that are flexible and forward-looking reap large benefits. Many farmers and ranchers join agvocacy campaigns to promote agriculture by educating consumers about how food is produced. In a market-based economy, consumers have the power to purchase whatever they find most desirable, and business firms that provide the desired goods will be the most profitable. Flexibility, adaptability, and a diverse portfolio of products allow food industry participants to remain productive and profitable during periods of rapid change.

Notes

1   The term food security is defined as "when all people, at all times, have physical, social, and economic access to sufficient, safe, and nutritious food to meet their dietary needs and food preferences for an active and healthy life" (FAO, 2002).
2   An interesting recent development in food consumption is the appearance of the "flexitarian." Flexitarians eat a primarily plant-based diet, but eat meat, poultry, and fish in moderation (Blatner, 2009). Blatner suggests that the flexitarian diet provides the benefits of vegetarianism without having to give up meat entirely. According to the author, flexitarians can lose weight, be healthier, prevent disease, and live longer without giving up meat.
3   These five questions are issues commonly studied in microeconomics, the part of economics that concentrates on the behavior of individual decision making units, such as business firms (sellers) and households (buyers).
4   The claim that fast food is inexpensive has been challenged. See Bittman (2011) for an interesting and well-written argument.
5   See Jayson Lusk (2013) for a strongly-stated and fascinating argument against government intervention in food consumption choices.
6   Information on agvocacy can be found on the AgChat Foundation (2013) website.
7   This term is used by Lang and Heasman (2004) who write that a defining characteristic of the productionist paradigm is a shift of food supply from local, small-scale production to concentrated production and mass distribution of foodstuffs (p. 19). The authors

continue, "The overarching goal of this paradigm was to increase output and efficiencies of labour and capital for increasingly urbanized populations" (p. 20). Lang and Heasman defined two possible visions of the future: (1) the Life Sciences Integrated paradigm, which includes genetic engineering (GM); and (2) the Ecologically Integrated paradigm, a holistic and systems approach to agriculture and the environment.

8 DDT is still used as an effective insecticide in many African nations.

9 Jonathan Haidt (2013) stated that markets are truly miraculous in their ability to provide consumers with what they desire. Haidt argues, "If God is commonly thought to have created the world and then arranged it for our benefit, then the free market (and its invisible hand) is a pretty good candidate for being a god" (Haidt, 2013, p. 303). He concluded, "When libertarians talk about the miracle of 'spontaneous order' that emerges when people are allowed to make their own choices (and take on the costs and benefits of those choices), the rest of us should listen" (Haidt, 2013, pp. 304–305).

10 Many of these food attributes are claimed by producers, but consumers have no way of knowing if the claims are true. Markets for food with this type of attribute are carefully explored in Chapter 10.

11 In international trade, nations that do not have restrictions on inputs may be at a competitive advantage.

5

CREATIVE DESTRUCTION AND THE CYCLE OF POLARIZATION

> It ought to be remembered that there is nothing more difficult to take in hand, more perilous to conduct, or more uncertain in its success, than to take the lead in the introduction of a new order of things. Because the innovator has for enemies all those who have done well under the old conditions, and lukewarm defenders in those who may do well under the new. This coolness arises partly from fear of the opponents, who have the laws on their side, and partly from the incredulity of men, who do not readily believe in new things until they have had a long experience of them.
>
> Niccolò Machiavelli, *The Prince* (1513)

Introduction

Previous chapters have provided evidence that many important and interesting issues in food and agriculture are polarized. Some of these issues are new, and the divisiveness may be temporary. Other issues such as agricultural chemical use and the use of biotechnology in food production remain controversial and contentious. This chapter seeks to explain how issues become polarized, and in many cases remain in a state of gridlock. The causes, consequences, and major features of polarization are described and explained.

Economic principles provide insight to these issues. Economists, utilizing the scientific method, abstract from the complicated and multifaceted aspects of reality, with the objective of simplifying the complex real world to explain and predict economic activity. Economists develop models, or abstractions, of issues that capture the most important features of the real world. At times, these models are only partially correct or are even incorrect. The scientific method uses hypothesis testing to advance: if a model explains or predicts well, the model is retained; if the model does not explain well, it is dropped. The advancement of science is the continual assessment and evaluation of models and hypotheses as evidence and experience accumulates.

Schumpeter (1962) emphasized the process of "creative destruction" as the major feature of a market economy. He argued that the creation and adoption of new ideas and ways of doing things often displace business firms, managers, and employees of existing products or production methods. In the short run, economic dislocation and individual costs can be large. However, in the long run, society progresses towards ever-higher income levels and longer life expectancies. Karl Marx (1848, 1857, 1863) wrote that creative destruction was inherent in capitalism, and continuously devalued existing wealth to make way for new wealth. Schumpeter, a free-market advocate, and Marx, a strong opponent of capitalism, agreed on the process of creative destruction. The process of creative destruction will be explored in detail to better understand how issues become polarized. Emphasis is placed on the characteristics of technological changes that often lead to divisiveness, the devaluation of existing wealth, the creation of new wealth, and polarization.

Theodore Schultz (1975) applied the idea of creative destruction to agricultural managers. He argued that all real-world market economies are characterized by enormous disequilibria, or the continuous movement from one product or technology or price to another. Schultz believed that the ability to deal with disequilibria is a scarce and valuable trait that allows some farmers to succeed while others fail or become entrenched in the status quo. Managers and other market participants who do not possess this trait are less capable of continued success, and are often required to change jobs or accept lower returns for their efforts. Kislev and Shchori-Bachrach (1973) called this skill "allocative ability": the ability to continuously allocate resources to their highest-valued use.

Simon Kuznets (1973) explored universal problems that arise from innovation in a market-based economy:

> Economic growth perforce brings about a decline in the relative positions of one group after another—of farmers, of small scale producers, of landowners—a change not easily accepted, and, in fact, as history teaches us, often resisted. The continuous disturbance of preexisting relative positions of the several economic groups is pregnant with conflict—despite the rises in absolute income or product common to all groups.
>
> *Kuznets (1973), p. 252*

Everett Rogers (1931–2004) was an American rural sociologist who devoted his long and productive research career to furthering the understanding of adoption and diffusion of new technology. Rogers' early work on the determinants of technology diffusion provided a useful model of the rate of adoption over time (Figure 5.1). Rogers (2003) described the diffusion process as started by innovators (considered to be 2.5 percent of the population that uses the innovation) and early adopters (13.5 percent).

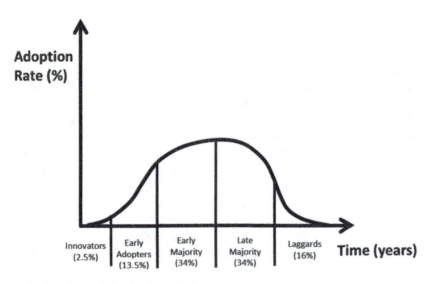

FIGURE 5.1 Rogers' distribution of adopters
Source: Rogers (2003)

The early adopters are followed by early majority (34 percent) and late majority (34 percent) adopters. Laggards are the last to adopt the innovation, and comprise 16 percent of the group. Given this pattern of adoption, the cumulative adoption curve of an innovation is a "S-shape," as shown in Figure 5.2. While the seminal model put forth by Rogers has been widely discussed, used, and extended by a host of writers, it may place too much emphasis on the percentage of individuals in each category. Rogers and other writers provided evidence for similarity across innovations, but there are likely to be differences in adoption and diffusion rates, based on the economic and personal benefits and costs of the new technology relative to the technology that is being replaced.

Rogers identified two major determinants of adoption: relative advantage and compatibility. Relative advantage refers to a comparison of the benefits and costs of adoption, and is an important approach to decision making. The idea of compatibility includes the important nonmonetary aspects of change, including the beliefs and values of an individual. Beliefs stemming from culture, politics, technology, and religion can, and often do, influence the ways that agriculturalists do things. For example, certain religious groups do not use electricity; many nations do not allow genetically modified organisms (GMOs); and many consumers do not eat meat products.

Rogers also identified two major causes of disadoption:[1] (1) disenchantment with the new innovation; and (2) replacement. Disenchantment may occur if an individual becomes less enthusiastic about an innovation after adoption than s/he was prior to the adoption. Disenchantment can occur for many reasons, including more information about the innovation as time passes, greater knowledge of compatibility, or smaller economic benefits than expected.

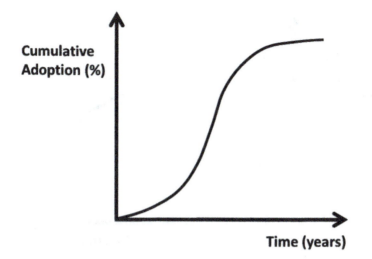

FIGURE 5.2 Cumulative technology adoption over time: aggregate diffusion
Source: Rogers (2003)

The work of Rogers and his followers provides a foundation for the understanding of individual adoption decisions. This model does not investigate aggregate diffusion, defined as the overall impact of individual adoption decisions. Aggregate diffusion is illustrated in Figure 5.2, where an example of the cumulative adoption rate, the sum of all individual adoption decisions, is measured over time. Rogers did not emphasize disadoption of an older technology that occurs simultaneously with the adoption of a new technology. The continuous process of creative destruction or the movement from the old to the new results in a cycle of innovation, as further considered below.

Background: early economic studies

Ernst Engel (1821–1896), a German statistician, was one of the first social scientists to quantify economic relationships. Engel (1857) used budget data from 153 Belgian families to formulate, or form the basis of, "Engel's Law" which states that the lower a family's income, the greater is the proportion of income spent on food.[2] The graphical representation of this law is shown in Figure 5.3. This graph is one example of an "Engel Curve," simply the relationship between income and the quantity of a good purchased.

Engel Curves provide three important antecedents to the study of divisiveness in food and agriculture. First, an Engel Curve is the precursor of a "life cycle" model, or how a variable changes over the life of an individual, nation, or business firm. If growing income is a typical characteristic of a family or nation, then Engel Curves capture how income increases affect consumer purchases. In many cases, consumption increases with initial income growth, levels out, then declines. Pasta

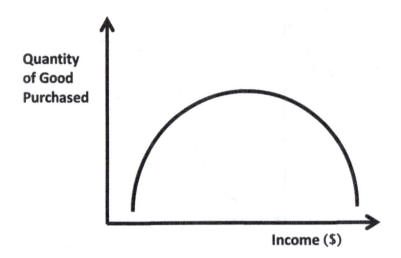

FIGURE 5.3 An Engel Curve

provides a classic example: as income rises from near zero, the amount of pasta purchased increases. However, with additional increases in income, the family shifts out of pasta and selects more expensive foods such as ground meat. After more income growth, ground beef might be replaced by more expensive cuts of meat. This results in the "inverted U-shape" of the Engel Curve in Figure 5.3.

A second reason why Engel Curves are important as a precursor to the work discussed here is the pattern of "increase followed by decrease" of a typical good. The "growth then decline" shape typifies adoption and disadoption of a particular method or technology over time. Technological change is the catalyst of both progress and disagreement in food and agriculture. Third, the Engel Curve is a flexible relationship often based on actual data: it can accommodate any type of relationship between changes in income and consumer purchases. Because of this wide applicability, Engel's Law and Engel Curves have remained a major feature in economic studies and theories. Engel Curves have been estimated using ever more sophisticated data, econometric models, and computational capability since Engel's initial studies in 1862. The concepts have held up well, resulting in one of the most important features of modern economics. The Engel Curve for beef, pork, and chicken holds important implications for food supply in the future, as emphasized by Schroeder *et al.* (1996) and Keyzer *et al.* (2005), who found that among low-income consumers, meat consumption increases as the low levels of income increase, then decreases as income reaches higher levels.

Simon Kuznets (1901–1985), a Russian American economist, developed a specific type of Engel Curve: one that illustrates the effect of income on inequality (Figure 5.4). Kuznets (1955) suggested that as per capita income increases, inequality increases at first, but later declines. Income inequality remains an important topic, recently evaluated by Chetty *et al.* (2014) and Piketty and Goldhammer (2014).

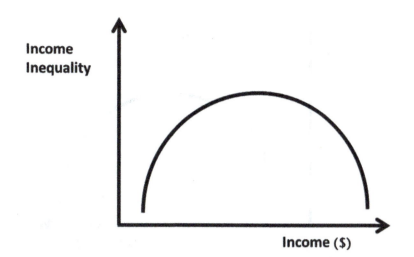

FIGURE 5.4 A Kuznets Curve

The inverted-U shaped curve of the Kuznets Curve mirrored Engel, and foreshadows this work. Grossman and Krueger (1991) studied air quality in a cross-section of nations across time, providing an empirical estimate of the relationship between income and environmental quality.

This type of Engel Curve became known as the "Environmental Kuznets Curve," or EKC, shown in Figure 5.5. Income growth results in environmental decay, until a turning point is reached, when further income growth results in environmental improvement. The EKC is intuitively appealing, but is likely to be more complicated in the real world. However, the EKC does a good job of depicting how the United States, Western Europe, and other high-income nations became polluted during industrialization, but due to environmental quality regulation and legislation, became cleaner in the post-industrial age. Currently, China is characterized by rapid economic growth, industrialization, and high and increasing levels of air pollution (*The Economist*, 2013a).

The inverted U-shape of the Engel Curve, the Kuznets Curve, and the EKC is an essential foundation for the study of innovation. Technological change, or a new way of doing things, is adopted over time: individuals and groups choose to adopt a new technology or innovation at different points in time. This idea is at the core of the study of adoption, a major branch of research in rural sociology and agricultural economics.

Through much of history, technological change has been a powerful source of economic growth and improvement in human well-being. Innovation has resulted in enormous increases in the production of food and fiber over time, and includes mechanization, plant genetics, and the use of fertilizer and chemicals in agriculture, just to name a few. Bioengineering, or genetically modified organisms (GMOs), global positioning systems (GPS), and precision agriculture are innovations that have resulted in huge productivity gains in recent years, and

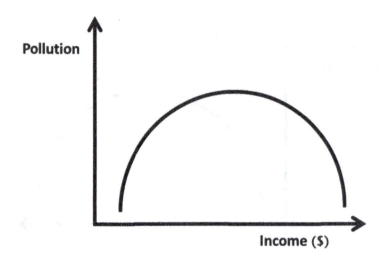

FIGURE 5.5 An Environmental Kuznets Curve

will continue to exert influence on how, and how much, food is produced in the future.

Diffusion of innovations

The study of technology adoption and diffusion emerged in the 1940s in rural sociology. Rogers' classic, *Diffusion of Innovations* (2003) contains the fascinating story of research in this area, first written in 1962, and updated in 1971, 1983, 1995, and 2003. The focus of early studies was the introduction of hybrid corn (maize) seed by the Iowa Agricultural Experiment Station in 1928. The hybrid corn provided a large boost in grain yields per acre, resulting in significant economic advantages to adoption. Ryan and Gross (1943, 1950) studied the rate of adoption, and the determinants of the adoption rate.

The Ryan and Gross studies yielded the classification of the five categories of adopters shown in Figure 5.1, and provided evidence for the S-shaped curve of technological diffusion among hybrid corn producers, as shown in Figure 5.2 (Ruttan, 1984, pp. 175–177). Zvi Griliches, an economist also at Iowa State University, produced two seminal studies of technological change, using data on the adoption of hybrid corn as an example (1957, 1958). Griliches emphasized the economic determinants of technology adoption: profits. The pioneering research by Ryan and Gross and Griliches formed the foundation from which a large literature has emerged, in both rural sociology and economics. Rogers describes how early work in technology adoption had a "pro-innovation" bias, and often lacked attention to the resistance to innovation. Early research was often geared toward assisting a farmer to adopt new technology, and tended to blame nonadopters for not making good decisions, rather than investigating the appropriateness of the potential adoption, or profitability (Rogers, 2003, Chapter 3).[3]

Determinants of the rate of adoption of agricultural innovations

New ideas and innovations in agriculture succeed or fail based on whether or not farmers or agribusinesses adopt the new way of doing things. Economic principles, together with previous research in sociology, suggest seven major determinants of the rate of technological adoption:

1. Availability of substitutes
2. Relative advantage
3. Adoption costs
4. Allocative ability of potential adopters
5. Vested compound interests
6. Compatibility, and
7. Timing.

Perhaps the most important determinant of technological adoption is the availability of substitutes. Truly useful new goods, services, and inputs have no suitable substitutes. Examples might include the cell phone, soil fertility evaluation, or RoundUp, an effective herbicide. If an innovation competes with a product that is already available, it will be less likely to be quickly adopted. The rate of adoption, therefore, depends on the existence and availability of alternatives. Truly innovative goods, production practices, and inputs are likely to be adopted more quickly, since they provide large potential benefits relative to less valuable innovations.

The economic approach emphasizes the benefits and costs of any decision or action. Following Griliches' studies (1957, 1958) of hybrid corn adoption, it is asserted that the relative economic advantage that a new technology provides is the most important determinant of the rate of its adoption: How will the innovation affect profits? The economic approach emphasizes the expected flow of economic benefits (EB) over the lifecycle of the innovation. If the economic benefits, or dollar value, of the enterprise with the adoption are greater than the economic benefits of nonadoption ($EB_A > EB_N$), adoption is more likely to occur than if profits are smaller with adoption ($EB_A < EB_N$). In many cases, farmers, agribusinesses, and researchers emphasize the benefits of a new technology, with little regard to the costs. Some individuals and groups support organic beef, free-range pork, or cage-free eggs, all of which increase production costs, and hence the price of food. The costs of adoption and implementation should also be considered in any decision to adopt new technology. No-till agriculture eliminates plowing a field by substituting planting the seeds of a new crop directly into the residue of the previous year's crop. No-till practices thus provide large cost-savings through less fieldwork, fuel savings, and conservation of soil moisture in arid regions. The equipment used to plant crops using this method can be expensive, resulting in a potential hurdle for adoption. Similarly, high perceived costs of precision agriculture, which uses satellites to guide the application rates of inputs such as chemicals and fertilizer, can lead to nonadoption.

The movement toward natural and organic meat can bring unanticipated expenses. When livestock producers attempt to produce beef without growth hormones or antibiotics, they often use the same production methods that they have used in their conventional beef operations. Optimal production practices may differ under natural and organic schemes, resulting in significant increases in costs. Particularly in the first years after conversion to new production practices, the costs of implementation can be high and unanticipated.

The meat and livestock industries would face truly enormous costs of changing the current meat production system of large slaughter facilities and concentrated animal feeding operations (CAFOs). These large facilities capture large economies to scale (lower per-unit costs) as production levels are increased. If consumers were to prefer less intensive production practices, the livestock industries investments in large, efficient facilities would be lost. In many situations, adoption costs are irreversible: a new feedlot would have to be shut down if consumers or government regulation required "free-range" meat.

Kislev and Shchori-Bachrach (1973) provided an economic model of the diffusion of innovations, where "[p]roducers with the highest skills (the better schooled, perhaps) will be first to adopt the innovation. Their advantage is spotting a good idea, experimenting with it, and solving the problems or adaptation to local conditions" (p. 28). Informal evidence for the importance of this ability is provided by the continuing high rates of return to investments in education. Large and increasing enrollment in colleges and universities, professional degree programs, and graduate schools demonstrate that "allocative ability," or entrepreneurship, is highly rewarded, and early adopters are most likely to earn profits from each new innovation. Indeed, Kislev and Shchori-Bachrach (1973) showed that as an innovation is adopted, the supply of the good being produced increases, driving price down. The result: early adopters are rewarded, but later their advantage erodes, resulting in the "innovation cycle."

Vested interests can thwart technological adoption when farmers, ranchers, or agribusinesses have "too much at stake" to make an investment in a new innovation worthwhile. In this case, the high costs of adoption and implementation due to previous irreversible investments would represent significant losses if adoption were to occur. Vested interests can be compounded when assets are durable: if an investment in plant or technology lasts many years, scrapping the existing production facilities could be expensive.

Barkley (1990) showed that compounding future benefits can alter economic and political decision making. When recipients view agricultural subsidies as permanent, they will devote more resources to defending current subsidy levels or increasing levels, compared to when the subsidies are considered temporary. When economic gains are durable, the dollar value of an asset is compounded, reflecting the value of all future benefits. These compounded asset values can influence technology adoption rates in cases where the losses of current assets would be lost if the adoption were to take place. Compound asset values are likely to be one of the major causes of polarization in food and agriculture: change can be costly for many agribusinesses that have large expected streams of economic benefits that rely on current assets.

Potential adopters can be swayed not only by financial asset values, but also by what Schultz (1975) called "human capital." This term refers to durable assets of knowledge, creativity, and entrepreneurial experiences that provide individuals with the ability to make decisions that produce economic value. If a corn producer has accumulated a great deal of education and experience producing corn with chemicals and fertilizer, s/he would have to give up, or lose, this investment in specific human capital if her/his activities switched to a different crop or product. These investments in specific human capital can be enormous, and often make it difficult for an individual or group to quickly and easily switch jobs, production practices, or ways of doing things. On the other hand, investments in general human capital (formal education) allow individuals to change jobs and careers: generalized knowledge and skills provide for greater opportunities in other jobs.

Humans often seem to prefer things as they have always been. The emotional and nostalgic costs associated with a change can be large, and often result in decisions to postpone adoption, or to not adopt at all. Although these emotional costs are subjective, personal, and difficult to measure, they can be one of the most important determinants of technological adoption rates.

Rogers (2003) emphasized the role of compatibility, or "the degree to which an innovation is perceived as consistent with existing values, past experiences, and needs of potential adopters" (p. 240). Many of the divisive issues in food and agriculture are a result of divergences in the perceived compatibility of an innovation: GMOs, lean, fine textured beef (LFTB), also called "pink slime," (discussed in Chapter 4), cloning, gestation crates in pork production, and pesticide use all qualify. Agriculturalists, including farmers, ranchers, agribusinesses, and researchers, are often "pro-efficiency," "productionist," or attracted to cost-saving and output-enhancing technological change. Indeed, it is this drive to become more efficient in production that has led to the continuing decrease in food costs, resulting in increases in the quality of life, improved health, and longevity. However, as seen in earlier chapters, efficient production practices are at times counter to some consumer desires about how their food is produced.

The compatibility of an innovation with currently used practices is subjective, and therefore difficult to measure in dollar values. Also, individuals often exaggerate the benefits or costs of an innovation in order to strengthen the case for or against it. Economists refer to compatibility costs as perceived social costs (SC). The social costs of adoption (SC_A) might include damage to the environment in the case of an agricultural chemical, or animal welfare issues in livestock production. The social costs of nonadoption (SC_N) could reflect environmental costs associated with a production practice that is currently used.

The final determinant of the rate of technological change is the timing of an innovation. The adoption rate of a useful, important innovation that provides large economic benefits depends on the stage when the innovation is introduced during the business cycle (recession, boom, depression). Also, the rate of adoption is influenced by when the innovation is introduced relative to other innovations. If producers have just invested in a new innovation, they might be less inclined to adopt a "new and improved" alternative that causes them to have to disinvest, or disadopt, in a recently acquired asset or experience. During economic downturns, innovation adoption rates typically slow, as there is less financial capital available for new investments. These seven determinants of the rate of adoption are summarized in a simple economic "model" in the next section.

A model of the rate of agricultural innovation adoption

A "model" reduces the complexities of the real world into a systematic representation that captures the most important aspects of the decision or action that needs explanation or understanding. The adoption of an innovation is shown in Figure 5.6. The bell-shaped curve on the left represents the life cycle of the first, or original, innovation (labeled A), introduced in time t_A. Individuals adopt this new way of doing things based on the perceived benefits, costs, compatibility, and timing, so that the time period from t_A to t_0 represents the same cumulative adoption pattern captured in Figure 5.2, following the original research in technological adoption and diffusion (Rogers, 2003).

At time t_0, a second new technology (B) is introduced. If the overall net benefits of B are large relative to A, it will be adopted, as shown in Figure 5.6. As adoption in B occurs (time t_0 to t_2), disadoption in A necessarily occurs simultaneously. For example, if 10 percent of vegetable production is organic, then 90 percent of vegetables must be produced using conventional (nonorganic) methods. The result is a 10 percent decrease, or disadoption, in conventionally produced vegetables.[4] The location and shape of the two bell-shaped curves in the model depend on the timing of the new innovations. If technological changes are introduced in rapid succession, no single technology will be completely adopted; some firms will move on to the next innovation before the old innovation reaches complete adoption. The width of each curve depends on the rate of adoption over time, which depends on one or more of the seven determinants described in the previous section.

In agriculture, economic conditions and societal values can have large effects on technological adoption. In Saudi Arabia, for example, the combination of oil wealth and a strong desire to be self-sufficient in food production have resulted in a highly productive, yet costly, investment in food production in the desert. One example is irrigation using desalinated water drawn from the Red Sea and Persian Gulf. This is expensive. Although the nation could import food at considerably lower cost, economic conditions and preferences in Saudi Arabia have led to a different set of technologies employed to produce food. Kislev and Shchori-Bachrach (1973) indicated that a rapidly growing economy causes innovation to occur, so the shapes (widths) of the curves in Figure 5.6 depend on the level of overall economic growth.

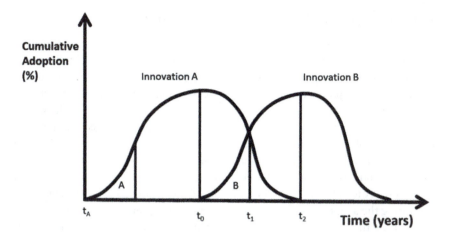

FIGURE 5.6 A model of agricultural innovation adoption

In what follows, a simple economic model of decision making is presented that follows a long tradition of economic models comparing the expected flow of future economic benefits to the expected flow of future economic costs. This economic approach is the foundation for most models of economic decision making. Sjaastad (1962) and Barkley (1990) used this framework to explain the migration of labor out of agriculture, and Barkley (1996) explored the durability of agricultural subsidies based on this framework. Recently, Onel and Goodwin (2014) expanded the framework to include option values in migration decisions. The relative economic advantage has the largest impact on the rate of adoption when the expected economic benefits of adoption are large relative to nonadoption ($EB_A >> EB_N$), and faster adoption rates are likely to follow.[5]

In some cases, perceived social costs can have a strong influence on adoption rates. If a nation finds an innovation to be incompatible with prevailing values and beliefs, the innovation may never be adopted. This has been the case for genetically modified organisms (GMOs, biotechnology) in parts of Europe and most nations in Africa. In these areas, the social costs of adoption are considered larger than the social costs of nonadoption ($SC_A >> SC_N$), resulting in a ban on GMO seeds in France and all African nations except Egypt, Burkina Faso, and South Africa.

To summarize, the extreme cases of large relative benefits ($EB_A >> EB_N$), and large relative costs ($SC_A >> SC_N$) lead to rapid adoption or nonadoption, respectively. These cases are often not controversial or interesting, since a large majority of citizens may strongly favor or oppose the innovation. Polarization, however, is likely to occur when expected economic benefits and social costs are relatively equal in magnitude: ($EB_A \sim EB_N$; $SC_A \sim SC_N$).[6] The simple model dev eloped here predicts that an issue is expected to be polarized when one group has large benefits (either economic or social) and a different group has large economic or social costs associated with the issue. As the US novelist Upton Sinclair wrote, "It is difficult to get a man to understand something when his salary depends on not understanding it" (Sinclair, 1935, p. 109).

A model of polarization in food and agriculture

The economic approach to adoption rates can be extended to form an explanation of how issues in food and agriculture become polarized. The model reflects any polarized issue, but is particularly useful for disputes in the food and agriculture sector, since food production has been subject to continuous technological change for all of its 10,000-year history. The upper half of Figure 5.7 replicates the rate of adoption of innovations in Figure 5.6: as innovation B is introduced and adopted, the adoption of innovation A declines. At time t_0 (Figure 5.7) innovation A is 100 percent adopted by the group under consideration (perhaps farmers in the examples). Innovation B is introduced at time t_0, and the process of switching from technology A to B begins. Adoption of B is 100 percent complete at time t_2.

During the adoption process, time t_1 represents the point in time when exactly one-half of the group in question is using innovation A and the other half is using B. For any controversial innovation, this is considered to be the point of maximum polarization.

In many cases, the adoption of B and disadoption of A represent significant financial decisions. Nonadopters of B might be sternly opposed to B, whereas early adopters of B could be earning significantly higher profits from using innovation B. If the economic benefits and costs are divided, the level of polarization could be high. Also, if social costs, compatibility, or emotional costs are involved, the polarization could be large. As was emphasized earlier in this chapter, the rate of adoption can be influenced by: (1) the rate of innovation; and (2) economic conditions. If innovations occur slowly, adoption curves are wide, as depicted in the top of Figure 5.8: adoption rates remain slow, since there are fewer innovations

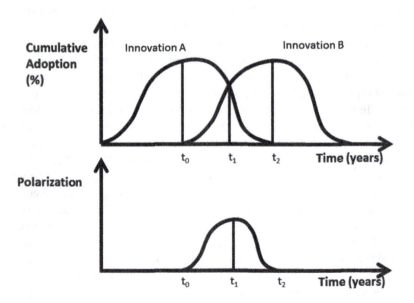

FIGURE 5.7 A model of agricultural polarization

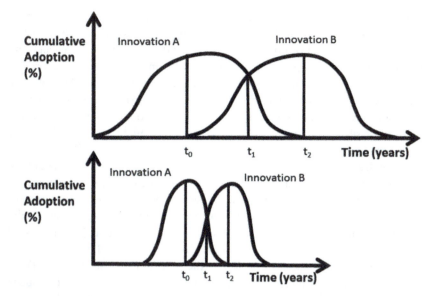

FIGURE 5.8 Impact of income growth on agricultural polarization

available in this case. This results in a longer period of polarization (the time interval between t_0 and t_2). Long-lasting social issues often reflect this: slavery, abortion, gun control, foreign policy, and the proper role of government are all issues that remained in a polarized state for extended periods of time.

When innovation is rapid, however, the adoption curves are narrow, as shown in the lower half of Figure 5.8. In this case, adoption occurs quickly, and polarization is less severe, since it is fleeting. An example might be cell phones: the benefits are large (EB_A >> EB_N), so adoption is relatively fast, resulting in a quick movement through the polarized phase. The length of the innovation cycle discussed here is closely connected to the business cycle. When overall economic activity slows during a recession, innovation cycles lengthen, since fewer innovations become available or fewer can be afforded by potential users. Thus, polarization is more likely to occur and remain during times of economic stagnation. Rapid economic growth results in an increase in the release of innovations, which can reduce the number and severity of polarized issues.

Innovators and early adopters: intensely pro-innovation

Agriculturalists the world over are typically pro-production. As such, most farmers, ranchers, and agribusinesses have a bias towards output-enhancing technological changes: they are pro-innovation. In high-income nations, government investments in agriculture have been large, effective, and durable. For example, throughout its history, the United States Department of Agriculture (USDA) led the effort to increase production, or "to make two blades of grass grow where only one grew before."[7] The US government investments in the Land Grant University complex (1862), agricultural research (1887), and the Cooperative Extension Service (1914) are considered a model of how to promote growth in productive efficiency and enhance agricultural output. The success of these institutions led to enormous productivity gains, and lower food costs. Agricultural producers, therefore, are often biased toward productive efficiency: innovations that reduce costs, increase output for a given level of inputs, or both. This "productionist" stance drives many of the most successful producers to develop new technologies and adopt new innovations quickly.

Recall that Rogers (2003) defined the innovators as the first 2.5 percent of the individuals in a system to adopt an innovation, and early adopters represent the next 13.5 percent. Although these quantitative definitions are more stringent than necessary for this analysis, the classifications provide a way to proceed in the adaptation of research on technology adoption rates to the polarization of food and agricultural issues. The innovators and early adopters are the first to adopt a new technology and appear to the left of the innovation cycle (Figure 5.1). In the adoption curve depicted in Figure 5.6, these two categories of adopters appear in area A for innovation A, and area B for innovation B. Rogers summarized his research:

> The salient feature of the innovator is venturesomeness, due to a desire for the rash, the daring, and the risky. The innovator must also be willing to accept an occasional setback when a new idea proves unsuccessful, as inevitably happens ... Thus, the innovator plays a gatekeeping role in the flow of new ideas into the system.
>
> *Rogers (2003), p. 283*

Early adopters are considered to be the "embodiment of successful, discrete use of new ideas" (Rogers, 2003, p. 283).

A great deal of agricultural economics research, both theoretical and empirical, has demonstrated that the major beneficiaries of technological change are innovators and early adopters: in many cases, there are large financial gains associated with new technology. To the extent that agricultural innovations reduce costs or enhance output, the first adopters will benefit the most. The innovators and early adopters, therefore, often form one pole of a divisive issue. This might be true for agricultural chemicals, growth hormones used in meat production, antibiotics, GMOs, gestation crates in pork production, and many other agricultural innovations that lead to productivity gains.

The public choice view (Box 5.1) implies that innovators and early adopters reap benefits, but only as long as other potential adopters do not adopt the innovation. Once adoption is widespread, production of the good using the innovation increases, resulting in downward pressure on price, and smaller gains to innovation. Interestingly and importantly, innovators and early adopters have a strong incentive to: (1) adopt an innovation early; and (2) keep others from

---

BOX 5.1: PUBLIC CHOICE

The field of public choice applies the theories and methods of economics to politics. The public choice view of politicians is that their behavior is motivated by self-interest, rather than the social good. The public choice literature suggests that small groups with concentrated economic benefits are more likely to have political power than larger groups (Downs, 1957; Olson, 1965). This counter-intuitive idea is due to the high costs of organizing larger groups, coupled with the low per-person gains to each member of a large group. Small groups have smaller costs of organization and mobilization, together with the possibility of large individual benefits. Therefore, small groups such as farmers and ranchers can have disproportionate power in politics, as can be evidenced by the large subsidies granted to agriculturalists in high-income nations.

---

adopting. If the early adopters can slow or halt the innovation adoption process before nonadopters enter, they can maintain higher levels of profits.[8] If the innovation is controversial, innovators and early adopters are likely to be the strongest political supporters of the innovation.

BOX 5.2: ORGANIC FOOD

Organic food provides an example of how a relatively small group of producers might earn high returns as long as the industry remains relatively small. Organic food commands a high price, based on a high willingness to pay by a relatively small but growing group of consumers. As the production of organic food increases, lower prices result in smaller returns to the original producers of organic food. Thus, to the extent that current organic producers can limit adoption of organic production practices, they can retain higher earnings. A rapid transition from conventional production methods to organically produced food would result in a loss of economic advantage to the early adopters of organic food production. In this case, there is a relatively small group of producers earning high rates of return, and a relatively small group of consumers who have a strong preference for organic food. Since organic food is more expensive than conventional food, consumers are typically in high-income brackets. Thus, the small size of producer and consumer groups allows them to have a large influence on the food industry.

This leads to a fascinating result of the polarization model: the innovators and early adopters of a technology can be co-dependent, or allied, with the opposition: current users of an innovation have an incentive to keep others from adoption. High returns to organic food would quickly diminish if there were to be a large shift out of conventional food production and into organic production practices.

BOX 5.3: GUN CONTROL

Gun control in the US is a nonagricultural example that is worthy of mention. Whenever an event triggers the likelihood of gun control legislation that seeks to restrict gun ownership, gun owners and the gun lobby increase their statements and marketing against gun control. This often results in a large increase in the purchase of guns and ammunition, and large increases in the returns to gun dealers and the gun industry. Oddly, the gun producers and dealers reap large economic benefits from the anti-gun lobby.

BOX 5.4: HARD WHITE WHEAT

Kansas is the "Wheat State," and produces a large percentage of the Hard Red Wheat (HRW) grown in the United States. Hard Red Wheat was originally brought to Kansas in 1871 from Russia by Mennonite immigrants. Elmer Heine, a wheat breeder employed in the Agronomy Department of Kansas State University, visited Australia in the 1960s and brought back wheat seeds of a class of wheat not typically grown in Kansas: Hard White Wheat (HWW) (Paulsen, 1998). A portion of the wheat grain grown in one year is saved back for seed wheat the next year. Thus, once a new wheat variety is released, it is difficult or impossible to control the quantity of the wheat produced, since wheat growers can determine how much wheat to retain for seed. Realizing the importance of maintaining exclusive rights to grow this new wheat, a wheat producers group was formed, with the idea of allowing only licensed growers to purchase and produce Hard White Wheat in Kansas. The economic theory was correct, with the exception of one fact: consumers found the two types of wheat to be what economists call "perfect substitutes." Flour tortillas and loaves of bread made with Hard White Wheat were indistinguishable from those made with Hard Red Wheat. The wheat growers had a great idea, but their efforts to corner the market were thwarted by indifferent consumers. Thus, Hard White Wheat had to be sold at the same price as Hard Red Wheat, or millers and bakers would purchase and use Hard Red Wheat instead. The story of Hard White Wheat in Kansas exemplifies the strong desire to keep an industry small in the attempt to keep prices and profits high.

Issues in food and agriculture that remain polarized over a period of time are likely to have two opposing groups locked in a debate that has large economic or social benefits or costs at stake. Many technologies that are currently under debate exhibit large private gains to early adopters. The members of this group often become strong proponents of the technology. Restated, early adopters are often opponents of the elimination of the technology. If the economic gains from use of the innovation are coupled with large start-up costs or implementation costs, the group of early adopters will have a large incentive to maintain the innovation. Somewhat counter to intuition, this group of motivated innovators can benefit from groups seeking to reduce the use or slow the adoption of an innovation. This brings the discussion to the second pole of a divided issue: the opposition.

The opposition: intensely anti-innovation

For many issues in food and agriculture, a large social gain is at stake, or perceived to be at stake. Many believe that agricultural chemicals are harmful to the environment and should be banned. Others may believe that animal agriculture is detrimental to the welfare of the animals raised for the purpose of meat consumption. For these groups, the perceived social gain from changes to conventional agricultural production practices is obvious, immediate, and worth investing in.

Many issues in food and agriculture have been characterized by successful opposition to a technology or innovation. Examples include the DDT ban in 1972, the elimination of finely textured lean beef (LFTB, or "pink slime") from the beef industry in 2012, and passage of the 2008 Proposition 2 in California, a law which requires that calves raised for veal, egg-laying hens, and pregnant pigs be confined in places that allow them to lie down, stand up, fully extend their limbs and turn around freely (Sumner *et al.*, 2008).

The opposition side of a debate can be characterized by public action, or political instead of economic solutions. In a market-based economy, consumers can purchase goods and services that they desire. If consumers wish to eliminate a certain characteristic of a good, or a production practice that is undesirable, they can stop the purchase of that product, or boycott, for a private solution. In many of these situations, the ability to organize, educate, and motivate consumers in large enough numbers is limited. Public choice theory suggests that the per-person gains associated with the elimination of a given technology are small, yet the social gains could be large, since all affected parties in a given jurisdiction could be made better off by a small amount. Since the per-person gains are small, these groups often rely on political strategies. If the opposition can receive 50 percent of the votes in a democratic referendum, nonmarket social policy could result.

The co-dependent nature of the opposition with the pro-innovation group should be highlighted. In the absence of the innovation, the opposition would not exist. In debates, the livelihood of full-time lobbyists, essayists, researchers, and pundits depends on the issue's continuation. This, together with the ability of the internet to magnify extremes of an issue, may be one explanation of why the number and magnitude of issues in food and agriculture have become increasingly polarized.

Summary and conclusions

Economic principles, together with the large literature on the rate of technology adoption rates, are used to derive a simple, useful model of polarization of food and agricultural issues. The model suggests that polarized issues are more likely to occur when there are large economic gains and losses that are of relatively equal magnitudes: a "balance of power." The maintenance of polarization requires two opposing sides with an economic or emotional stake in an issue.

Many issues in agriculture are characterized by large economic benefits concentrated on a small group. In many cases, a technology or innovation produces financial gain to the innovators and early adopters. These groups have a large incentive to promote their own continued use of the innovation. Forward-looking possible adopters may also benefit from slowing others from adopting the innovation, to maintain their own exclusive benefits.

Opposition groups are typically motivated by perceived social gains rather than potential private losses. These groups face significant organization and mobilization costs in their efforts to reduce or eliminate an opposed production practice or technology.

The polarization model provides an explanation of the causes, consequences, and major features of polarization in the food and agricultural sector. The model is based on economic determinants, but includes many characteristics of an issue that are often considered to be "noneconomic." These include compatibility, emotion, nostalgia, and personal commitment to a given course of actions.

As will be seen in the following chapters, the polarization model predicts that important issues can be depolarized through rapid innovation and the process of creative destruction. It should not come as a surprise that the new innovations that eliminate the current polarized debates will inevitably lead to new and different future polarizations. The innovation curves in Figure 5.6 will not stop at A and B, but will continue as time passes with future innovations in an unending process of technological advancement. The costs of polarization are greatly reduced in periods of rapid adoption of new ideas, production practices, and ways of doing things. However, rapid adjustment is also subject to transition and implementation costs. When confronted with these costs, it can be tempting to defend the status quo, or even become nostalgic about a more desirable past. However, overwhelming and abundant evidence suggests continuous improvement: the present is better than the past, and the future will be better than the present. Future polarized issues will be less severe than current ones, just as the issues that we face today pale in comparison to slavery, child labor, democracy, and environmental issues.

Notes

1 The term, "disadoption" refers to choosing to not use a given technology or innovation. It differs from depreciation and obsolescence in that disadoption refers to an active decision not to use the technology, idea, or innovation in question.
2 George Stigler (1954, p. 98) noted, "This was the first empirical generalization from budget data."
3 Ruttan (1984) provides an excellent summary and analysis of this research and the implications.
4 This is a simplification, and assumes that the two innovations are mutually exclusive, sum to 100 percent of a production system, that other resources devoted to production are held constant, and output rates are fixed. These simplifying assumptions are necessary to make the graphical model easier to interpret, with no loss in generality.
5 The symbol ">>" means "much greater than" and "<<" refers to "much less than."
6 The symbol "~" refers to "of approximately equal magnitude" or "is approximately."
7 This adage is commonly associated with the United States Department of Agriculture. However, it originates from Jonathan Swift's *Gulliver's Travels* (1726, Part II, Chapter 7): "that whoever could make two ears of corn, or two blades of grass, to grow upon a spot of ground where only one grew before, would deserve better of mankind, and do more essential service to his country, than the whole race of politicians put together."
8 The desire for exclusive rights to sell a good is pervasive in our economy: government licensing of taxis, public utilities, and medical doctors are examples. This is also how producer protection from imported goods arises. Domestic producers lobby for tariffs, import quotas, or nontariff barriers such as quality or food safety requirements. These barriers keep foreign food out of a nation, resulting in higher prices for domestic producers, discussed in Chapter 7. Immigration policy is similarly affected by early adopters. In this case, early migrants strive to keep out new immigrants to a nation, to protect jobs or perceived economic benefits.

6

INDUSTRIAL AGRICULTURE AND ECONOMIES OF SCALE

Only after considerable further investigation will we know whether or not reform in the packing industry is necessary. It is conceivable that such monopoly elements as exist yield desirable results. A less extreme possibility is that results are undesirable but not sufficiently bad to bother about.

William H. Nicholls (1940)

Consumers are the big winners in vertically coordinated modern agricultural markets; they have access to an incredibly wide range of products reflective of their increasingly diverse tastes, and at low cost. The less efficient producers and intermediaries are the big losers.

Crespi *et al.* (2012)

Introduction

On March 12, 2010, US Attorney General Eric Holder and US Secretary of Agriculture Tom Vilsack traveled to Ankeny, Iowa to participate in a meeting aimed at the reduction of "anticompetitive practices" in the broadly defined agricultural industry. Over 800 persons attended. The seriousness of the event was captured by the unprecedented joint efforts of the US Department of Justice (DOJ) and the US Department of Agriculture (USDA). Holder claimed, "You will see an historic era of enforcement that will almost inevitably grow with the partnership that we have established" (Neuman, 2010). Holder opened his talk by stating, "reckless deregulation has restricted competition in agriculture," and,

We all know that one of the greatest threats to our economy is the erosion of free competition in our markets. And we've learned the hard way that recessions and long periods of reckless deregulation can foster practices that are anti-competitive and even illegal.

Murphy (2010)

Vilsack confirmed the alarming situation by saying, "If we have a system that is not fair, is not making it easier for midsized [farm] operations to stay in business and therefore is leading to further declines in the number of farmers, then that's something we need to address" (Neuman, 2010).

A major topic at the meeting was Monsanto's market share in corn and soybean seeds: the biotech company sold 93 percent of all soybean seeds and 80 percent of all corn seeds in 2009, the year before the meeting (Whoriskey, 2009). Concentration in the meat packing industry was also emphasized, because four companies (Tyson, Cargill, Swift, and National Beef Packing) produced 85 percent of US beef, and four firms (Smithfield, Tyson, Swift, and Cargill) controlled 66 percent of the pork packing industry (Murphy, 2010; Crespi *et al.*, 2012). The largest four poultry companies processed 51 percent of all broilers in 2010 (USDA/GIPSA, 2013). According to Tom Laskawy, founder and executive director of the Food and Environment Reporting Network, an independent news organization that produces articles and information about food, agriculture, and environmental health, "When you get that kind of market power, abuse becomes rampant. Indeed, ranchers all around the country now agree that it's impossible for them to get a fair price for livestock" (Laskawy, 2011). This view has been common among food advocates for decades. As early as 1919, the US Federal Trade Commission (USFTC) accused the five largest meat packing firms of manipulating markets, restricting throughput, harming producers and consumers, and eliminating competition (Myers *et al.*, 2010).

The Ankeny meeting in 2010 did not lead to major legislative, regulatory, or commercial changes in the structure of the food and agriculture industry. Two years later, the GIPSA 2012 annual report stated, "[f]uture changes in concentration are expected to follow the patterns of the last 5 years" (USDA/GIPSA, 2013, p. 35). The ongoing rhetoric about the unacceptable behavior and performance of food and agribusiness industries has apparently not generated or been followed by actions undertaken to alter or ameliorate the problems. How could such a major problem be so resistant to reform over such a long period? One answer is the constant technological change that makes large volumes more cost effective, and thus profitable, for agricultural and food businesses. As volume increases, producers in almost all sectors of agriculture can succeed by increasing size, merging, and concentrating their activities.

Market concentration in food and agriculture

Agricultural and food industries have experienced large and increasing concentration among: (1) agricultural commodity buyers, such as food processors; (2) food manufacturers; and (3) grocery retailers (Kaufman, 2000; Rogers, 2001; Sexton,

2013).[1] The term "concentration" in this context refers to the extent to which a small number of firms control the sales or purchases in a specific industry or market (US Government Accountability Office [USGAO], 2009, p. 1).[2] The concentration ratio (CR) is generally defined as the percent of the industry's business, sometimes referred to as "market share," performed by the largest four firms (CR4) and by the largest eight firms (CR8). A high concentration ratio indicates that only a few firms are controlling or can control a market. A low ratio indicates the reverse: no single or small collection of firms does sufficient business to influence the market.

The average four-firm concentration ratio (CR4) in 15 key food-manufacturing industries was 56 percent in 2002, up from 45 percent in 1982 (USGAO, 2009). Crespi *et al.* (2012) report similar updated concentration ratios for 2007. The livestock processing industry has been singled out as a highly concentrated industry in which the top four firms slaughtered 64 percent of all US hogs in 2007, up from 32 percent in 1985, and the beef processing CR4 increased from 41 percent in 1981 to 84 percent in 2007 (Johnson and Becker, 2009). Grocery stores (chains) have also become more concentrated over time, with the average grocery retailing CR4 for 2006 for 229 metropolitan statistical areas equal to 79.4 percent (Sexton, 2013).

BOX 6.1: THE SUPERMARKET REVOLUTION: GROCERY STORES IN LOW-INCOME NATIONS

As economic growth and development occurs, food markets typically shift from fragmented, local markets such as village markets with both wholesale and retail functions to larger, centralized wholesale markets (Reardon *et al.*, 2003; Humphrey, 2007). Research by agricultural economist Thomas Reardon has focused on this process, which he states tends to occur first in dry goods such as grains and later in perishable, "fresh" products, including fruit, vegetables, meat, fish, eggs, and milk. The process of integration of fresh food markets into supermarkets has occurred in Africa, Asia, and Latin America as markets have become larger due to urbanization and improvement in transportation. Reardon *et al.* (2003) explored the major causes of the worldwide increase in the number of supermarkets. On the consumer side, urbanization and the entry of women into the workplace increased the convenience of supermarkets for many families. Large-scale supermarkets have lower processed food prices and greater food variety, based on cost savings from high-volume food procurement. Reardon *et al.* (2003) also emphasized that growth in refrigeration, access to automobiles, revolutions in logistical technology, and improved inventory management have contributed to lower food prices in supermarkets.

Reardon and his colleagues reported that the supermarket sector in Africa, Asia, and Latin America is "increasingly and overwhelmingly multinational (foreign-owned) and consolidated" (p. 1143). Rapid growth in foreign investment in the retail grocery sector was mainly due to global retail multinationals, including Ahold (Netherlands), Carrefour (France), and Walmart (US). Due to cost savings that arise from large volumes, the supermarket sector has become increasingly consolidated across the globe. For example, the top five chains per country comprised 65 percent of the supermarket sector in Latin America; 40 percent in the US; and 72 percent in France (Reardon *et al.*, 2003, p. 1143). Reardon *et al.* (2003) concluded that, "The consolidation takes place mainly via foreign acquisition of local chains (and secondarily by larger domestic chains absorbing smaller chains and independents)" (p. 1143).

Many observers and analysts are concerned with the impact of supermarkets on small farmers, since many of the companies demonstrate a preference for working with relatively fewer, modern suppliers (Swinnen, 2007; Humphrey, 2007). Food retailing in the UK has become consolidated over time, where food sales have transitioned from small independent shops to supermarket chains, including Tesco, Sainsbury's, Asda-Walmart, and Safeway (Tulip and Michaels, 2004).

A second feature of agricultural and food markets is increasing vertical coordination (also called vertical integration), referring to contracts or mergers between producers and processors. Contracts comprised over 39 percent of the value of US agricultural production in 2008, up from 28 percent in 1991 and 11 percent in 1969 (MacDonald and Korb, 2011). Contracts assure and improve efficiency in production (Sexton, 2013; Key and McBride, 2003). For example, the poultry industry is almost completely characterized by processors contracting with producers by defining and specifying nearly all conditions under which the birds are raised. In modern broiler producing facilities, the farmer does not own the birds, and production and economic decisions (what to feed, when to feed, how many birds per square foot of space, etc.) are nearly all defined by the processor (Goodwin, 2005).

Other agriculturally related firms and businesses have similarly high concentration ratios. Agriculture, food processing, and the retail grocery industries are each concentrated in a small number of large firms. The movement towards more concentration and ever-larger firms and industries has been present for the past several decades. Based on current trends and anticipated technological change, this movement is likely to continue.

BOX 6.2: POULTRY PRODUCTION IN THE UNITED STATES

The US poultry industry is large and growing. Until the 1940s, a majority of US farms had chickens mainly for use by the farm family. At that time, new technology and new breeding practices led to the growth of commercial poultry farming. Starting in the 1980s, broiler consumption has continued to increase due to new methods of growing and processing chickens and increasing human dietary concerns about fat and cholesterol. The combined value of production of broiler, egg, turkey, and chicken sales was $34.7 billion in 2010. Over 68 percent of the total value was broilers, eggs were 39 percent, turkeys 13 percent, and chickens 1 percent. The number of poultry farms grew 70 percent between 1987 and 2007, from 86,000 to nearly 148,000 (USGAO, 2009, p. 17). Even with the near doubling of poultry farm numbers, the market share of the four largest poultry producing firms increased from 27 to 57 percent during the 1982 to 2006 period (USGAO, 2009, p. 18).

Broilers are housed in confinement facilities for protection, disease control, and efficient use of labor and land. A typical poultry farm in the US is on 160 acres, has 70,000 birds per house, with three to four houses per farm. Each house turns out 6.5 "crops," or nearly 450,000 birds per year. Most poultry houses are dimly lit to reduce cannibalism among the birds and to encourage growth. The birds are fed on a nutritionally sound diet composed mostly of ground corn and soybean meal. Most poultry production occurs in the Southeastern US: the top three poultry-producing states are Georgia, Arkansas, and Alabama. In 1925, a 2.5 pound chicken required 16 weeks and almost 12 pounds of feed to reach saleable weight. Today, a chicken more than twice that weight grows in less than half the time and consumes only 11 pounds of feed – less than 2 pounds of feed for each pound of weight gain (Tyson, 2013).

Poultry consumption has grown relative to beef and pork consumption since the 1980s. In 2010, broilers represented 43 percent of all beef, pork, and poultry consumption in the US (USDA World Agricultural Outlook Board, 2012). The domestic market places higher value on white meat, and export markets are used for dark meat. The growth of poultry consumption has led to the poultry industry becoming complex and highly vertically integrated, meaning that one business owns several links in the supply chain. For example, Tyson, the largest chicken processor, owns firms that specialize in broiler breeding stock, hatcheries, broiler houses where the birds are raised, poultry processing plants, and distribution networks for poultry products.

The meat industry in the UK has become more concentrated, and as a result the number of slaughterhouses has declined from over 3,000 in 1967 to 520 in March 2001 (Tulip and Michaels, 2004).

Economies of scale

The major cause of the large scale of industrial food production is what economists refer to as "economies of scale." Economies of scale exist when the per-unit cost of production decreases as output is increased. Economies of scale are prevalent in nearly all production processes in which at least some of the costs can be spread over more units of output. The idea dates back at least to Adam Smith, who evaluated larger returns to production obtained from the division of labor (Smith, 1776). Although economies of scale, or decreasing costs per unit of production, are a characteristic of nearly all businesses, the large fixed costs needed for beef processing, food manufacturing, and retail grocery stores make economies of scale a major factor in their economic organization. Fixed costs are payments for inputs that must be paid regardless of how much output is produced. A farm purchased using borrowed money incurs an annual fixed cost in the form of a mortgage. The farm operator must pay the annual mortgage payment even if the farm produces no product (no revenue) at all. The same is true of taxes, insurance premiums, heavy machinery, and buildings. Payments for these must be made regardless of the level of output. This necessity forms an incentive for the business manager to produce as much as possible so these fixed costs can be spread over as many units of output as possible. The beef packing industry is used to help explain the concept in Box 6.3.

BOX 6.3: BEEF

Beef has been consumed since prehistoric times, and is currently the third most commonly consumed meat globally, after pork and poultry. Cattle were domesticated around 8000 BCE as draft animals and as a source of meat, milk, and leather. The United States, Brazil, and the People's Republic of China are the world's three largest beef producers and consumers. Two basic processes are used to raise cattle for beef. Either they are grass-fed on pasture, or they are grain-fed in confined pens, or feedlots. Feedlots, or concentrated animal feeding operations (CAFOs), typically feed cattle a ration of grain, protein, roughage (usually hay or silage), vitamins and minerals. The world's largest exporters of beef are Brazil, Australia, and the United States. Beef production is also important to the economies of Paraguay, Argentina, Ireland, Mexico, New Zealand, Nicaragua, Russia, and Uruguay (United Nations Food and Agriculture Organization [UNFAO], 2013).

Beef in a human diet is an excellent source of complete protein and minerals such as zinc, selenium, phosphorus, iron, and B vitamins (NCBA, 2014). Even so, recent health concerns have developed surrounding beef consumption. A short list of these concerns includes cancer, cardiovascular disease, and coronary heart disease. Some cattle in the US are fed on pastures fertilized with sewage sludge, and as a result may carry dioxins. The sludges are known to include E. coli contamination and bovine spongiform encephalopathy (BSE or, colloquially, "mad cow disease"). Given the importance of beef in the US diet, consumers continue to weigh the culinary and nutritional advantages of beef consumption with the food safety, environmental, and health concerns that arise in modern, concentrated beef production (NCBA, 2014).

BOX 6.4: MEAT PACKING IN THE UNITED STATES

The meat packing industry is made up of firms that slaughter, process, package, and distribute meat from animals such as cattle, pigs, sheep, poultry, and other livestock. The industry is primarily focused on producing meat for human consumption, but it also yields a variety of by-products including hides, feathers, dried blood, and, through the process of rendering, fat such as tallow and a number of protein meals used primarily in animal feeds. The meat industry is the largest agricultural sector in the US. Total meat and poultry production in 2011 exceeded 92.3 billion pounds. The meat processing industry alone employed 487,600 people in 2010 (American Meat Institute, 2013).

The meat packing industry has changed greatly in the past 30 years. Much of the change came after the industry-wide movement of packing plants to the Great Plains, where large numbers of feedlots are located. New meat packing companies such as Iowa Beef Processors (IBP, now owned by Tyson) brought new technologies and captured economies of scale in large plants located in areas where labor unions did not have a strong history. This, coupled with increasing worker speed and productivity, cut labor costs while the consolidation and mergers of plants provided new sources of profits to large firms that operated their large facilities on small margins. Over the past three decades the industry has been criticized for its hiring practices, hazardous working conditions, and low pay. The average earnings of meat processing workers in 2010 was $11.27 per hour, about 30 percent less than the average wage for all manufacturing jobs in the US at that time (US Department of Labor, 2013).

In beef processing, the slaughterhouse facility is an example of an asset that requires a large fixed cost. The large facility costs must be paid before a single kilogram of hamburger or a single leather hide can be produced. Large quantities of output allow spreading these fixed costs across many units to lower the per-unit cost of production.

TABLE 6.1 Per-unit costs decline with size: Hypothetical beef packing plant

Plant cost = $20 million	
Annual beef	*per-unit production cost*
(mil kg)	*($/kg)*
0	–
2	10
4	5
6	3.3
8	2.5
10	2

A hypothetical example is shown in Table 6.1 and Figure 6.1. The cost of constructing this new packing plant (slaughterhouse) is assumed to be $20 million.[3] If this new plant produces only one kilogram of beef, the cost of producing that single kilogram would have to be high enough to cover the entire fixed cost of the plant: $20 million. If production is increased – perhaps by increasing the speed of the production line – the per-unit costs decline, from $10 per kilogram for two million kilograms of beef to $2 per kilogram if the plant produces 10 million kilograms of beef. This simple example shows that as the plant's output increases, spreading these fixed costs allows the cost per unit of output to fall.

The principle of economies of scale helps explain the large and increasing scale and concentration levels of many industries, including food and agriculture. And, although the example is hypothetical, real-world meat industry economies of scale "are usually attributed to a larger firm's ability to divide tasks among more specialized workers, to use the most advanced technology, and to spread fixed costs across a larger volume of output" (Barkema *et al.*, 2001).

Substantial evidence demonstrates large gains in efficiency from larger plants and firms. A Government Accountability Office Report (USGAO, 2009) concluded that "[e]mpirical economic literature has not established that concentration in the processing segment of the beef, pork, or dairy sectors or in the retail sector overall has adversely affected commodity or food prices" (USGAO, 2009, p. 27). The careful analysis by the GAO found no evidence of market power (USGAO, 2009, p. 28). This report fits into a well-established cycle in the analysis of industrialized agriculture. First, concern over increasing concentration is expressed by consumers, farm interest groups, or politicians. Next, the allegations are investigated, and evidence demonstrates that, indeed, concentration levels have increased over time. Finally, evidence is nearly universal among economists and federal investigators that the impact of vertical integration, contracting, and concentration is likely to be beneficial to farmers, consumers, and the economy as a whole. This is explained in what follows.

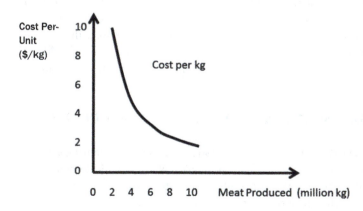

FIGURE 6.1 Graph of economies of scale: Hypothetical beef packing plant

Nicholls (1940) presented evidence that the packing industry exhibited illegal market power starting in 1890 (Nicholls, 1940, p. 225). Market power refers to the ability of a firm to charge a higher-than-competitive price on sales, or lower-than-competitive price on purchases. Allegations against the packers included acts in restraint of competition in the purchase of livestock, sale of meats, and conspiracy to secure rebates from the railroads (US Congress, 1919, p. 73). Economists' views of monopoly power have remained the same since the seminal findings of Harberger (1954), who concluded that monopoly power (market power) resulted in a loss of consumer well-being of approximately one-tenth of 1 percent of total market value, or about $2 per capita at the time of the study. These results have been remarkably consistent over time: economic studies confirm that the advantages of cost efficiency outweigh the potential damaging effects of market power among food and agricultural industries.

Studies show large gains in efficiency from both larger plants and larger firms. Multi-plant firms gain economies of scale by spreading administrative and management costs across more plants. Multi-product firms can gain cost advantages by producing different products: if the products are complementary, economists call these gains "economies of scope." Efficiency gains that result from economies of scale are the cause and the result of some of the most intense polarizations in the food and agricultural industries. The cost savings of large-scale or "industrial" agricultural production (commonly called "Big Food" by its opponents) provides significantly lower food costs to consumers because of economies of scale in the meat processing industry. Hamburger, steak, pork chops, and boneless chicken breasts have become less expensive over time. These gains benefit consumers (recall Chapter 4).

The opposition to larger plants and larger firms comes from individuals and groups opposed to market power, or industry concentration. This opposition is characteristic of typically "American" distrust of concentrated power and/or authority, a cultural ethos that was a major motivation for the American Revolution, and the basis of the constitutional democracy, as highlighted in Chapter 3. The concern that large firms could use and abuse market power is legitimate: firms with market power can charge prices above production cost to consumers, or offer prices lower than production costs to suppliers. Therefore, the concentration of industry based on economies of scale is the cause of a fundamental tradeoff between: (1) lower costs of agricultural products; and (2) potentially abusive market power.

BOX 6.5: GLOBAL ECONOMIES OF SCALE IN DIET

Globalization and international trade have increased dramatically in the past several decades, due to rapid and significant decreases in communication and transportation costs, and trade liberalization policies among most nations. Food, nutrition, and diets have also become globalized in two important and interesting ways (Khoury et al., 2014). First, diets have diversified in some nations. For example, as other foods have become more available in China, rice has declined as a portion of the average consumer's diet. In high-income nations such as the US and those nations in the EU, consumers are eating more imported foods such as mangoes (Khoury *et al.*, 2014). Second, the global diet is becoming more reliant on a small group of global "mega-foods," such as wheat, potatoes, dairy products, and palm oil. These two trends in global diets reflect a fundamental tradeoff between diversity and homogeneity of diets.

Global dietary preferences are in a transition towards "Western" diets, which include meat and dairy products, wheat, temperate vegetables and fruit, and sugary beverages. This movement towards homogenization of global diets reflects economic forces that lead to economies of scale in food production and consumption. The drivers of mega-foods include globalization and urbanization, the development of commodity transportation systems and multinational food industries, improvement and standardization of food quality and food safety, mass media, smaller family size, the growth of supermarkets, fast food, and processed foods (Kearney, 2010; Popkin, 2006). Technological change and policies in high-income nations have also led to a smaller number of crop commodities. These changes include the development and adoption of modern agriculture production techniques including mechanization, investments in breeding and adoption of high-yielding crops as a development strategy, and subsidies for a narrow range of crops.

Global mega-foods include soybeans, sunflowers, and palm oil, which have each increased in worldwide diets during the period 1961–2009. Low-income nations have been characterized by a transition to diet "Westernization," including a movement towards energy-dense foods such as animal products, plant oils, and sugars, and away from cereals, pulses, and vegetables (Kearney, 2010). Concern has developed over the possibility that economies of scale in food production and consumption could lead to less stability, less resilience to weather and nature, and lowered levels of food security. Therefore, the globalization of diets has resulted in a tradeoff between lower food costs provided by global economies of scale and the potential problems of the homogenization of diets worldwide.

Industrial agriculture and polarization

Consumer groups and others frequently make strong allegations and accusations about "Big Food" or industrialized agriculture. Regulation and reform of food companies exists, but it has done little to slow the continuing increases in concentration and consolidation of the agricultural, food processing, and grocery industries. The "economics of information" helps to explain why. For a food activist or concerned consumer, the cost of holding strong views against large food companies is small. Anti-corporate views may be prevalent because of the low cost of holding these views, rather than because of the accuracy of the views themselves. Holding and publicizing strong opinions opposing "factory farming," "industrial agriculture," or "multinational food corporations" costs little to nothing. Explaining the truthfulness and correctness of such strong claims is more expensive in terms of time, energy, and the difficulty of collecting, organizing, and analyzing evidence in favor of and against the claims.

Viewing the problem another way suggests that business firms subjected to regulation or reform could be subject to potentially large costs. The impacts of "breaking up" concentrated industries in the attempt to foster competition are important and interesting. For businesses characterized by economies of scale, industrial reform may result in smaller firms operating at significantly lower levels of efficiency, and incurring the concomitant increase in production costs. Consumers would pay higher prices for food.

Economists have traditionally claimed the need for a "competitive" industry to include many firms producing the same product. This classical view of a competitive industry has been replaced with the idea that competition can occur in industries with any number of firms. In the newer definition, the level of competition refers to how rapidly firms respond to price changes made by rival firms. Some industries have few firms, but high levels of price competition. Grocery stores in a specific location might be an example. If a competing grocery store quickly matches its rival's prices, there could be high levels of competition with only two firms. In the extreme, competition can exist in an industry with only a single firm (monopoly), if there exists a potential rival that could quickly enter the market and compete with the single existing firm. Economists call these "contestable markets," or industries characterized by a small number of firms, but high levels of competition due to the possible entry of rival firms.

Contestable markets are characterized by: (1) no entry barriers; (2) no sunk costs; and (3) access to the same level of technology.[4] In many food markets, if a single firm exhibits market power, it is possible that a rival firm could enter the market, resulting in a competitive price. The theory of contestable markets was used by economists including Baumol et al. (1982) to defend deregulation and market-based policies for industries that were traditionally regulated: communication, transportation, and banking.

Even more expensive than assessment of food industry allegations are the potential unintended consequences of regulatory reform of the food and agricultural industries. Regulations or industry reform could result in costly movements away from large-scale farms and processing facilities. Although large-scale firms cause social objections, breaking up large farms and firms would come at significant societal cost from losses of economies of scale leading to higher food prices. Any regulation or law that would cause movement towards smaller-scale agriculture must be carefully considered.

Even though a small number of firms produce and sell a large percentage of meat industry output (Ward, 2002), numerous economic studies have found high levels of price competition among firms in the meat industry (Ward, 2010). Ongoing disapproval of the meat packing industry has led to much study, reflection, and investigation of anti-competitive allegations. Most available studies conclude that large-scale operations provide economic benefits in the form of lower food costs, with a relatively small cost attributable to potential market power.

Industrialized agriculture, food processing, and retail groceries are not without greed, scandal, and corruption. However, it is unlikely that these large entities have a worse record or greater probability of ethical oversight than small firms and institutions. Temple Grandin reflected, "I see badly managed big and badly managed small ... It's not so simple to say, 'big is bad.' Big can learn from small, and small can learn from big" (Welshans, 2014).

Depolarizing industrial agriculture: a way forward

Industrial agriculture continues to be characterized by two opposing forces: (1) consumer and political groups that find flaws and abuse of power in large food and agricultural firms; and (2) a large and growing body of economic evidence that says the status quo may be superior to the alternative that includes more but smaller firms, more processing plants, and more grocery stores. The longevity and intensity of the polarized debate concerning industrial agriculture are exceptional. They are based on emotional, deeply felt issues concerning how food is produced and consumed. Depolarization of the issues of industrialized food could be achieved through recognition of both benefits and costs of large-scale agriculture, rather than a unipolar view that "big" is either "all good" or "all bad."

British economist E. F. Schumacher explored the increasing scale of production in his popular 1973 book, *Small is Beautiful: Economics as if People Mattered*. He concluded that large-scale organization is problematic, since large public or private bureaucracies result in impersonality, insensitivity, and a desire for power (Schumacher, 1973, p. 4). Schumacher emphasized that human activity could be enhanced by consideration of higher motivations such as spirit, morals, and meaning, rather than merely the acquisition of wealth and materialism. Schumacher explored the duality of size and found that there is no single answer:

> For his different purposes man needs many different structures, both small ones and large ones, some exclusive and some comprehensive. Yet people find it most difficult to keep two seemingly opposite necessities of truth in their minds at the same time.
>
> *Schumacher (1973), pp. 65–66*

Schumacher's view of looking at both sides of the scale issue is an important component of depolarizing large-scale issues in food and agriculture.

Depolarization of industrial agriculture could be enhanced through the pursuit of three tenets: (1) recognizing that criticism, both constructive and destructive, leads to improved future outcomes; (2) openness and transparency can mitigate polarized issues more effectively than secrecy and defensiveness; and (3) education and knowledge are powerful antidotes to polarization. One of the recurring themes of this book is that the political and economic systems of the US were founded in the belief that open debate, dialogue, and disagreement lead to superior policies and ways of doing things. People, cultures, and nations who close themselves off from the rigorous debate brought about by interactions with rivals and adversaries make the mistake of shutting down feedback and information crucial to improvement and continued success. Thomas Friedman puts it this way:

> It is not that closed societies can't innovate, it is simply that the chances of them doing it consistently are much, much lower. When you live as an open society your strength comes precisely from that openness and the undying spirit of innovation and entrepreneurship it constantly nurtures.
>
> *Friedman (1999), p. 230*

This is particularly true for groups that attempt to close themselves off from those who adhere to different and possibly opposing ideas. The ongoing need for all businesses to maintain continuous investigation of evidence based on ever-changing information and knowledge results in a dynamic path toward positive changes. The application of this conviction to large-scale agriculture suggests that food industry activists who criticize the food industry may be one of the major sources for future success of the industry. Firms and industries that take criticism and assessment into account in their decision making will certainly adopt, grow, and be more successful at meeting consumer wants and needs in the long run than those who do not.

Critics of industrial agriculture will continue to challenge the food industry in ways that cause it to upgrade policies, practices, and products to make them more favorable to consumers, while eliminating those actions that cause public relations problems and consumer anger. One method of maintaining the continuous, constructive flow of information and challenge is by adopting policies of openness and transparency. For example, farms and food processors that provide open processing facilities and tours to all interested individuals and groups do a great deal towards shutting down inaccurate claims. This is true for all farms and firms, from California strawberry farms to Nebraska meat packing plants. The idea is simple: by becoming open, any undesirable practices will need to be modified or eliminated. When activities and policies that do not meet the general high standards of ethics, animal welfare, and food safety are made public, the activities and policies will need to be changed. What may appear to be a potentially damaging policy could become a progressive program of improved public relations and consumer satisfaction (recall the "pink slime" example in Chapter 4).

While a policy of openness and transparency may appear idealistic and even "anti-agriculture," it has been recommended by Temple Grandin, one of the beef industry's most respected thinkers and advocates.[5] In her 2008 book, *Humane Livestock Handling*, Grandin suggests that openness can improve accountability to consumers since production practices become known to the public. Grandin emphasizes that the policy of openness allows the opposition to hold less severe views based on facts rather than speculation. Transparency increases public engagement with the industry, and leads to superior outcomes.

In one controversial strategy, animal activists gained entrance to meat packing plants by taking jobs at the plants for the express purpose of uncovering abuses by publicizing videos taken in the meat industry's facilities. As a reaction, five states have enacted "ag-gag" laws, which make these undercover operations illegal. Economists with experience in regulatory attempts to restrict human behavior suggest that such laws might have unintended consequences, including causing more difficulties than the original problem. Grandin (2008) suggests that meat packers should be open to all: "We've got to show what we do. We've got to get over being bashful. We've got to open the door and let the public see it" (Lowe, 2012; Schlosser, 2012). Grandin supports fast food restaurants McDonald's and Wendy's, who require their suppliers to treat animals humanely (Garner, 2009).

Retail groceries and economies to scale

Retail grocery stores have become larger, primarily due to the entrance of Walmart into the grocery market in 1988. The impacts of large-scale grocery stores are much the same as those in food processing and farming; large scale results in lower food costs to consumers, and the possibility of market power. Given the huge popularity and success of Walmart, it is evident that many consumers are content with lower costs, although many consumer groups remain strongly opposed to Walmart.

BOX 6.6: WALMART

Walmart is the largest retailer in world history, with millions of global customers. Sam Walton, the founder of the company, opened his first Walmart discount store in 1962, with the vision of saving customers money and helping them live better. According to the Walmart website, Walton's secret was simple: give your customers what they want. From a single store in Rodgers, Arkansas, Walmart has grown to over 10,000 stores in 27 countries, employing over 2.2 million workers, and serving over 176 million customers a year. The size of an average Walmart store is 108,000 square feet (over 2.5 acres), and each store employs about 225 people (Walmart Corporate, 2014).

One important feature of Walmart's success is logistics: how to transport goods from producers to customers across the globe. Walmart has one of the largest private distribution operations in the world, with over 40 Regional Distribution Centers. Each one is over one million square feet in size, and operates around the clock, supporting between 75 and 100 stores within a 250-mile radius. Walmart's innovations in transportation and logistics allowed the retailer to lower costs through expansion of the distribution network. A second major factor behind Walmart's success is the development and use of technology to track its inventory, causing reduced supply chain costs (Walmart Corporate, 2014).

Economies of scale and the environment

Environmental consequences are another potential impact of large size in agricultural and food production. Polarization has occurred in how meat is produced. Beef feedlots are criticized for potential environmental degradation and use of pharmaceuticals, and hog confinement operations are often criticized on the basis of animal welfare measures.

BOX 6.7: FEEDLOTS: CONCENTRATED ANIMAL FEEDING OPERATIONS (CAFOs)

A feedlot or feed yard is a type of animal feeding operation (AFO) used for finishing beef cattle prior to slaughter. The large beef feedlots, sometimes referred to as concentrated animal feeding operations (CAFOs), have thousands of animals in pens. Regardless of the size of the facility, the animals eat a diet composed mostly of grain. The first known feedlot was designed and built on the south side of Chicago by Gustavus Swift in 1876. It was followed by hundreds of similar facilities in the 1950s and 1960s when feed became widely available and lower transportation costs made it possible to locate feedlots on or near grain farms. In the 1980s, meatpackers located their plants next to the feedlots in the Central and Southern Great Plains.

Cattle destined for the feedlot feed on pasture until they weigh about 650 pounds at approximately 12 to 18 months of age. At that time, the animals are transferred to a feedlot, where they continue to grow (they are fattened) for approximately three to four months, gaining up to 400 additional pounds before slaughter. The grain diet provides marbling, or fat deposits, desired by consumers. However, a high grain diet lowers the acidity in the animal's rumen, and antibiotics are necessary to maintain animal health.

Feedlot operators have become increasingly attentive to the environment. Odor, water quality, air quality, and land utilization are all factors that feedlot operators must consider. Most feedlots require some type of governmental permit and must have plans in place to deal with the large amount of waste that the animals generate. The Environmental Protection Agency (EPA) has authority under the Clean Water Act of 1972 to regulate all animal feeding operations in the US. In some cases this authority is delegated to individual states. Feedlots contribute to greenhouse gases, due to the methane produced by the animals. Feedlot operators also consider animal welfare through attention to practices considered sound from an ethical and economic standpoint (NCBA, 2006).

BOX 6.8: SWINE CONFINEMENT

Until the 1990s, swine production was typically carried out on farms as a supplement to crop enterprises. Hogs were used to add value to corn when corn prices were low (Pitcher, 1997). No major improvements in genetics, productivity, or consumer acceptance occurred. In the 1990s, swine operators began to earn higher returns, which led to industrialization, economies of scale, and rapid gains in productivity. The number of hog farms decreased by approximately 70 percent from 1987 to 2007, a time when the number of large operations grew demonstrably. Modern swine operations frequently have more than 2,000 pigs. Today's producers strive to minimize production costs and optimize productivity and product quality. Environmental impacts including waste and odor must be managed effectively. North Carolina, for example, has a two-year ban on all new construction and existing swine facilities as a result of public concern over waste management issues (Pitcher, 1997).

The USGAO (2009) concluded, "Large processing plants achieved cost economies by ensuring a smooth and undisrupted flow of hogs allowing managers to operate their plants at near full capacity." For all plants, large and small, average total cost, or the cost per unit of output, increases sharply as volumes are reduced (Muth *et al.*, 2005, p. E5–6).

BOX 6.9: ANTIBIOTICS IN MEAT PRODUCTION

In the US and other meat-producing nations, antibiotics (also called antimicrobial drugs) are incorporated into animal water or feed to promote weight gain (Key and McBride, 2014). These antimicrobial pharmaceutical products are used at the sub-therapeutic, or prophylactic, level, meaning that the drugs are not used to treat a sick animal, but rather to maintain health and efficiency in healthy animals (Wade and Barkley, 1992). This use differs from the treatment, control, or prevention of disease.

The use of antimicrobials is controversial, because of concern about the overuse of antibiotics in livestock production, which could lead to the development of antimicrobial drug-resistant bacteria, since many of the drugs fed to livestock are the same as those used in human health care (US Food and Drug Administration [USFDA], 2012). The US Government Accountability Office (USGAO, 1999) reports increased consumer concern for antibiotic effectiveness due to: (1) over-prescription by medical doctors; (2) improper use by patients; (3) routine use in meat production; and (4) resistant strains of bacteria (USGAO,

1999). Several European nations have banned the use of antibiotics for growth promotion (Dibner and Richards, 2005). In the US, sub-therapeutic antimicrobial drugs are widely used, but growing concern by consumer groups and regulators has led to the implementation of a voluntary strategy to promote the judicious use of antibiotics in food-producing animals (USFDA, 2012).

This policy promotes voluntary measures of limiting antimicrobial drugs and incorporation of veterinary oversight in the use of the drugs. The key component of this policy is the phasing out of antibiotics used for weight gain or improving feed efficiency (converting feed into muscle). Research by Key and McBride (2014) indicates that the use of sub-therapeutic antibiotics increased hog enterprise efficiency by 2 percent. This is consistent with previous research. The authors concluded that a national ban on sub-therapeutic antibiotics would result in higher meat prices.

BOX 6.10: ANIMAL WELFARE

Many consumer groups are increasingly concerned about animal suffering during the production of meat and livestock products. Temple Grandin (2010, p. 39) has provided "core standards" based on the beliefs that: (1) animals have basic needs; and (2) a failure to fulfill these needs places animals under unnecessary stress. These standards include (National Research Council, 2010, pp. 242–243):

- Animals must be given opportunity to care for, interact with, and nurture their young.
- Animals must be able to build nests during farrowing.
- Animals must have sufficient space to move, exercise, and socialize with herd mates.
- Animals must have a dry area where they can lie down at the same time without soiling their bellies.
- Animals require clean air, including nonexcessive ammonia levels.

Many livestock producers, researchers, and observers have argued that farming practices that yield healthy, unstressed animals promote production and profitability (Grandin, 2008). In some cases, consumers are willing to pay for food that has been produced with animal welfare standards. However, Michael Carolan (2011) points out that "[f]armers are understandably concerned that more strict animal welfare standards will cost them in the long run because of a lack of consumers' willingness to pay for more humanely obtained animal products" (p. 158).

Summary and conclusions

Many food and agricultural industries are characterized by highly concentrated market structures, in which a small number of large firms produce a large percentage of the industry's product. Concentration has been present in the meat processing industry for over 100 years. Agricultural industries are often concentrated. Recently, grocery retailing has become concentrated as Walmart and other large, low-cost companies have entered the grocery market.

Concentration is caused by economies of scale, which occur when a firm has large fixed costs. These large costs result in decreasing average (per-unit) costs as firm size increases. Farmers, consumer groups, food activists, and others have continuously (and at times voraciously) called for regulation or reform of large agribusiness firms, yet very little has been done to slow or halt the continuing increase in the degree of concentration. This is explained by the huge economic advantages brought about by economies of scale – lower food costs for consumers and greater efficiencies for producers.

The dissipation of the continuous and extreme polarizations that surround industrialized agriculture are likely to require recognition that: (1) criticism and challenge can lead to improved future outcomes; (2) openness and transparency mitigate opposition more than secrecy and defensiveness; and (3) education and knowledge are powerful antidotes to polarization.

Notes

1 Sexton (2013) provides an outstanding and accessible summary of market power in modern agricultural markets.
2 The term "consolidation" is similar to "concentration," but generally refers to the organization of farms, food processors, or retail stores into fewer, larger firms (USGAO, 2009, p. 1). The term "concentration" refers to the extent to which a small number of firms control most of the sales or purchases in a specific industry or market (USGAO, 2009, p. 1).
3 The numbers in this example are simple, round numbers to make the example easy to follow and understand.
4 No real-world industry perfectly fits these three conditions for a contestable market. However, many industries are characterized by significant levels of competition due to the possibility of entry by existing or rival firms (Baumol et al., 1982).
5 Grandin is also known for her triumph over autism. This story is told in her autobiography, *Thinking in Pictures: And Other Reports From My Life With Autism* (2006).

7

EXTERNALITIES, PUBLIC GOODS, AND AGRICULTURAL SUBSIDIES

The traditional approach has tended to obscure the nature of the choice that has to be made. The question is commonly thought of as one in which A inflicts harm on B and what has to be decided is: how should we restrain A? But this is wrong. We are dealing with a problem of a reciprocal nature. To avoid the harm to B would inflict harm on A. The real question that has to be decided is: should A be allowed to harm B or should B be allowed to harm A?

Ronald Coase (1960), pp. 87–88

Introduction

Agriculture provides plentiful and nutritious food for a growing global population, but agricultural production processes also result in a wide range of environmental impacts – some beneficial and some harmful. Beneficial amenities beyond the production of food might include open spaces and rural scenery, features highly valued by many individuals in an increasingly urban society. The agricultural sector also produces food security for much of the world's population. Food production, however, also contributes to environmental problems including nitrate and pesticide runoff, odor from animal agriculture, soil erosion, and human health issues stemming from pesticide application (Lichtenberg, 2002). Agricultural productivity depends on a natural resource base (land, water, space, etc.) that links it to food producers, processors, and consumers who may also generate problems that affect other people and processes.

Modern, science-based agriculture is characterized by the development and adoption of new technologies that greatly improve the human condition. However, these new technologies, including agricultural chemicals, fertilizer, genetics, and machines, are not perfect. Nor are they always neutral with respect to human activity and well-being.

The production of crops and animals also has three unique features that cause it to diverge from the competitive industry ideal described in Chapter 3. These features create the potential for market failures within the agricultural and food processing sectors. First, agriculture is a major user of resources, including chemicals, fertilizer, land, and water. Second, much of agricultural production has a crucial intertemporal characteristic. Resource use decisions have long-term consequences, so resource use today inevitably alters resource availability in the future. Third, many people desire to live in a nation that maintains rural landscapes and rural communities as well as some assurances regarding agricultural viability into the future.

Since the industry creates both positive and negative outcomes, it is a strong candidate for economic analysis that investigates both the benefits and costs of all decisions, systems, and ways of doing things. The systematic approach of economics (weighing costs against benefits) is highly useful in both private and public policy decision making, since many individuals do not see issues and events as possessing both good and bad characteristics.

Chapter 3 emphasized the major advantages of a market-based system of economics: efficiency, prosperity, and gains in longevity. The discussion also pointed out the potential for market failure, or situations where markets do not provide socially optimal outcomes. Market failures stem from market power, externalities, and public goods, as will be defined and explained below. Market power was discussed in Chapter 6. This chapter discusses externality issues in agriculture. Economic theory provides elegant analyses, background, and a strong case for effective public policy. However, real-world policies for the market failures that surround externalities and public goods are challenging to formulate and costly to regulate, enforce, and evaluate. Given that public policies redistribute income and wealth through resource use programs, it is little wonder that the policies relating to agriculture are controversial.

Externality

Externalities are present when the actions of one person affect another person. The external effects can be positive, such as when person A's bees, which are raised for their ability to produce honey, pollinate person B's fruit orchards. Or they can be negative, as when toxic chemical runoff finds its way into a downstream neighbor's water supply. Markets do not always provide an optimal outcome in such situations, and the external events are referred to as "market failures." Externalities will be analyzed in detail, and possible solutions to negative externalities associated with agricultural production will be explored.

BOX 7.1: ECONOMIC THINKING APPLIED TO STRONG OPINIONS REGARDING RISK

Many environmental and consumer groups, including the Environmental Defense Fund, the National Resource Defense Council, the Environmental Working Group, and Greenpeace, oppose the use of agricultural chemicals.

The claims against agricultural chemicals are often bold and acrimonious. Because of this, changes in how food is produced and processed can be, and often are, polarizing. But such claims are easily made, because it is costless to have an opinion. An actual major change such as a chemical ban, however, is often much more costly than an opinion or a claim. Such a change requires more thought, analysis, and careful review. While chemical use may require regulation, eliminating chemical use comes at substantial costs (Zilberman, 2012). When care is taken to communicate the full costs of policy changes, many individuals change their views from extreme to moderate. For example, in many cases some chemical use is warranted to maintain low food costs. Externality issues, that is, inadvertently harming others, can often be resolved through greater levels of knowledge and communication. When benefits and costs are explained to individuals and groups on both sides of an issue, agreement or compromise often follows. For example, the Environmental Working Group (EWG), a "think tank" headquartered in Washington, DC, provides careful monitoring, evaluation, and reporting of health risks associated with chemicals typically found on fruits and vegetables (EWG, 2013b).

BOX 7.2: AGRICULTURAL CHEMICALS

Chemicals are widely used to enhance agricultural productivity. Higher yields per acre are obtained when synthetic organic pesticides are used to control unwanted pests, including weeds, insects, and plant diseases. The agronomic and economic benefits of chemical use are large for farmers, food processors, and consumers, but chemical use has unintended environmental effects that can be harmful to human health. Adverse health can be short term due to direct chemical exposure, or long term due to chemical residues in the environment. The possibility of undesirable side-effects is used to justify government intervention into agricultural chemical use. Intervention usually takes the form of regulation and enforcement of chemical production, distribution, and use (Waterfield and Zilberman, 2012).

The use of agricultural chemicals has grown rapidly since World War II (Osteen, 2003) with nearly 75 percent of all herbicides used to control weeds in fields of corn, cotton, and soybeans (Zilberman *et al.*, 1991). Global pesticide expenditures were estimated at approximately $32 billion in 2001, and US expenditures on pesticides were $11 billion in the same year (Kiely *et al.*, 2004). Waterfield and Zilberman (2012) reported that the huge growth in chemical use is due to ease of use, limited information requirements, and the speed of effectiveness.

Agricultural chemical use is contentious, and is often the subject of intense and emotional debate. Farmers who use a variety of chemical-laden products to produce "conventional food" are often pitted against organic food producers, consumers, advocates, and activists who desire food produced with no chemical application. To regulate chemical use, governments can use taxes on chemicals, quantitative restrictions, outright bans, or tradeable permits. Tradeable permits, also called "cap and trade" policies, place a mandatory cap on emission levels, while providing businesses with a degree of flexibility in how they comply. According to the US Environmental Protection Agency (USEPA, 2013), successful cap and trade programs reward innovation, efficiency, and early action and provide strict environmental accountability without inhibiting economic growth. Examples of successful cap and trade programs include the nationwide Acid Rain Program, and the northeast region nitrous oxide program (USEPA, 2013).

Bans on use make up the main form of agricultural chemical regulation in the US. They prevent use of those chemicals that have been found to be harmful to the environment or human health. The economic approach to regulation assesses the benefits that arise from chemical use, typically higher output levels, and/or prevention of yield loss due to pests. These agronomic gains are valued in dollar amounts to identify the economic value of chemical use. Similarly, the costs associated with chemical use are estimated, and a dollar value is derived for environmental and potential human health risks. Analysts often focus on the availability of substitutes, and identify alternative sources or methods of pest management. The value of a chemical will depend crucially on substitutes available to solving the pest problem. An effective chemical with no close substitutes will be more valuable, and more likely to avoid bans than one that has alternatives.

In some cases, chemical use results in pest resistance. Resistance is an unintended consequence of controlling that part of the pest population that is able to survive treatment and often leads to a new group of chemical-resistant pests. Individual pests that survive in this way become an increasingly large fraction of the pest population, and the effectiveness of existing chemicals declines over time (Waterfield and Zilberman, 2012). Palumbi (2001) estimated the annual cost of pest resistance to be between $2 billion and $7 billion in pesticide expenditures and yield losses.

Optimal chemical policy is defined by comparing of the estimated economic benefits with the potential environmental costs of chemical use. Efficient regulation of agricultural chemicals is difficult due to the complexities of measurement and knowledge about the levels of chemical residues in the air, water, food, and soil. Not only are these levels difficult to measure, but the levels differ widely across space and time, making a quantitative targeted reduction (e.g. 45 percent of usual use rates) inequitable. Measurement and monitoring are costly and challenging. Nor is that all. Even if chemical levels could be quantified accurately, the impact of the chemicals on the environment and human health would need to be known in order to plan and implement effective public policies. The linkages between agricultural chemicals and their impacts on ecosystems and human health are notoriously difficult to uncover and understand.

International trade adds another layer of difficulty to chemical policies since chemicals used in some nations and banned in others lead to differences in production costs, providing an economic advantage to countries where it is possible to use chemicals that are banned elsewhere. In spite of these challenges, the use of agricultural chemicals will likely continue as population growth increases the demand for food and continual discovery, development, and the adoption of safer, more effective pesticides occurs.

A numerical example shows the benefits and costs of agricultural chemicals (Zilberman and Marra, 1993). The example is general enough to extend to most negative externalities that might occur in agriculture, including airborne odors from confined animal feeding operations (CAFOs) or chemical runoff in downstream waters. Suppose a corn farm is located next to a vineyard where grapes are grown. The corn farmer applies herbicides to kill weeds in the corn fields, but the chemical drifts and causes damage to grape production in the adjacent vineyard. The herbicide is effective at killing weeds, and increasing the productivity of the corn crop, but it is also (unfortunately) effective at killing grapes, thus decreasing profits for the grape grower. Suppose further that the vineyard owner has no legal recourse against the corn producer. The corn farmer receives economic benefits from spraying: weed reduction results in higher corn yields, and increased profits, as shown in columns (1) and (2) in Table 7.1. As is typical for production processes, the first spray provides the largest increase in profits, followed by further profit increases, but at a declining rate for subsequent sprayings. The fifth spray costs more than it earns in profits, as seen in the bottom row of columns (2) and (3) of Table 7.1.

TABLE 7.1 Effects of corn farmer herbicide on corn and grape profits

(1) Sprays	(2) Corn profits	(3) Corn Δprofits	(4) Grape damage	(5) Corn profits – damage	(6) Grape profits = 100 – damage	(7) Grape Δprofits	(8) Corn + grape profits
0	100	—	0	100	100	—	200
1	160	60	20	140	80	–20	240
2	200	40	30	170	70	–10	270
3	220	20	45	175	55	–15	275
4	230	10	60	170	40	–15	270
5	220	–10	75	145	25	–15	245

Economic analysts reach their conclusions by referring to the marginal (incremental) changes in benefits and costs associated with each additional application of chemical spray. Column (3) shows the marginal benefits from each additional spray application, or the additional profits associated with an additional spray (Δprofits). These are called marginal benefits: the additional benefits of increasing the level of an economic activity (spraying in this case) by one unit. The grape grower faces additional costs from each spray due to the herbicide drift. Each additional spray concentrates more chemical on the grapes, resulting in increasing damage, as shown in columns (4) and (7) of Table 7.1. Each additional spray results in greater damage to the grapes, causing unintentional economic harm to the vineyard owner. The dollar value of damage for each spray is shown in column (4).

The marginal cost of each spray application to the grape grower is the additional dollar reduction in profit that comes with increasing the level of spray by one unit (Δprofits), shown in column (7). Note that the marginal benefits to the corn farmer in column (3) are the rate of change in corn profits (column 2) and the marginal costs of the grapes produced shown in column (7) are the (negative) rate of change in total costs (column 4). The corn farmer would prefer to use four sprays, and the grape grower would prefer no sprays at all. If the grape grower had no legal recourse to stop the spraying activity, then the corn farmer would spray four times, earn $230, and cause an externality equal to a loss of $60 to the grape grower. Column (6) shows the impact of spraying on grape profits: the value of the grapes equals $100, and the damages (column 4) are deducted from $100 to achieve the grape grower profit level net of herbicide damage (column 6).

The externality can be "internalized," and the market failure resolved in any of three ways: (1) a tax; (2) government regulation such as imposing a quantitative restriction on spraying; or (3) private bargaining, between the corn farmer and the grape grower.

First, consider the tax. A tax used to "internalize" an externality, or account for the cost of the externality, is called a Pigouvian Tax named after a British economist Alfred C. Pigou (1877–1959). As early as 1932, Pigou studied the possibility of using such taxes for regulatory purposes (Pigou, 1932). If a tax set equal to the cost of a negative externality is levied on the person or firm that creates the externality, the person who creates the negative externality will change his behavior so that the externality will not be created. This solution justifies taxes on goods that may be "overconsumed" because the overconsumption is responsible for the negative effects. Overconsumption of this kind can easily occur in cases dealing with agrochemicals such as pesticides and herbicides, fertilizer, or water pumped from a commonly held aquifer. If these goods are used at levels higher than optimal, a Pigouvian tax can lower the use to the economically optimal level.

Table 7.1 shows a hypothetical situation in which a Pigouvian tax is used to regulate chemical use. If the tax is set equal to the damage, the resulting impact on corn profits is found in column (5). With the tax, net profits are highest for three sprays, a reduction of one spray from the original no-tax case. Corn profits under the tax are maximized at $175, and the damage inflicted on the grape grower is

$45. The example shown in Table 7.1 demonstrates how government regulation in the form of taxes, quantitative restrictions, or outright bans of chemical use could reduce or eliminate externalities. One important characteristic of the example is that a ban on herbicide use would result in an overall loss of $130 in profit reductions to the corn producer from the ban's effect on the use of four sprays. In this case, damages to the grape grower would be reduced by $60, and the net loss to both farmers would equal $70 (130 − 60 = 70). Therefore, the "optimal" level of chemical use is greater than zero. Society (in this case the two farmers) is better off with some positive level of chemical use, and an accompanying positive, but lower, level of pollution, or externality. This result is often surprising to individuals who have not investigated the costs of banning or eliminating risks to society. The analysis does not suggest that all individuals desire a positive amount of pesticide use. Instead, it suggests that society is better off when a positive amount of pesticide is used. The benefits of this action outweigh its costs.

The analysis becomes deeper and more interesting when the two affected parties can bargain with each other or strike a private deal. This possibility was first discussed by Ronald Coase (1910–2013), a University of Chicago economist (Coase, 1960). Coase suggested that market failures due to externalities would not occur if property rights were well defined. If the two affected parties were allowed to bargain with each other, the optimal solution would occur without government coercion, regulation, or the costs associated with monitoring and enforcement. This non-intuitive solution to externalities was initially met with disbelief by other economists (*The Economist*, 2013b). By 1991, however, "Coasian Bargaining" was highly regarded, widely used in public policy, and Coase was awarded the Nobel Prize in Economic Sciences for his contribution. Coase hypothesized that in an idealized world of full information, low transactions costs, and complete enforcement of property rights, externalities would be resolved and the socially optimal allocation of resources (the optimal level of resource use) would occur regardless of who was granted the property rights (Coase, 1960). Table 7.1 provides an example. Rather than legislating a tax or a restriction on use, the role of government is changed to granting the "right to pollute" to one of the two affected parties: either the corn farmer (sprayer) or the grape grower, whose crops are damaged by the herbicide drift.

First, suppose that the corn producer has the right to use herbicides with no penalty. As before, the corn farmer would spray four times to maximize profits at $230. If the grape grower could bargain with the corn farmer, the grape grower would be willing to pay up to $15 to have the number of sprays reduced from four to three sprays (column 7). The reduction of chemical application by the corn farmer would reduce corn profits by $10, and the grape grower would gain $15. The grape grower would voluntarily pay at least enough to fully compensate the corn farmer for lost profits from herbicide reduction. In this situation, the corn farmer has the property rights, and a mutually beneficial agreement results in three sprays per year. Further reduction from three to two sprays would not occur, since the gains in the form of reduced damages to the grape grower ($10, column 7) are less than the lost corn profits ($20, column 3).

If the grape grower has the rights to limit all spraying, he would allow zero sprays to maximize grape profits at $100 (column 6). However, the corn farmer would gain $60 for the first spray, $40 for the second spray, and $20 for the third spray. For the first three sprays, the grape grower would lose $20, $10, and $15, respectively. For each of the first three sprays, the corn farmer would be willing to pay the grape grower enough to compensate fully for the herbicide damage, and still make the chemical use profitable. For the fourth spray, however, the corn farmer would gain $10, and inflict damage equal to $15. This spray would not be worth a bargain being struck or even discussed, since the grape grower would require more ($15) than the corn farmer was willing to pay ($10). Therefore, the optimal number of chemical sprays is equal to three sprays per year, the same result as was achieved when the corn farmer owned the right to spray. The optimal number of sprays was equal to three, regardless of who owned the property rights, as long as the affected parties could bargain with each other. This unexpected solution requires full information, low transactions costs, and enforceable (and enforced) property rights. These conditions are not always present in the real-world agricultural sector.

Coase's approach to externality problems has resulted in major changes in public policy and the regulation of externalities. In many situations, Pigouvian taxes, quantitative restrictions, and bans have been replaced by "tradeable permits." In the usual Coasian situation, public policy sets a maximum amount of pollution in the environment, then sells "licenses to pollute" to the highest bidder. The market mechanism encourages efficiency and innovation, providing benefits over older forms of regulation that mandated certain practices or banned the use of pollutants. The major Coasian conclusion is that many externality issues are resolved every day through private bargaining agreements between parties without government intervention or involvement. Typically, these situations occur when the number of affected parties is low and the transactions costs of bargaining are low. Examples include the Nature Conservancy and the American Farmland Trust, which purchase land in order to preserve it (Zilberman and Marra, 1993, p. 232). The Environmental Defense Fund (EDF) also emphasizes market-based solutions: "We use a uniquely effective approach, drawing on science, economics, partnerships and bipartisan outreach. We solve problems by bringing together insights from many disciplines and diverse groups of people" (EDF, 2014).

An intermediary solution instead of one extreme or the other characterizes outcomes of Coasian bargaining. This is a useful approach to depolarization issues dealing with agriculture and food issues. Bargaining can result in socially desirable outcomes. Extreme positions taken by those who refuse to bargain result in an extreme position that is good for some, but at the expense of others. To move affected parties toward bargaining, Coase suggested defining property rights clearly, and lowering transactions costs.

Coasian bargaining between affected parties is a popular solution among economists, since the solution relies on private incentives, and the outcome is voluntary and mutually beneficial. The herbicide example in which the corn farmer's herbicide drift harmed the neighbor's grape crop provides additional understanding.

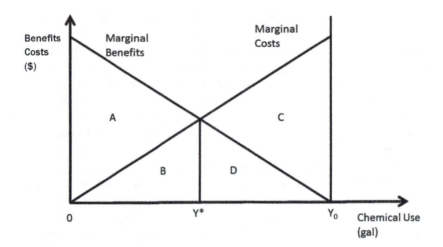

FIGURE 7.1 Graph of effects of corn farmer herbicide on corn and grape profits

Consider Figure 7.1. Recall that the corn farmer uses chemicals to increase his farm's productivity and profits. This practice, however, imposes costs on a nearby vineyard. As in most production processes, marginal benefits to the corn farmer are subject to diminishing returns: the first gallon of chemical applied is the most productive, and each successive gallon provides lower marginal (additional) revenue (Figure 7.1). At Y_0 gallons, all of the productivity (and therefore monetary) gains are exhausted. Now consider the grape grower's situation. As chemical use on the neighboring farm increases, the damage to the grapes also increases at an increasing rate, since higher levels of chemical result in greater marginal damages (Figure 7.1).

The externality occurs because the corn farmer desires to use Y_0 gallons of chemical to maximize profits, whereas the grape grower desires zero gallons of chemical use. The outcome will depend on who has the legal right to use the chemical. If the corn farmer owns the right to apply chemicals, Y_0 will result, whereas if the neighboring grape grower has the legal right to limit pesticides, zero chemical use will result. Coase suggested that if the costs of negotiation (bargaining) are low, then the optimal use of chemicals will result, regardless of which party owns the property rights. Suppose that the corn farmer owns the right to use chemicals, and applies Y_0 gallons. This will cost the vineyard owner BCD dollars, since the total costs of damage are equal to the additional costs times the quantity used (Y), or the area under the Marginal Cost curve. To reduce the quantity of chemical use to $Y^\star$, the grape grower would be willing to pay any amount up to CD dollars (the total value of economic damage from using $Y_0 - Y^\star$ gallons of chemical), and the corn farmer would be willing to accept any payment above D dollars (the economic gains from using $Y_0 - Y^\star$ gallons of chemical). At $Y^\star$, the grape grower's willingness to pay (Marginal Cost) is equal to the corn farmer's willingness to accept the payment to reduce chemical use (Marginal Benefit). Thus, the optimal quantity of chemical applied to the corn is $Y^\star$.

If the grape grower owns the right to chemical use, and could legally halt all chemical use by the corn farmer, the initial value of chemical use will be zero. However, if the corn farmer can negotiate with the grape grower, s/he will be willing to pay up to AB dollars (the economic benefit of chemical use for Y★ gallons), and the grape grower will accept any dollar amount above B dollars (the amount of economic damage caused by Y★ gallons of chemical use). In this case, the equilibrium quantity of chemical use is also Y★ gallons. It should be emphasized that this is truly an unexpected result: private bargaining will result in the optimal use of chemical (Y★), regardless of who owns the right to use or prevent the use of the chemical.

Coase's contribution suggests that in many externality cases, there is no need for government regulation or market intervention. In particular, if the costs of negotiating are low, the best solution to many externality problems may be to let the affected parties negotiate a solution. According to the analysis described here, this will result in the socially optimal level of resource use. It is important to note that the optimal level of chemical use is greater than zero, a result that some dedicated environmentalists and organic agriculture advocates will not accept. Some individuals and groups may advocate zero use of agrochemicals, fertilizer, and other agricultural inputs that have environmental consequences. This position ignores the societal benefits from more efficient food production, resulting in lower food and fiber costs.

Challenges of agricultural externalities

Imposition of a tax has limitations. It may be difficult to measure the level of externality, or to know the appropriate tax level to charge to achieve a desired outcome. Perhaps the biggest drawback to Pigouvian taxes is the measurement issue associated with externalities, including: (1) physical measurement of the externality source, such as the presence of a pollutant, which differs across time and space; (2) economic damage caused by the externality, which can be highly variable; and (3) societal preferences for non-market goods such as clean air, clean water, or human health. The measurement problem makes policy decisions related to resources and the environment challenging. To complicate the decision further, most environmental policies are interconnected, and have possible effects on other environmental goals and resources. However, there is a need for policies even if inexact, due to the potentially large negative externalities associated with agricultural production: soil erosion, water quality, future water availability, human health, and the like.

Negotiation is often expensive enough to eliminate the possibility of a Coasian bargaining process. In agricultural resource issues, the costs of negotiation are often high, because of the large number of affected parties and the need for accurate measures of benefits and costs associated with the externality. Coase (1960) concluded that "transactions costs are costly, sufficiently costly at any rate to prevent many transactions that would be carried out in a world in which the pricing system worked without cost." Saying this, Coase was the first to point out a serious limitation to using Coasian bargaining in real-world situations.

A possible (but hypothetical) Coasian situation might go as follows. Suppose that many individuals are negatively affected by use of agricultural chemicals and fertilizers in fields near their homes. They may not be able to negotiate effectively with a tightly knit and well-organized group of agricultural producers. Getting all affected parties to work together in a negotiating session could increase the costs associated with solving the problem in this way. Because of the large number of affected people there may be a role for government regulation of resources (chemicals) used in agriculture or for the government to assign a negotiator to assist in a Coasian-like "bargaining" process. In reality, agriculture is heavily regulated by the government: input bans, quantitative restrictions, taxes, and subsidies are pervasive. This type of regulation reflects the high costs of developing and enforcing agreements between affecting and affected parties. Similarly, it should be emphasized that government regulation is not costless, and these costs are often overlooked in policy analysis. It is possible that government policies aimed at internalizing externalities could lead to costs higher than those of the externalities themselves (Caplan, 2008).

Coase used the economic way of thinking to help resolve externalities. Unfortunately, the real world is too complex to apply Coase's analysis to many externalities that arise in food production: water pollution, soil erosion, odor from concentrated animal feeding operations (CAFOs), human health issues, and dozens of others. Why? Because the transactions costs are high given the large number of affected individuals and groups.

BOX 7.3: BETA-AGONISTS IN MEAT PRODUCTION: ZILMAX AND OPTAFLEXX

Zilmax and Optaflexx are brand-name pharmaceutical products known as beta-agonists, or non-hormone growth promoters, fed to cattle to add weight and reduce fat content in the meat prior to slaughter (Polansek and Huffstutter, 2013). These two pharmaceuticals were tested extensively during the early 2000s, and in 2007 gained approval from the US Food and Drug Administration (USFDA) for use in feedlots. The economic benefits of the growth promoters are large: on average, cattle that are fed beta-agonists gain 24 to 33 additional pounds in their last 20 days in a feedlot (Kay, 2013). Temple Grandin, a livestock industry leader, publicized her concerns about the potential harmful effects of beta-agonists on animal welfare: lameness and heat stress (Polansek and Huffstutter, 2013). Kay (2013) reported that feedlots were reluctant to use the growth promoters, and beef processors were even more reluctant to accept cattle fed with the recently developed feed additives. Kay (2013) also reported that Tyson and JBS USA, the nation's two largest beef processing companies, "began accepting [beta-agonist fed cattle] in 2011 after intense debate within each company." One year later, over 75 percent of all cattle on feed were fed either Zilmax or Optaflexx. The beef industry became eager to use beta-agonists once it was learned that consumers found their use acceptable.

Merck, the manufacturer of Zilmax, halted sales in 2013. Interestingly, using Zilmax does not cause any known food safety issues. Consumer concern was solely about animal welfare. Zilmax shows the beef industry being proactive: not only did the beef processors and Merck halt a public relations issue before it got started, but the action also captured a part of the beef export market from nations unwilling to accept beef products produced with Zilmax. Many nations have banned beta-agonists, and the continued export market requires removing Zilmax from the production process. Optaflexx, produced by Eli Lily's Elanco Animal Health, is a substitute for Zilmax. The future of Optaflexx use depends crucially on nations that import beef and pork from the US. In the era after pink slime (see Chapter 4), the beef industry is actively searching to find ways to handle issues that involve consumer perceptions and market relations.

Agricultural externalities can also be resolved by government compensation of farmers for reductions in use of chemicals, fertilizer, or soil-eroding practices. In US agricultural policy, the compensation often takes place through financial incentives. The Conservation Reserve Program (CRP), for example, pays farmers to take highly erodible acres out of production. Some conservation and environmental objectives are achieved through "cross-compliance," which forces farmers to comply with environmental objectives in order to qualify for agricultural subsidy payments. In the UK, this type of program is referred to as a "compensation scheme," and numerous schemes provide financial incentives to producers to help eliminate externalities and meet environmental objectives.

Public goods

Public goods provide another example of market failure in agricultural production. Agricultural benefits such as food security and rural landscapes are "nonexcludable." A good is excludable if nonpaying consumers can be stopped from consuming the good. A hamburger is an excludable good. The purchaser receives the hamburger, making it unavailable for others to buy. A good is nonexcludable if it is not possible to prevent nonpaying consumers from gaining access to the good. Fresh air, public parks, and beautiful vistas are nonexcludable goods. Since farmers cannot exclude citizens from enjoying a safe, nutritious, and secure food supply, consumers do not pay for these benefits. Since no payment is made for scenery and open space, farmers are "undercompensated" for these attributes. Therefore, the supply of farms and food is lower than it would be for an excludable good such as a hat or an automobile.

Traditionally, economics and economists focus on excludability and rivalry as public good attributes. Rivalry refers to the impact of one consumer's consumption of a good on others. A rival good is one where one person's consumption prevents simultaneous consumption of the good by others. Most tangible goods (hot dogs, bicycles, easy chairs, and cell phones, for example) are rivalous. Intellectual property and radio signals are nonrivalous, since all interested consumers can gain access to these goods at the same time. A modern treatment of public goods focuses on the commonality between public goods and positive externalities (Caplan, 2008). Education is a public good that creates a positive externality: higher levels of education provide benefits to others in society, such as lower crime levels and higher employment rates.

Agricultural research and development (R&D) is a public good: the rate of return on public investments in agricultural R&D is high (Alston, 2000; Alston *et al.*, 2009). Since the results of agricultural research are often nonexcludable, research in agriculture is "underproduced." Rural landscapes, food safety, and food security also exhibit characteristics of public goods: nonexcludability and nonrivalousness. Economists, most often skeptical of government intervention, believe that externalities are at times used as a rationale for government intervention into markets. However, externalities can be used to justify government ownership of industries that exhibit positive externalities (have public good characteristics), and ban goods that produce negative externalities. If public goods such as education and agricultural research are underproduced, a subsidy may make more sense than government ownership of schools and research institutions. To the extent that private firms are most often more efficient than government-owned entities, a subsidy could provide benefits without the costs of government ownership.

Measurement of the benefits of public goods is particularly difficult and determining consumer willingness to pay for such benefits is a major challenge for social scientists. Survey respondents, for example, often overstate their true willingness to pay for goods such as rural landscapes and food security. After all, it is costless to claim a large willingness to pay, and it could have strategic implications for public policy: policy makers could increase subsidy levels based on exaggerated estimates of willingness to pay claims. If a survey forced citizens to pay their stated willingness to pay it would, in most cases, be much lower than the initial stated claim. This is only one difficulty associated with measuring the benefits of public goods. Subsidies to agricultural producers are common in high-income nations such as the US, Australia, Japan, and the EU. There is much controversy associated with these subsidies, since the farmers who receive the subsidies are, on average, much wealthier and have much higher incomes than the taxpayers who pay for the subsidies. Some argue that agricultural subsidies are justified since agricultural goods are underproduced. Underproduction is a result of a positive externality associated with rural landscapes, food security, and confidence in a safe food supply.

Economic analysis of agricultural policy

Agricultural subsidies appear to be an anomaly in a democracy, since the majority is being taxed, and the proceeds are distributed to a small group. It seems that such a policy could not garner majority approval in a democracy. The economic way of thinking can be applied to virtually any situation, decision, or policy. When economics is used in this way, it is referred to as "public choice" (see Box 5.1), and has made significant contributions to understanding public policy formation and outcomes (Shughart, 2008). Economists focus on decisions made by policy makers, based on the policy makers' incentives to accumulate political support and be re-elected. In this view, politicians will support policies that have large and observable political benefits and small or near-invisible political costs.

Agricultural subsidies in the US are no exception and are used here as an example. Currently, the US government subsidizes farmers at a rate of approximately $5 billion annually (Environmental Working Group, 2013a). The number of recipients is small. In 2010, only 838,391 farms (38 percent of all US farms) received government subsidies (Environmental Working Group, 2013a). The per-farmer benefits are concentrated among a small number of large farmers: the top 10 percent of the recipients received 75 percent of all subsidies. The costs of the subsidies are spread across a large taxpayer group: each individual taxpayer pays a small part of the total subsidy bill. According to the US Internal Revenue Service (IRS), there were slightly over 145 million tax returns filed in 2011. The average taxpayer cost of the farm subsidies is less than $35 per year (5 b/145 m). Since the costs of the subsidies are spread over a large number of persons, and the benefits are concentrated on a relatively small group, this type of legislation is often called "special interest legislation," and is ubiquitous among democracies. Taxpayer costs are small enough that, traditionally, there is no major opposition to the subsidies.

Economic analysis provides a reason: the costs of political opposition are larger than the small per-taxpayer cost of the programs. Why devote time, energy, and expense to opposing a program that costs each taxpayer only $35 per year? In recent years, this has changed as more is learned about who actually receives the agricultural subsidies. The subsidy recipients lobby strongly to maintain the subsidies. The bulk of the payments are made to wealthy farm owners, with higher levels of income and wealth than taxpayers: the average household income for farmers was over $87,000 in 2011 (Schnepf, 2013). In that same year, the median income among all US households was $50,054 per annum (US Bureau of the Census, 2013a).

Debate over US farm legislation in 2013 was heated (see Box 10.1), with the major point of disagreement being the funding levels of: (1) food stamps, which subsidize the poor; and (2) farm subsidies which, as noted, go generally to wealthy households. The economic way of thinking about agricultural subsidies suggests that, to the extent that agriculture is a public good, the subsidies provide a way for society to promote family farms and a safe, nutritious food supply. The argument against subsidies is that taxpayers fund a large monetary award to farm owners, who have higher incomes than the taxpayers.

Optimal level of polarization

This chapter has suggested potential solutions to polarized externality issues. One of the major results of the discussion led to an intermediary solution between two extreme views. This common-sense solution is surprisingly evasive in situations characterized by intense emotions and strongly held views. The economics-based approach suggests that negotiations between the opponents can lead to a compromise (a Coase solution) that benefits the greatest number of persons.

The optimal negotiated solution characteristically results in a positive level of externality, rather than an all-or-nothing solution. Not only are there optimal levels of pollution, odor, and agricultural chemical use, but there is also an optimal level of polarization in a society. Although this may appear to be an unusual claim, polarization can be a useful force in society.

As has been emphasized, polarization can be a helpful force in a process of change or adjustment. If there were no disagreements or polarized issues, society would stagnate and the status quo would prevail indefinitely. Externalities are ubiquitous, challenging to resolve and perhaps necessary for progress. Polarization, combined with institutions that provide for resolution of divisive issues, is a major prerequisite for rapid economic growth. The democratic process also forces all issues to be considered by numerous individuals and groups. James Madison summarized the role of factions: "Liberty is to faction what air is to fire, an aliment without which it instantly expires, but it could not be less folly to abolish liberty, which is essential to political life, because it nourishes faction, than it would be to wish the annihilation of air, which is essential to animal life, because it imparts to fire its destructive agency" (Madison, 1787).

An "optimal" level of polarization would be one that allowed progress to occur, with adoption of new technologies at a pace that enabled optimal benefits to be gleaned by society. The optimal level of polarization would also provide checks and balances against the risks of new innovations that could cause environmental damage or adversely affect human health. As difficult as controversy, rancor, and divisiveness can be in the short run, they play an important role in providing the necessary culture for growth and change in the long run. As will be shown, creative destruction in food and agriculture often creates solutions that replace the need to resolve the debate. All newly introduced agricultural technologies, including machinery, chemicals, fertilizer, and genetically modified crop varieties and animal traits have met with opposition when first introduced. As the benefits to society became more obvious, these innovations became accepted and widely used. Today, society is determining the future of agricultural inputs such as growth promoters in meat production. Not all new innovations are acceptable by society: DDT and Zilmax are examples of agricultural innovations that had huge benefits, but large negative externalities resulted in bans.

Summary and conclusions

The major result, and intentional outcome, of agriculture is food, fiber, and fuel production. By its nature, however, agriculture also produces both positive and negative externalities. These consequences include rural landscapes, and a safe, secure, nutritious food supply, which many individuals value at a rate higher than the cost of food. Negative externalities include air and water pollution, soil erosion, odor from CAFOs, and potential human health issues resulting from chemical and pharmaceutical use in food production.

Potential solutions to the externality issues include taxes, quantitative restrictions, outright bans, or negotiation and bargained solutions. Well-defined and enforced property rights can result in a solution to externality problems by providing affected parties with the legal right to end the externality. Coase suggested that under ideal conditions, the same optimal, bargained results would occur regardless of who was entitled to the right to use chemicals. Real-world externalities, however, are often much more complicated. One major difficulty of real-world negotiations is typically the large number of affected parties: the costs of forging a solution becomes challenging when large numbers are involved. Similarly, measurement, regulations, and enforcement are challenges to optimal solutions of issues like chemical use, fertilizer runoff, antibiotic and hormone use in meat production, and other agricultural practices and policies.

The externalities of agricultural production can also be positive. Such characteristics are often called public goods. Public goods are underproduced, since the market return to the producers of the good does not include the full value of the good to society. The governments of high-income nations often subsidize agriculture as a method of compensating farms for the public good, or positive externality, attributes of agriculture.

Although agricultural externalities are pervasive and complex, economics and economic analysis often provide solutions. The comparison of benefits and costs, when applied to political decisions, is the basis for the field of study called public choice. Public choice asserts that the major motivation behind decisions and actions of all voters, politicians, and bureaucrats is self-interest. Although the true motivations of political actors may be public-minded, the theory of public choice provides useful explanations about public policy. Agriculture is heavily subsidized in all high-income nations, including the US and the EU. Public choice suggests that the political benefits of these subsidies are large, even though only a small number of farmers are the beneficiaries. This is a classic explanation of special interest legislation. The costs of the program are widely dispersed across a broad base of taxpayers, each of whom pays a small amount. The benefits of the program are concentrated among a small group of politically active individuals. Therefore, the political benefits in terms of support and money are often larger than political costs.

The Coasian bargaining solution provides a major implication for the study of the depolarization of food and agricultural issues. In many cases, the optimal societal solution lies somewhere between the extremes. This is not always the case, in situations where damages are greater than benefits (DDT, Zilmax) or cases where benefits dominate perceived costs (GMOs and legal herbicides such as RoundUp).

Coasian analysis provides a way to study polarized issues by emphasizing that many externalities can be resolved through: (1) carefully defining and enforcing property rights; and (2) allowing for the process of negotiation between affected parties. When policy makers grant entitlements to one side or the other, or mandate specific rules about how to achieve environmental or social goals, sub-optimal outcomes can result. The economic way of thinking suggests that the same kind of bargaining process used in the purchase and sale of goods can be used to resolve polarized differences arising from external effects of food production and consumption. Optimal solutions derived from the economic approach often mimic Aristotle's suggestion: everything in moderation.

Modern agricultural inputs such as chemicals, fertilizers, pharmaceuticals, and machinery are likely to be pursued in a fashion that balances the need to feed a large and growing world population with the need to preserve and maintain our natural resource base for future generations. To do this, a positive level of modern inputs is likely to provide societal benefits, but care must be taken to include external environmental effects into decision making about the optimal levels of resource use change over time, based on new innovations and new evidence of economic benefits and environmental costs.

8

PRODUCT BUNDLING

Bringing together divergent consumers

Rule 1: The customer is always right. Rule 2: If the customer is ever wrong, re-read Rule 1.

Stew Leonard, CEO of Stew Leonard's, the world's largest dairy store

Introduction

Market prices reflect changes in production and consumption, as explored in Chapter 3. Production change in agriculture often reflects enhanced technology, or changing climate and weather conditions. Consumption changes often accompany changes in income, and the ability to purchase more expensive products. Changes in consumer preferences can lead to stronger desires for new products, such as healthier food or food with positive environmental characteristics associated with it. The profitability of a new product changes over time. The product lifecycle (Figure 8.1) demonstrates how profit levels of a typical food product change over time, based on the process of creative destruction.

As new products are introduced, business firms must determine if they would like to produce and sell the new product. This requires the trait that Schultz (1975) called "the ability to deal with disequilibrium." Entrepreneurs must decide if the opportunity to purchase and sell the new product represents a fad (temporary sales), or a trend (permanent sales). Farmers, ranchers, and agribusinesses must separate the "signal from the noise," or the true shifts in consumer desires and purchases from temporary changes in sales. In rapidly changing markets such as food and agriculture, this can be an ever-present challenge. The following list identifies some common choices or decisions for producers and consumers of agricultural products.

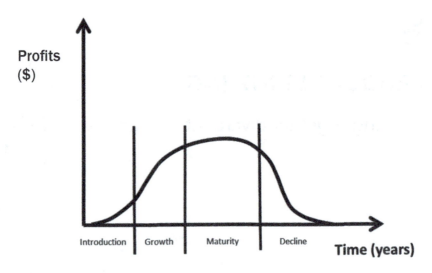

FIGURE 8.1 Product lifecycle

- Conventional or organic produce?
- Low-carbohydrate or high-carbohydrate diet?
- Low sodium, low fat, low calories or low cost?
- Natural, antibiotic-free or hormone-free meat?
- Gluten-free or grain-based diet?
- Environmentally-friendly products or energy-intensive goods?

All of these relatively new innovations in food markets must be considered by a firm desiring to remain successful in a market-based economy. Consumers have hugely divergent opinions, attitudes, purchasing power, and desires. The modern grocery store has thousands of food choices.

Consumer sovereignty

As shown in Chapter 3, consumer choices drive value in a market economy, and product value determines what is produced. Therefore, consumer desires must be taken seriously by producers interested in remaining economically viable. Whether consumers desire organic celery or conventional steak, the most successful producers are those who meet consumer needs. In a market-based economy, consumers are "royalty," in the sense that production only occurs to meet consumer needs and desires.

Consumer tastes and preferences can shift rapidly, capriciously, and serendipitously. Recently, behavioral economists have provided evidence that consumer behavior is subject to many irrationalities or irregularities. One common characteristic of consumer choice is the halo effect, which describes a cognitive error that occurs when judgments of an object or an attribute are clouded by the overall impression that it presents. An example of the halo effect is consumers continuing to desire organic food in spite of evidence that shows that it may not be either more or less healthy than conventional food.[1] The perception that the food is "good" overrides the evidence and runs counter to science. Regardless of scientific merit, consumers become vegetarians based on the idea that there will be less world hunger if all consumers become vegetarians.

Many issues in food and agriculture may be subject to the halo effect. Food is not only important, but life-sustaining. Research has shown that once the positive perceptions of organic food, local food, or environmentally-friendly production practices are set in place, consumer beliefs on overall food quality increases (Blair, 2012; Grunert, 2006). These research results suggest that consumer objectives and purchasing habits are likely to be deeply engrained, making changes in food purchase habits difficult to change. Consumer food preferences are based on tradition, culture, and history. Dietary preferences and restrictions have a long history, dating back to the Garden of Eden and forbidden fruit. The third book of the Hebrew Bible, Leviticus, warns against pork, shellfish, and many other types of food. Thus, new food products and changes in food consumption patterns and trends may require strong marketing efforts to overcome religious teaching, or strong consumption habits.

Related to the halo effect is the nirvana fallacy, also called the perfectionist fallacy. It characterizes a situation where potential solutions to problems are rejected because they are less than perfect. In food choices, consumers may reject changing purchase habits when a perfect solution is not possible. If organic food represents only 10 percent of all food consumed, some individuals may not purchase it because of their perception that such a small purchase will not make a difference. They may believe that one more purchase may not cause a major shift in agricultural production processes. One solution to the nirvana fallacy is to find middle ground, or a balance, between competing objectives. It may be worthwhile to make an effort to change the status quo rather than merely accepting it, even if it is difficult to recognize that a change has occurred. Thus, consumers may decide that "every little bit helps," and promote their own view of food and agriculture, whether it be organic/local or conventional/industrial food.

Product bundling

What can producers do to deal with price changes, market changes, creative destruction, the halo effect, and the nirvana fallacy? What can producers do about the apparently growing division between the group of consumers who desire conventional, inexpensive food and those who prefer more costly organic food? Continuing success depends on the ability to deal with market disequilibria. The ability to adopt new, more profitable products is paramount. The ability to let go of outdated, less profitable practices and products is also important. Firms in competitive industries must adopt new technologies and new products to remain competitive with other firms. In addition, firms in highly competitive, rapidly evolving industries must continuously adopt new products to keep up with ever-changing consumer tastes and preferences.

Adoption of new products allows food and agribusiness firms to continuously upgrade their profit potential. Bundling two or more products together to be sold as a single good is a frequently used business strategy. Bundling examples include meals at fast food restaurants; bundled cable television, phone, and internet services; and automobiles equipped with multiple attributes in "packages." The economic reasons behind bundling provide both an explanation for why bundling commonly occurs, and why it is a major potential source of depolarization of numerous agricultural issues. As shown in the following example, the success of bundling depends on consumers with different tastes for different components of the bundle. Bundling brings consumers together by causing consumers to buy two products when they have interest in only one of the bundled goods. When consumers have different willingness to pay for different products, bundling can increase profits.

BOX 8.1: CHIPOTLE MEXICAN GRILL

Chipotle Mexican Grill, typically called "Chipotle," is a highly successful restaurant chain known for affordable burritos made from fresh, natural ingredients. Chipotle was founded in 1993, selling burritos in a single restaurant in Denver, Colorado. Five years later, Chipotle operated 16 restaurants in Colorado, and McDonald's became an investor in the Chipotle firm. When McDonald's sold its share of Chipotle in 2006, the chain had over 500 locations (Chipotle Mexican Grill, 2013). In 2007, the *Wall Street Journal* called Chipotle "arguably ... the country's most successful fast food chain in recent years" (Adamy, 2007, p. 1). The combination of good food and concern about how the food is produced has resulted in growth. In 2010, Chipotle served approximately 750,000 customers each day (Lean, 2010). By 2012, the restaurant operated at over 1,400 locations, with revenues of over $27 billion (Chipotle Mexican Grill, 2013).

In 1999, Chipotle owner Steve Ells began purchasing free-range pork. Since free-range, natural pork is more expensive than conventionally-produced pork, burrito prices increased. However, the inclusion and identification of free-range, natural meat on the menu also resulted in an increase in burrito sales (Kaplan, 2010). By 2001, Chipotle expanded free-range pork to a mission statement, "Food with Integrity," including emphasis on naturally raised meat, organic produce, and hormone-free dairy products (Barnes, 2009). Food with integrity focuses on "using ingredients that are grown or raised with respect for the environment, animals and people who grow or raise food" (Chipotle Mexican Grill, 2013). "Food with Integrity" is the core of Chipotle's marketing efforts, and is described on the company's website (Ragas and Roberts, 2009, p. 51).

Chipotle is committed to using as much free-range, natural meat as possible. However, given the magnitude of the restaurant's success, it is often unable to find sufficient supplies of natural, free-range meat. This has led to public relations issues, as Chipotle has attempted to provide food produced within certain guidelines. Since this type of food is relatively new, the increasing demand for Chipotle has been larger than the producers' ability to supply the restaurant's needs. Currently, the restaurant is in the process of attempting to purchase all of its needed ingredients from producers who meet "Food with Integrity" conditions, while keeping customers informed about the true source and nature of meat and other ingredients used to produce the Chipotle products.

BOX 8.2: SUSTAINABLE CLOTHING: NIKE AND ORGANIC COTTON

Clothing in high-income nations is often advertised or labeled with identifying tags or logos such as "Made in USA," "Sweatshop Free," and "Made with Organic Cotton." Organic cotton is a natural fiber grown without the use of synthetic chemical pesticides, fertilizers, or defoliants. The production of organic cotton is increasing rapidly, as conventionally produced cotton is chemical-intensive, requires a great deal of water, and in some cases is characterized by poor labor conditions. Beginning in 1997, Nike, a highly successful footwear and athletic clothing manufacturing firm in Beaverton, Oregon, began to purchase certified organic cotton for use in producing garments. Certification is provided by third-party accredited auditors primarily in China, India, Turkey, and the USA. In fiscal year 2011, Nike estimated that 90 percent of the firm's cotton-containing apparel was produced with a minimum of five percent organic cotton (Nike, 2012). Nike hopes to use a blend of at least 10 percent organic cotton in all cotton-containing apparel by 2015. This goal is intended to match increasing demand for organic cotton with limited but growing production. Nike also offers some items that contain 100 percent organic cotton (Nike, 2012).

Nike joined the Better Cotton Initiative (BCI) in 2011 (BCI, 2013). The BCI establishes standards for the management of inputs such as pesticides, fertilizer, and water. It also strives to improve profits and working conditions for cotton farmers. According to the BCI website, "[e]nsuring humans profit at the same time as the environment is our constant goal. It's also sound business." Research by Hainmueller and Hiscox (2012) employed a large-scale field experiment to show that labels with information about fair labor standards had a significant positive impact on sales, even in stores where consumers are typically only concerned with prices. Better Cotton is an attempt to be a mass-market commodity, to capture increasing returns, and keep the price of Better Cotton equal to conventionally produced cotton (BCI, 2013).

An example illustrates how bundling works, why it is prevalent, and how it could work to depolarize many issues in food and agriculture. One of the most familiar bundling examples is fast food restaurants, which commonly bundle burgers, fries, and drinks into a "meal." In Figure 8.2, a fast food restaurant can determine if it should bundle burgers and beverages, or sell them separately, based on revenues. To measure and quantify consumer demand for a good, economists define "willingness to pay" (WTP) as the dollar amount that a consumer will offer to purchase a good.[2]

These maximum prices appear for two hypothetical consumers in Figure 8.2. Here, two hypothetical consumers have a WTP for: (1) a burger; (2) a beverage; and (3) the bundle. Notice that the WTP for the bundle is simply the sum of each consumer's WTP for each item separately. In this example, costs of production are ignored in order to focus on revenues. This simplifying assumption does not alter the results of the bundling example, as revenues could be labeled as "profits," or "net revenues," and the outcome of the model is the same in both cases.

If burgers and beverages are sold separately, total revenues reflect the price multiplied by the quantity sold. Recall that a customer will not purchase an item if the price is above the WTP. If the burger price is set at $5/burger, only consumer A buys, and revenues equal $5. If the restaurant prices the burger at $3/burger, both A and B purchase one burger, and revenues equal $6. To maximize revenues, the firm will set the burger price equal to $3/burger. Likewise, if beverages are sold separately, and price is set equal to $2/beverage, both A and B buy one drink, and revenues equal $4. If the beverage price is set at $3/beverage, only B buys, and revenues equal $3. Consumer A does not purchase a drink in this case, since A's WTP is less than

Willingness to Pay ($/unit)

	Burger	Beverage	Bundle
Consumer A	5	2	7
Consumer B	3	3	6

Sell Burgers only:
1. If P = 5, only A buys, revenues = 5
2. If P = 3, A and B buy, revenues = 6

Sell Beverages only:
1. If P = 2, A and B buy, revenues = 4
2. If P = 3, only B buys, revenues = 3

Items Sold Separately Revenue Total = 6 + 4 = 10

Sell Bundle:
1. If P = 7, only A buys, revenues = 7
2. If P = 6, A and B buy, revenues = 12

Bundle Revenues Total = 12

FIGURE 8.2 Bundling burgers and beverages

the price. The revenue-maximizing price of beverages equals $2/beverage, and the maximum revenues accruing from the sales of burger and beverages separately is equal to $10 ($6 from burger sales, and $4 from the sale of beverages).

Bundling combines products into a single good: "burger plus drink." The consumer WTP for the bundle is simply the sum of the WTP for each item separately. If the bundle is sold at a price equal to $7/bundle, only consumer A buys, and revenues are equal to $7. Alternatively, if the bundle price is set at $6/bundle, both consumers purchase the bundle, and revenue increases to $12. This example shows that profits can be increased by offering two products together as a single good. The mechanism that causes bundling to increase revenue is the divergence between consumer WTP for the two goods. If the consumer values for the two products are inverse, or opposite, bundling will always increase revenues. Restated, if A would pay more for burgers than B ($5/burger vs. $3/burger), and B would pay more for beverages than A ($3/beverage vs. $2/beverage), then bundling provides the opportunity for greater revenues.[3]

Bundling works because consumers are diverse. The greater the divergence in customer valuation of goods, the better bundling works. This characteristic makes bundling a strong potential force in depolarizing food issues associated with food characteristics, or attributes, on which consumers place different values. To the extent that polarization reflects divergence in willingness to pay, bundling is one approach that occurs spontaneously in a market economy, and brings different consumers together. The example in Figure 8.3 shows how burrito lovers who do not care about how their beef is produced could end up happily eating natural beef burritos. The example also demonstrates how consumers with concerns about animal welfare, antibiotics, and hormone use in beef production might end up in a restaurant known for delicious burritos.

The example simply replaces the beverage in the "meal bundle" example in Figure 8.2 with "natural beef" in Figure 8.3. Consumer A is a burrito lover, characterized by a high WTP for burritos. However, consumer A is relatively uncaring about the natural beef attribute: A is WTP only $1 for natural beef. Although the natural beef attribute is typically not sold separately, natural beef could be considered as an "add on," such as guacamole or sour cream. When sold in combination, burritos and the natural beef attribute increase revenues, from $13 when sold separately to $16 when natural beef is sold with burritos as a bundle (Figure 8.3).

The profit motive naturally and spontaneously brings together people with different views. Only the most adamant anti-natural beef consumers would boycott the restaurant. The bundling process has been used extensively for organic food, natural food, healthy food, and numerous other food attributes that consumers increasingly demand. In fact, consumer desire for environmentally friendly (sometimes called "green") products has caused most business firms to consider providing consumers with goods and services that are healthy and green. Hu *et al.* (2010) show evidence that "consumers' knowledge of sustainable restaurant practices and environmental concerns were important determinants of consumers' intentions to patronize green restaurants" (Hu *et al.*, 2010, p. 344).

	Willingness to Pay ($/unit)		
	Burrito	Natural Beef Attribute	Bundle: Natural Beef Burrito
Consumer A	8	1	9
Consumer B	5	3	8

<u>**Sell Burritos only:**</u>   1. If P = 8, only A buys, revenues = 8
2. If P = 5, A and B buy, revenues = 10

<u>**Sell Natural Beef Attribute:**</u>   1. If P = 1, A and B buy, revenues = 2
2. If P = 3, only B buys, revenues = 3

Items Sold Separately Revenue Total = 10 + 3 = 13

<u>**Sell Bundle:**</u>   1. If P = 9, only A buys, revenues = 9
2. If P = 8, A and B buy, revenues = 16

Bundle Revenues Total = 16

FIGURE 8.3   Bundling burritos and a natural beef attribute

BOX 8.3: BUNDLING PUBLIC RELATIONS WITH PHILANTHROPY: GOLDEN RICE

Golden Rice is a genetically modified rice variety that incorporates beta-carotene (Vitamin A) into the edible part of the grain. Golden Rice was developed by agronomists with the idea of providing fortified food to regions where there is an acute shortage of Vitamin A in the diet.[4] Vitamin A deficiency can cause blindness and death, and affects millions of individuals each year. The idea for Golden Rice was first conceived in 1984, and the first field tests were conducted by Louisiana State University in 2004. The Bill and Melinda Gates Foundation provided funding for further development of Golden Rice in 2005, and field trials are now underway in the Philippines.

Genetically Modified Organisms (GMOs) were developed to enhance food production. GMOs have been successful in creating more food with fewer inputs such as pesticides and herbicides, but continue to face opposition on several grounds from many groups and nations. Biotechnology companies such as Syngenta and Monsanto have been strong proponents of Golden Rice, arguing that Golden Rice was the first biotech crop that was unarguably beneficial. Monsanto and Syngenta provided free licenses for growing Golden Rice, so farmers will not have to pay royalties for the seed. Golden Rice is intended to help the poor, but has also been promoted as a public relations effort to help promote the image of biotechnology (Charles, 2013). Thus, Golden Rice is an example of bundling products to increase acceptance, or at least decrease opposition, to biotechnology.

BOX 8.4: SUSTAINABLE INTENSIFICATION

All commentators agree that global food production will need to increase significantly in the coming decades (World Bank, 2007; Pretty *et al.*, 2011). Pretty *et al.* (2011) emphasized that there are divergences and disagreements about how this should be accomplished. One possibility is bringing new land into production, but this gives rise to increased environmental degradation. Another solution is to repeat the approach of the Green Revolution with enhanced research and outreach expenditures and efforts. Other groups promote biotechnology, and yet others simply advocate organic food as the solution. No matter which solution, or combination of solutions, is chosen, agricultural activity will need to intensify (Pretty *et al.*, 2011; Garnett and Godfray, 2012).

Sustainable agricultural intensification is defined as producing more output from the same amount of land while reducing the negative environmental impacts. At the same time intensification contributes to natural capital, and to the flow of environmental services (Pretty, 2008; Pretty *et al.*, 2011). Therefore, intensification can be considered a "bundle" of enhanced outcomes in both agricultural production and environmental objectives. Advocates of sustainable intensification seek to spread and enlarge successful processes and projects where "science and farmer inputs into technologies and practices that combine crops–animals with agroecological and agronomic management" (Pretty *et al.*, 2011, p. 6).

Garnett and Godfray (2012) report that the phrase "sustainable intensification" has been controversial, as both critics and some advocates claim that the term refers to a particular system, or group of systems of production (p. 6). This debate reflects a major polarization in how food is to be produced in the future. Some observers believe that sustainable intensification is an appropriate description of the existing high-input, high-output modes of production found in high-income nations. Others interpret the term to be aligned with agroecology, a concept that connotes a preference for organic practices. Garnett and Godfray (2012) list and describe several related terms that have been put forward to define sustainable intensification (pp. 19–20):

- ecological intensification
- agroecology
- permaculture

- organic agriculture
- ecofunctional intensification
- climate-smart agriculture
- eco-efficiency, and
- technological optimism.

All of these concepts combine agricultural production and sustainability objectives into a "bundle." In the midst of controversy about the most effective way forward, the major conclusion of Garnett and Godfray (2012) is the need for more discussion, debate, and scientific knowledge into both objectives: increased production and enhanced sustainability. The authors conclude with the statement:

> [I]t must be recognized that values shape stakeholders' different attitudes to the food system and their views on what the way forward should be. More deliberate exploration of these different values will help society obtain a deeper and shared understanding of what the challenge is and of what solutions might work.
>
> *Garnett and Godfray (2012), p. 51*

This conclusion for the sustainable intensification debate provides an example of the idea that bringing together individuals and groups with divergent preferences can lead to superior outcomes and reduce the degree of polarization in food and agriculture.

Once bundling takes place, scale economies can occur, bringing the price of the products with desirable characteristics down, as discussed in Chapter 6. For example, when Walmart entered the organic produce business in 2006, the price of organic food was lowered. This benefited Walmart customers who desired organic food, but many organic producers complained. This has led to a new controversy in food and agriculture: "Industrial Organic" (Pollan, 2006a). As has been shown, profitable innovations such as organic food result in entry of competing firms, and lower prices. In a market-based economy, high profits are typically short run in nature: when other firms see the profit potential, they enter the industry, increasing the supply of the good, and driving down price and profit levels. Many polarized issues in food and agriculture are due to the issue of scale (Chapter 6). Many consumers like to think of organic food as produced by a small family farm, but in actuality, a great deal of organic food is produced by large businesses.

Summary and conclusions

A market-based economy is similar to nature: business firms are subject to: (1) changes beyond their control; and (2) competition that results in the survival of the fittest. Successful firms drive out businesses that are unable to compete. Market changes bring about changes in producer and consumer behavior, guiding resources to their highest return. In the process, consumers get what they most desire, surpluses of unwanted goods cause lower prices and diminished future production, and shortages result in higher prices and enhanced production. Thus, market changes are self-correcting. Similarly, food and agricultural markets constantly evolve towards higher profits, which automatically bring diverse groups together. The profit motive causes bundling of disparate products and attributes, resulting in an ever-changing composition of products and consumers that are brought together.

Often, when new products such as phones, computers, or applications are introduced, some consumers are skeptical. Once the right product bundle is introduced, however, in many cases skepticism recedes. Likewise, once green bundling takes place, many consumers and firms benefit from changes in consumer preferences and the diversity of consumers.

Notes

1   See Forman *et al.* (2012).
2   Consumer willingness to pay is also sometimes called a "reservation price." This refers simply to a price above which a consumer will not purchase a good.
3   The relative valuations are "inversely correlated." If consumer values are similar to each other, the values are positively correlated, and bundling does not increase profits.
4   Food fortification, also called food enrichment, is a process of adding micronutrients, such as essential trace elements and vitamins, to food. At times, it is motivated by profit (breakfast cereal products), and at other times it is a public health policy aimed at reducing dietary deficiencies (Golden Rice).

9

TRADE, GLOBALIZATION, AND LOCALISM

No nation was ever ruined by trade.

Benjamin Franklin

The road of isolationism and protectionism ... ends in danger and decline. I am for free commerce with all nations, political connection with none.

Thomas Jefferson

Instead of indulging into a fruitless debate about what strategy would be appropriate in agriculture, it would be much more rewarding in looking at the best way forward for a given country, a given ecology and economy. Looking for sustainable and equitable farming methods means in my eyes to refrain from any kind of ideological debate and concentrate on pragmatic decisions in order to find the best solution for a given region. Roads to success in these areas are many, and we must pursue them all.

Klaus Ammann, Director, Botanical Garden, University of Bern

Introduction

Specialization and gains from trade are the foundation of the study of economics, and form the cornerstone of the market system. The idea of comparative advantage explains how firms become more efficient, how society operates, and how an economy grows. It is difficult to overstate the importance of specialization and trade, particularly in a globalized world where coffee is produced in Brazil, cell phones in China, clothes in Vietnam, and software in the US. Food and agricultural products have been traded between nations for millennia, and disputes have often arisen about what goods, what quantities of goods, and in what form, a nation should import into and export from a region or nation. These trade disputes are condemned by economists, who almost universally favor free trade because it expands the quantities and qualities of goods and services available to consumers. Breakfast in Minnesota would be much different in the absence of coffee imported from Central or South America, orange juice squeezed from fruit grown in Florida, California, or Mexico, and bananas from Costa Rica. Trade allows a region or nation to specialize in the production of goods that are most efficiently produced in the area. California's Great Central Valley, for example, has some of the best growing conditions for agricultural products in the world. California producers can grow nearly all commercial crops, but specialize in vegetables, fruit, and nuts – the crops that provide the highest returns for the resources employed to produce them. Not everyone wins from trade, however. Globalization and trade result in winners and losers, and many producers and consumers are made worse off from trade, even though the overall societal benefits from trade are positive.

Specialization and trade allow regions or nations to increase the size of firms and industries to capture economies of scale. This lowers the per-unit costs of production, and allows goods and services to be produced at their lowest cost per-unit, in the most productive location.

At the international level, free trade between two nations results in benefits to both trading partners. However, it must be emphasized that not every individual or group benefits from trade, and the strong economic arguments in favor of trade are not always heeded by nations for this reason. The driving force behind trade is diversity of skills, climate, workers, technology, and production practices. The theory of specialization and trade extends not only to trade of goods between nations, but is a useful explanation for the dynamics of ideas, innovations, and technology over time.

A great number of polarized issues in food and agriculture are due to movements toward and away from free trade between nations. Trade can disrupt a nation's economic activities, as imported products replace domestically produced goods and services. Producer and consumer groups made worse off by trade will oppose it, since their economic position is harmed. However, the overall benefits to society are positive: the gains are larger than the losses. This result allows economists to conclude that trade may be disruptive in the short run, but eventually provides economic advantages. Trade, in this sense, fits the theme introduced in Chapter 5: creative destruction can be costly in the short run, but is beneficial in the long run. Creative destruction in a globalized economy is faster, bigger, and more volatile as each industry now competes with other individuals and groups throughout the entire world.

Trade and globalization are controversial, as many individuals and nations have strong preferences for goods produced in their own nation. Trade is often used as a political tool to express pleasure or displeasure with another nation. For example, in 1980 the US placed a grain embargo on the former Soviet Union as a consequence of that nation's attack on Afghanistan.

BOX 9.1: GRAIN EMBARGOES

In 1980, the US placed an embargo (ban) on sales of grain to the Soviet Union (USSR). The embargo was motivated by the need to retaliate for the Soviet invasion of Afghanistan. The embargo lasted from January 1980 to April 1981. Even though it was a significant political event, later research indicated that the embargo had very little impact on the affected nations. The reason is simple: the Soviets purchased grain from other nations. Reed (2001) stated that embargoes do not have a large impact on the nations involved. The food distribution pattern might change, but the overall production and consumption patterns do not change. For example, the USSR could buy grain from Mexico, and Mexico could purchase grain from the US. This makes sense in an efficient global economy where the incentive to buy low and sell high is strong. Grain merchandisers find ways to purchase grain from the low-cost producers and sell it to the consumers with the highest willingness to pay (WTP) for the grain.

As globalization proceeds and nations become more interconnected, the likelihood of retaliatory food trade barriers becomes smaller. A nation that is dependent on other nations is less likely to use embargoes on its trading partners.

Food safety concerns are often the stated reason behind restrictions or limitations on trade. Many highly intelligent and well-meaning leaders have called for "self-sufficiency" as a societal goal. Gandhi (India) and Mao (China) both believed that there were limits to trade. Many economic development experts call for food self-sufficiency, rather than specialization and trade. Recently, the idea of self-sufficiency has gained popularity in the "local food" movement, a desire to purchase food that is produced close to home. In what follows, the enormous gains that come from specialization and exchange are explored, as well as the causes and consequences of trade barriers, or policies intended to protect local groups from the impacts of globalization. This leads to a discussion of how polarized trade issues can be ameliorated through trade agreements. Several timely and important examples of gains from trade in agricultural production methods are presented and evaluated, including sustainable intensification, genetically engineered organic food, ecological economics, and reduced tillage practices.

Absolute advantage

Adam Smith, often considered to be the "father of modern economics," published a path-breaking book in 1776 entitled *An Inquiry into the Nature and Causes of the Wealth of Nations* (Smith, 1776). One of the major contributions of the book was an explanation of absolute advantage, or specialization in what an individual, firm, or nation produces at lower costs per unit than other individuals, firms, or nations. Smith's concept makes sense: if one person is good at producing food, and another is good at making clothing, both will be better off by doing what they do best and trading with the other. Smith's idea is at the heart of a market economy, and also the catalyst of modern economic growth. To the extent that production can be specialized by the division of labor, the total output of a nation will increase. Smith also famously suggested that this occurs naturally, with no incentive necessary other than self-interest. Individuals, families, and groups will specialize in the production of goods with their absolute advantage to increase their own economic well-being.

In his description of absolute advantage, Smith was speaking of efficiency in producing output: quantities of resources (labor, steel, water, glass, coal, etc.) must be given up (used) to produce a good or service. For example, if England could produce 10 metric tons of wheat in one growing season, and France could produce 20 metric tons of wheat with the same resources, then France would have the absolute advantage in the production of wheat. Smith's theory of trade suggested that France produce wheat, and England produce a good for which it had an absolute advantage – sheep, wool, and textiles at the time. Both nations could be better off by utilizing resources in the most efficient way, producing the good that was least expensive for that nation to produce.

The explanation of why trade occurs provides a powerful insight into how economies work and how nations and individuals specialize in a mutually advantageous way. It also explains how families, firms, and nations can gain through specialization of tasks, and how national wealth can be increased. Smith concluded that the only limit on how much specialization could take place is the "extent of the market," or the total demand for the product. In large and highly sophisticated economies, the gains from specialization are enormous. Imagine how a town or a region or a state would look if every individual had to produce her/his own food and clothing rather than rely on farmers, ranchers, and processors to do it. Self-sufficiency, while surely having some satisfying features, would not allow all individuals to participate in the economy in the way that is most productive.

As important, correct, and useful as the theory of absolute advantage is, the theory was extended by David Ricardo in 1817 to a more general theory, called comparative advantage, which explains additional interactions between individuals and nations (Ricardo, 1971).

Comparative advantage

Ricardo's theory is called "comparative advantage." The theory is an extension and refinement of the explanation of how a modern economy functions. It differs from absolute advantage by emphasizing not absolute productive ability, but instead the ability and efficiency of producing one good relative to another. The explanation used here explains comparative advantage. Several simplifying assumptions are used to make the point. Overwhelming evidence shows that Ricardo's theory holds even in more complex and realistic settings, and provides a powerful explanation of how all economies function, including traditional, modern, agrarian, and industrial economies.

Comparative advantage occurs when a nation (or individual, or region) can produce a good at a lower cost (using fewer resources) relative to other nations. If a nation can produce a good at lower cost, it will export this good and will import goods that are produced by other nations at costs lower than possible in the importing nation. Both trading partners benefit from buying low and selling high. Upon first reflection, it appears that everyone wins when trade is based on comparative advantage. This, however, is not always the case. As stated earlier, not all individuals are made better off from trade, even when both trading partners as a whole (nations, regions, etc.) benefit. If the US imports sugar from the Dominican Republic, this drives the price of sugar in the US down, making US sugar producers worse off, even while it makes US consumers better off. As will be shown, the net benefits to domestic consumers are larger than the losses to producers, so the overall gain from trade is positive. As a result, trade is not universally favored. Likewise, a nation could lose its comparative advantage when a still lower-cost nation joins the trading group. For example, China has been a low-cost producer of a huge number of consumer goods until recently, when other nations such as Malaysia, Myanmar, and Sri Lanka have begun to produce many goods at even lower costs.

The individuals or groups that are made worse off due to trade often seek to stop international trade to avoid competition from lower-cost producers in other nations. These affected parties are often able to lobby governments to impose trade restrictions and avoid economic hardship. These outcomes can be seen in the following example. Although the example centers on trade between two persons, the concepts are easily extended to trade between regions or nations.

The ubiquity and generality of Ricardo's concept of comparative advantage are widely recognized. Suppose Alan and Barbara are the only two individuals in a region. They produce and consume only two goods: grain and meat. The combinations of each good that each individual can produce in a given time period (perhaps one week) are called that person's production possibilities, as shown in Table 9.1. If Alan devotes all of his time to the production of grain, he can produce 40 kilograms in one week. If he devotes all of his time to meat production, he can produce 20 kilograms of meat.

In one week, Barbara can produce more of either of the goods than Alan: 50 kilograms of grain or 100 kilograms of meat. Barbara has an absolute advantage in the production of both grain and meat. Smith's theory of absolute advantage, suggests that gains from trade are not possible in this case. Barbara is more productive than Alan in both products, so why should she trade? Ricardo's extension of the theory of absolute advantage to the more general theory of comparative advantage shows that both Alan and Barbara could be made better off through specialization

TABLE 9.1 Production possibilities: Maximum weekly output

	Grain (kg)	Meat (kg)
Alan	40	20
Barbara	50	100

and trade, even if Barbara can produce more of both goods than Alan. This holds true for trade between nations, and explains why resource-rich and highly productive nations trade with nations that have fewer resources and operate at lower levels of productivity.

If Alan and Barbara do not trade, the quantity of each good consumed by each person must be equal to the amount produced by each of them: both individuals are self-sufficient. Both, however, could be made better off through specialization and trade. Assume that both Alan and Barbara prefer eating both grain and meat, and each spends half of the week in the production of each good. This is just one of many possibilities for the two individuals. They are limited only by their production possibilities (Table 9.1) and could produce any combination of the two goods that they desire. The result is shown in Table 9.2, where Alan produces and consumes 20 kilograms of grain and 10 kilograms of meat, and Barbara produces and consumes 25 kilograms of grain and 50 kilograms of meat. Table 9.2 also indicates the total quantity of each good produced and consumed in this two-person economy: 45 kilograms of grain and 60 kilograms of meat.

Comparative advantage allows both parties to consume more than they produce, by allowing each person to specialize in the production of what they do best. Table 9.2 shows one possibility that increases the amount of both grain and meat available to both Alan and Barbara. If Alan specialized completely in grain, he could produce 40 kilograms per week. Barbara could shift most of her time (7/10 of the week) to meat production, and produce 70 kilograms of meat ($0.7\star100 = 70$). Barbara could then spend the remaining 3/10 of her week producing 15 kilograms of grain ($0.3\star50 = 15$). If Barbara suggests to Alan that she trade 15 kilograms of meat for 15 kilograms of grain, Alan will quickly agree, since the "price" of trading Barbara one unit of grain for one unit of meat is better (more productive) than his own cost of producing meat. Without trade, Alan must give up the production of two kilograms of grain to produce one kilogram of meat (recall the production possibilities in Table 9.1).

Weekly consumption of both goods is higher for both Alan and Barbara after specialization and trade, a result that shows the benefits from trade. With specialization, the two individuals together produce 10 more kilograms of grain (55–45) and 10 additional units of meat (70–60). Both persons benefit, since after

TABLE 9.2 Comparative advantage: Specialization and gains from trade

	No trade: weekly production & consumption		Specialization: weekly production		Trade: weekly consumption	
	Grain (kg)	Meat (kg)	Grain (kg)	Meat (kg)	Grain (kg)	Meat (kg)
Alan	20	10	40	0	25	15
Barbara	25	50	15	70	30	55
Total	45	60	55	70	55	70

the trade each can consume more of both goods. Trade would not take place unless both parties benefitted. This idea is worth emphasis: free trade is always mutually beneficial, otherwise the trade would not occur. This is as true for simple swaps of tee shirts, as it is to the international trade of manufactured goods, computer software programs and services, and ideas about how to do things, such as produce meat and grain. If trade is voluntary and not coerced, it must benefit both parties. However, for international trade between nations, while trade is beneficial for trading partners (individuals or nations), it will leave some individuals and groups worse off.

Specialization brings benefits to both parties. Even though Barbara has an absolute advantage in both goods, Alan has a comparative advantage in grain, since Alan's cost of producing one kilogram of grain (= 0.5 kilogram of meat) is less than Barbara's cost (= 2 kilograms of meat). This same principle applies to nations trading in millions of kilograms of meat and grain. And it holds even if one nation has large cost advantages. Many people in the US, for example, have concerns that China has drastically lower labor costs and less strict environmental regulations than the US, so could have a comparative advantage in all goods. This is not true, however, since US workers continue to be highly productive in highly skilled work, and the US continues to produce many exported goods.

The belief that exports are more desirable than imports is another common, yet erroneous, belief about international trade. Exports diminish the domestic supply of a good and increase the domestic price. Domestic producers are made better off, while domestic consumers are worse off in the exporting nation. Similarly, domestic consumers benefit from imports, as the price of imported goods is lower than the domestic price with no imports.

The only reason to export a good is to be able to import goods that are more desirable. In the extreme case, a nation that only exports and does not import would amass huge amounts of foreign currency, but would not use it to purchase and consume more goods and services.

Opposition to trade due to protection from import competition

The potential benefits of trade result in large amounts of food flows between nations. In 2011, the US imported over $16 billion (USD) of fish and shellfish, $12 billion of fruit, and over $100 billion in total agricultural imports (USDA/ERS, 2013). At the same time, the US also exported large quantities of agricultural products. In fact, the US exports more agricultural products than it imports (USDA/ERS, 2013). These trades only take place because both buyer and seller (importer and exporter) were made better off. Given these large apparent benefits, it is difficult to imagine why individuals and groups would oppose trade. A great deal of opposition to trade, also called protectionism, is due to potential economic loss from trade. While individuals or groups that are hurt by trade appear to have solid reasons to oppose trade, the overall economy is hurt by restrictions in voluntary trades. From an economic perspective, since the benefits of trade exceed the costs, it should be undertaken, even though there are losers.[1]

Now return to Alan and Barbara. Suppose that Alan prefers to produce some meat and some grain, as in the specialization example shown in the first two columns of Table 9.2. If Alan shifts some of his working hours to grain, as in the middle two columns, he may be less happy as a specialized grain producer than he was as a diversified meat/grain producer. Extending this example to the national level, if a group of meat producers in a country characterized by Alan's production possibilities had to give up their traditional method of making a living, they may be less happy after trade, even though the nation as a whole is made better off.

Imported goods such as coffee, sugar, and avocados make these goods more available, and therefore lower the price for consumers in the importing nation. It is easy to imagine much higher prices for these goods if they were grown in the United States instead of in tropical climates. Given this outcome, the domestic producers of imported goods are likely to oppose imports, since their ability to remain in business is threatened by trade. These producer groups could approach Congress to pass laws that restrict or ban international trade in these goods. In the US, sugar and corn producers successfully lobby to maintain strict quantity limits, or quotas, on the amount of sugar legally imported into the country.

Similarly, the producers of exported goods benefit from increased exports, since the added demand increases the value of the good. Agricultural productivity in high-income nations has led to situations of food production exceeding food consumption. This has been true in North America, Western Europe, Japan, and Australia in the past 50 years. Food producers in these nations often seek export subsidies to remove the surplus food and maintain higher prices.

The arguments for protectionism often seem to make sense when only one side of the issue is heard. For example, many will sympathize when US sugar producers explain that their livelihood will be taken away by imported foreign sugar, and that the production methods and treatment of labor in sugar-producing nations is poor. These appear to be logical statements, and who wants to support poor working conditions in the Caribbean? Likewise, much of the clothing worn in high-income nations is produced in "sweatshops" in low-income nations with low wages and poor working conditions. However, while each of the protectionist arguments may make sense individually, if each of the special cases were to be enacted, the economy could no longer take advantage of free markets and free trade. After all, it is the ever-evolving nature of creative destruction (Chapter 5) that allows for innovation and growth. Protectionist policies can shield domestic producer groups from import competition and once trade barriers are put in place, it is difficult to remove them.

Free trade results in a great deal of creative destruction, since producers must compete not only with rivals within their own nation, but also potential rivals worldwide. The global competition provides the incentives for all nations to remain competitive in the production of goods and services with a comparative advantage. The major beneficiaries of free trade are consumers, who are provided with goods and services at the lowest possible cost at the quality desired.

Diversity and trade

Northern nations with temperate climates will specialize in grain and meat production, and benefit from trading with nations in tropical climates that specialize in fruit and vegetable production. Consumers in the Northern Hemisphere can now purchase fresh fruit and vegetables year-round, as the growing seasons in the Southern Hemisphere provide fresh produce during the northern winters. This is also true of individuals, groups, and firms: teams are often more effective if they include a diversity of personalities, knowledge, and experiences.

Dynamic gains from trade

Trade often increases the size of the market for many firms, allowing them to take advantage of returns to scale (Chapter 6). Using trade to double the size of an industry's market can allow the industry to become larger and take advantage of lower per-unit costs of production. Such gains can accumulate over time. One of the most favorable attributes of international trade is the global competition that it brings to each trading partner. With globalization and trade, it is no longer good enough to be the low-cost producer in one region or one nation. Each producer must be the low-cost producer in the world marketplace. These advantages to trade – sometimes called dynamic gains from trade – are most important in the long run, when resources are continually re-allocated towards efficient production methods and places.

Specialization of production often leads to static gains, meaning that trade provides a one-time increase in national income. Dynamic gains occur when trade increases the rate of growth in national income, and happens when global competition results in the innovation and investment in new technology, and inputs result in a process of creative destruction. Wacziarg and Welch (2008) conducted an econometric study of trade among dozens of countries for the period 1950–1998. The study led them to conclude that dynamic gains from trade are more difficult to measure, but are, in general, much larger than static gains from trade. The authors found that trade liberalization increased the rate of growth in GDP from 1.5 to 2 percentage points in the studied countries. Although this may appear to be small, over ten years of compounding, this becomes a 22 percent increase in GDP attributable to trade.

Self-sufficiency

Within broad limits, each nation can determine the level at which it interacts with the rest of the world. On the surface, self-sufficiency has been seen as a laudable goal for many individuals, nations, and cultures. It seems to make sense to be self-reliant, and in charge of one's own destiny. As an economic policy, self-sufficiency has been limiting. Mao Zedong believed in local self-sufficiency and attempted to implement policies in China to eliminate food transportation between regions, and imports of food from other nations (Lardy, 1983). The policy failed, since some areas of China were better suited to food production than others. Mao's resistance to the idea of local specialization based on comparative advantage was costly to the people of China. The nation's agricultural output declined from the 1960s until the household responsibility system was put in place in 1981 (see Box 3.2).

The local food movement is similar to a policy of self-sufficiency, regarding locally produced food as superior to food imported from other regions or nations. The arguments for local food appear to be rational, but careful investigation reveals that local food may have unanticipated costs, in addition to its obvious benefits. An economic decision about food purchases would be based on the amount of societal resources used in the production of the good, regardless of the location. For example, it is possible to produce tomatoes in Minnesota but the expense of growing them in greenhouses is higher than the cost of production plus transportation to obtain tomatoes from California.

If local food has unique qualities that consumers desire, then local food fulfils the wants and needs of local consumers. If consumers learn more about the production and characteristics over time, and find that local food does not meet their objectives, consumers can purchase food products from other locales. From an economic perspective, the price of food reflects the amount of resources used to produce the good (Lusk and Norwood, 2011). Even though food produced long distances from consumers may require fuel for transport, it may use fewer total resources to grow and transport it than the locally produced alternative.

This is called a "make or buy" decision: if it is less costly to produce a good domestically, then a nation could be most efficient producing the good. If it is less expensive to purchase the good than produce it, a nation is better off importing the lower-cost product.

Revenues from tariffs

A tariff is a tax levied against imported goods. Many governments use tariffs to generate the revenue needed to support general government expenditures. Politicians and government leaders are drawn to this type of trade policy, because the individuals paying the tax are not citizens of the nation receiving the revenue. Domestic consumers are made worse off, but the higher prices that they pay are not immediately transparent. Agricultural products have been subject to trade barriers and tariffs in many nations over a long period of time.

Preferential Trade Agreements (PTAs)

A Preferential Trade Agreement (PTA) is a bloc of trading nations that gives preferential access to certain goods from participating (member) nations. Typically, the PTA reduces or eliminates all trade barriers between member nations. This is often the first stage of movement toward complete economic integration between member nations, or a free trade area (FTA). The General Agreement on Tariffs and

Trade (GATT) is a group of nations founded in 1947 to promote freer trade between nations. There were 23 original members of the GATT, which was replaced by the World Trade Organization (WTO) in 1995. The WTO is committed to reducing trade barriers between nations.

The member nations of the North American Free Trade Agreement (NAFTA) – a large and modern PTA – have also agreed to lower trade barriers. At times, member nations will break the agreement to place a tariff or import restriction on a product. This type of behavior typically occurs for political reasons, or to protect domestic producers rather than from recognizing comparative advantages among members.

Trade agreements provide a powerful insight into the reduction of trade disputes and polarized issues involving international agricultural trade. Nations that join a free trade area (FTA) agree to reduce and then eliminate trade barriers over time, with the objective of increasing economic benefits or advantages to all member nations. If successful, such areas will result in large overall benefits of economic integration. These gains provide a powerful motivation for nations to join free trade agreements, and FTAs have proliferated since the 1970s.

Trade agreements result in economic gains, but, as in other trading situations, they also adversely affect some industries that now face competition from other nations. Groups who benefitted from trade barriers, the protected industry, are made worse off from a trade agreement that eliminates the trade barrier. Policies that compensate workers and industries that have been negatively affected by trade can alleviate some of the necessary restructuring. When the US opened its automobile markets to imports, domestic steel and US auto workers suffered lower wages and fewer employment opportunities. To the extent that the workers could be compensated with retraining programs and safety nets for lost wages and salaries, the transfer to free trade could be made easier and beneficial (or less harmful) to some individuals and groups.

The intuition behind using economic integration as a solution to protectionism has had advocates since the time of the American Revolution. James Madison (1751–1836), writing under the pseudonym "Publius" in "The Federalist Number 10" (1787), put forth a potential solution to the major issue of forming a new nation (Madison, 1787). His solution focused on the existence of political "factions." Madison's "faction" included "a number of citizens united and activated by some common impulse." Madison believed that such factions, or special interest groups, operated in their own interest and ignored the rights of other citizens and the common good. He wrote that factions are an inevitable outcome of human nature: "As long as the reason of man continues fallible, and he is at liberty to exercise it, different opinions will be found." He also stated that factions should not be eliminated. Instead, Madison believed that a republican form of government would alleviate the problem of factions. Minority factions would be defeated in a regular vote, so posed no problem. Republics that extend over larger numbers of citizens and larger territories could therefore deal more effectively with majority factions.

Madison claimed that larger republics encompass a greater variety of parties and interests, making it less probable that a factious majority could be found or act. With a large electorate, interests will be varied and no single set of interests would dominate. By voluntarily joining a free trade agreement, a member nation is attaching itself to a group of nations that will not allow any single nation to use protectionist policies. If, for example, sugar producers have enough political power to receive protection from import competition in one nation, they will be less likely to be able to retain this privilege in a larger group of like-minded nations. This is particularly true if some of the member nations are sugar exporters, harmed by sugar protection policies. Trade barriers have been reduced dramatically in the post–World War II era. During this period, globalization has increased dramatically: trade has increased, trade barriers have dropped in number, and free trade agreements have proliferated.

A large portion of the growth in national incomes has been due to the movement toward free trade with other nations (Gwartney, 2009). As nations join in larger and larger agreements, Madison's arguments for "large republics" become reality as nations lower trade barriers. The process can appear to be slow, however, as dramatic changes often require time and disaffected groups and individuals often need to be compensated for their losses.

Food safety

As incomes rise, consumers become more interested in food quality and food safety. Many nations have put in place sophisticated regulatory systems to maintain domestic food safety. It is much more difficult, however, to enforce food safety regulations for imported goods. Technical barriers and rules on imports help reduce the spread of diseases, pests, or other problems associated with imported food.

BOX 9.2: TECHNICAL BARRIERS TO TRADE: FOOD SAFETY

Food entering a nation from abroad raises concerns about pests and diseases harming domestic consumers or agricultural production. Examples of harmful pests that have entered the US include aphids, gypsy moths, and fire ants (Reed, 2001). Because of this, countries place strict controls and regulations on imported food. However, technical barriers to trade may also be a form of protectionism, since a nation could under the guise of food safety impose trade barriers to protect domestic producers from foreign competition.

Avocados from Mexico were banned from the US during the period 1914–1997, due to a fear that Mexican avocados might introduce seed weevils into the US. Although Mexico is the largest avocado exporter in the world, US producers were successful in banning imports for a long period of time. Even today, avocados from Mexico cannot be imported into California, where avocados are grown.

Similarly, the European Union (EU), a free trade area, has banned US meat products from entering the EU due to the use of growth hormones. As China has transformed from a centrally controlled economy to a market-based economic system, the US has increased imports of food from China, leading to concerns about food production practices and the potential impact on human health and nutrition. Technical measures such as sanitary and phytosanitary (SPS) regulations are important in protecting plant and animal health. Member nations of the WTO are allowed to set their own regulations provided they are based on a scientific risk assessment, and are not trade barriers (Peterson *et al.*, 2013).

BOX 9.3: THE EUROPEAN UNION AND GENETICALLY MODIFIED ORGANISMS

Genetically modified organisms (GMOs) are plants or animals that have genetic material altered or inserted into them. Modified plants, also called genetically engineered (GE) plants, have been a major source of worldwide controversy for many years. Plants have been genetically altered in many ways, beginning with natural and conventional crossbreeding which crosses and combines plant traits through pollination. "Genetic modification" originates with the work of Gregor Mendel, who, in the mid-1800s, conducted experiments that led to the modern understanding of genetics and then to using different methods of combining plant traits. The goal of both conventional and genetic modification is to alter the plants to make certain favorable characteristics such as higher yield, or pest resistance, a permanent part of the plant's genetic makeup. More recently, plant scientists have introduced genetic material from other plants and animals into food plants. The first commercially produced GE food, the Flavr Savr tomato, came onto the market in 1994. US consumers have been eating GMOs since that time, and a large percentage of the nation's feed corn and soybean crops are now genetically modified. Genetic engineering of agricultural crops can increase yields and resistance to different diseases caused by pathogens and parasites. Higher yields, lower pesticide use, and decreased fertilizer requirements are characteristics of GE crops that are beneficial to society.

Even given the beneficial traits, the production and use of GE crops have been accompanied by numerous ethical and safety concerns. It is possible, but not yet proven, that GE crops contain toxins or allergens not contained in conventional food. Food based on GE crops has been consumed for over two decades by millions of consumers, with no apparent ill effect. Even so, the potential for damage to the environment or to human health caused by

GE crops remains. Some growers and consumers are concerned that genetic material will flow into and harm related nontransgenic crops. Ethical concerns involve religious issues, corporate control of the food supply, intellectual property rights, and the level of labeling needed to make genetically modified products more transparent. As with any new technology, there are potential risks from using GE methods. Plant scientists as well as policy makers must be thoughtful and careful about the introduction of new GE plants into the marketplace.

The debate over genetically engineered food is long lasting, contentious, and unlikely to be resolved soon. However, as GE crops continue to be grown without problems in the US, it appears likely that most other nations will eventually adopt GE food. In 2012, Mark Lynas, an outspoken opponent of GE food, changed his mind about genetic modification, and publicly embraced GMOs after being one of their strongest opponents for many years (Lynas, 2013).

Gains from trade from complementary paradigms in production agriculture

The underlying theme of specialization and trade is the ability of individuals, groups, and nations to benefit from the diversity of different people in different locations. Benefits from specialization and trade also exist in ideas, innovations, and production practices. Agricultural production can be optimized by targeting the best management practices in each specific location where food and fiber is or can be produced. Even within a single wheat or corn field, today's GPS-guided production technology allows for "precision agriculture" to optimize the quantity of inputs applied to every small plot – in some cases, as small as one square meter – of land within the field.

Some of the major controversies in agriculture could be reduced by combining, or trading, ideas and innovations. Genetically engineered (GE) organic food provides one example of potential success in this area. Ronald and Adamchak (2008) effectively present a case for combining genetic engineering with organic food production practices to "create a new generation of plants that will dramatically reduce our dependence on pesticides, enhance the health of our agricultural systems, and increase the nutritional content of our food" (p. ix). The authors provide evidence that organic agriculture can help address the environmental degradation associated with conventional agriculture. However, the question is whether or not organic agriculture can meet the growing global demand for food and fiber (p. 37). This objective could become closer to realization to the extent that GE could "increase resistance of plants to insects, diseases, and nematodes, and help plants adapt to environmental stresses such as drought, flooding, cold, and salt" (p. 37). Merging the benefits of GE with the attributes of organic farming, currently illegal under USDA organic labeling rules, would provide gains from trade that could provide benefits to food and agriculture. Paarlberg (2009, 2010) argues that GE could make a positive difference in Africa, where the need for increased food production is greatest.

Genetic engineering practices in plant breeding could combine with a number of other production practices to enhance food production throughout the world. Several other recent innovations in production agriculture include:

- Sustainable intensification, as described in Box 8.4, combines an ecosystem approach to increasing food production while enhancing the environment. This is a strategic objective of the United Nations Food and Agriculture Organization (UNFAO), and brings together the best attributes of crop management technologies to increase productivity and profitability in a sustainable fashion (Pretty, 2008; Pretty et al., 2011; Garnett and Godfray, 2012). This bundle of economic and environmental objectives provides a useful foundation upon which to build a truly sustainable agricultural future.
- Precision agriculture uses global positioning systems (GPS) to observe, measure, and respond to variability in crops within a specific field by combining recent developments in satellite technology with variable rate application of chemicals and fertilizers to enhance output while minimizing input use. This merger of available knowledge into innovative production practices allows farmers to increase yields, decrease input costs, and improve environmental conditions simultaneously. The high level of technology allows producers to meet multiple objectives (Oliver et al., 2013; Bongiovanni and Lowenberg-Deboer, 2004; McBratney et al., 2005).
- Ecological economics combines aspects of ecology with economics to better understand the impact of agriculture on the environment. The term "eco-efficiency" was endorsed by the 1992 Earth Summit in Rio de Janeiro as an approach for the private sector to obtain sustainability. Specifically, eco-efficiency refers to "competitively-priced goods and services that satisfy human needs and bring quality of life, while progressively reducing ecological impacts of goods and resource intensity throughout the entire life-cycle to a level at least in line with the Earth's estimated carrying capacity" (World Business Council for Sustainable Development [WBCSD] 2014). The major objective is to create more value with less impact.
- Reduced tillage practices leave residue from the previous year's crop on the soil surface. Instead of plowing, farmers plant seeds directly into the residue. This practice reduces fuel, labor, and machinery costs significantly. In arid climates, reduced tillage helps retain soil moisture (Triplett and Dick, 2008; Soane et al., 2012). Reduced tillage decreases erosion and runoff. This practice is widely used in the Midwestern US and Latin America, but not in Europe (Soane et al., 2012).

By combining ideas and innovations, these relatively new approaches to farming have provided yield enhancements and lower per-unit input use. These solutions based on diversity are similar to the product bundling examples explored in Chapter 8.

Summary and conclusions

Specialization and gains from trade provide the foundation for economic growth and development. By allocating resources based on comparative advantage, large gains can accrue. Trade between individuals, regions, and nations can increase the overall well-being of trading partners. However, some individuals and groups will be made worse off from trade. If these economic agents could be compensated for their losses, then trade could make the largest possible contribution to economic growth. Trade of ideas and innovations also leads to large potential gains, and the more divergent the ideas, the larger are the potential gains. Diversity provides the cause and motivation for specialization and gains from trade. Individuals, firms, and nations that take advantage of the differences in people, climate, culture, and ideas will benefit the most in finding gains from specialization and trade.

Note

1   The only legitimate economic reason for import barriers is if the importing nation is large enough that it can use market power to restrict imports, causing a decrease in world price (Reed, 2001).

10

NEGOTIATING RESOLUTION

Game theory

> Locally grown food is the new organic and small farmers are the latest cause celeb.
>
> Stew Leonard, successful grocer

Introduction

Polarized issues in food and agriculture are typically the result of two or more groups whose well-being or livelihood depends on or can be threatened by the actions of other individuals or groups. Beef producers are affected by the actions of animal welfare groups or vegans seeking to enlarge the number of consumers who do not purchase animal products. Farmers who use chemicals are affected by environmental groups and government agencies seeking to decrease or eliminate the use of pesticides, herbicides, or fungicides used in the production of some crops and animals. These groups are interdependent in the sense that one group's actions result in reactions from other groups. Such issues polarize when the actions and reactions by affected parties cause economic and political damage. When producers, consumers, and policy makers incorporate interactions and interdependencies of all affected parties into their decision making, it can depolarize controversial issues in food and agriculture.

As new food products are developed, farmers and food processors must decide if it is in their best interest to produce the new product or not. In many cases, the most profitable course of action depends on the actions of others, outside a firm's control. Game theory provides a useful and informative way of improving decisions by including the anticipated actions of others during the decision making process. For example, beef producers who incorporate consumer reactions to how beef products are produced may make more effective long-run decisions than those companies that do not. Consumer groups seeking to change how food is produced may have a strategic advantage if they use game theory to find common ground with their adversaries. Game theory shows rivals that observation and cooperation, rather than retaliation, may lead to the best outcome. In many situations, polarized issues in food and agriculture can be resolved through consideration of long-term costs and possible consequences of rivalry and retaliation.

To decision makers, the interdependence of stakeholders often results in strategic interactions. A chemical company must think through the effects of its own decisions, the expected outcomes for other groups, and their possible reactions to this "second round" of decisions. These groups are involved in a "game," defined as a decision-making situation in which the participants make strategic decisions: person A considers person B's response before making a decision. Strategic decisions of this kind take into account all players' actions and possible responses. This way of looking at the world is called "game theory," and is a powerful and useful way to organize thoughts about how to make decisions that result in or respond to responses by others.[1] Game theory provides insights into the best possible course of action, incorporating the action's original impact and reactions or expected reactions of other affected parties. It is easy to imagine how important it is for decision makers of all types to evaluate carefully the possible reactions of all affected parties in strategic thinking. If polarized groups incorporated the opposing viewpoint, progress could be made towards depolarization of issues in food and agriculture, as will be shown in what follows.

Strategic decisions result in payoffs which are the outcomes that generate benefits or costs to the players (stakeholders). These payoffs can be summarized in a "payoff matrix," which shows the benefits or costs accruing to each player given her/his decision and the decision of her/his competitor. A simple game of product choice is illustrated by the payoff matrix in Figure 10.1.

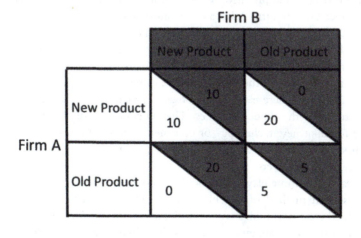

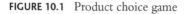

Payoffs in $ (million)

FIGURE 10.1 Product choice game

This game formalizes a hypothetical situation similar to issues that arise in the food and agriculture industry when a new product is made available. Suppose that two firms are currently selling an "old" product, and split $10 million, the total amount of consumer willingness to pay in this market. Both firms earn $5 million selling the old product. Suppose a new product doubles the size of the market to $20 million. As a result, the "first mover" (that is, the first firm to produce and sell the new product) earns all new product revenue, and the competitor earns nothing.

If both firms produce and sell the new product, they split the market evenly at $10 million each. These payoffs are shown in Figure 10.1, where the payoffs to Firm A are shown in the lower left triangle of each quadrant, and the payoffs to Firm B are in the shaded upper right triangle. If both Firm A and Firm B continue to sell the old product, they are in the lower right quadrant, where each firm earns $5 million. To summarize: if either A or B sells the new product, the outcome is shown in the lower left (Firm A) or upper right (Firm B) quadrants, indicating the winner-take-all nature of this strategic game. If both firms produce and sell the new product, the outcome is shown in the upper left quadrant, where the firms split the market evenly, and each firm earns $10 million.

The earnings in this situation depend not only on the firm's (either A or B) own decisions, but also on the actions and reactions of other firms. How do firms decide what to do? There are two ways of thinking about a solution. The first is called a "dominant strategy." A dominant strategy is one that is optimal no matter what the opponent does. To find Firm A's dominant strategy, consider Firm A's decision in light of the decision made by Firm B. If Firm B chooses to produce and sell the new product (left column of the payoff matrix), then Firm A can choose between the new product, which would earn $10 million, or the old product, which would result in zero profits. Firm A will select "new product" if B chooses "new product." Similarly, if Firm B selects "old product" (right column), Firm A will again select "new product," since 20 > 5. Firm A has a dominant strategy in "new product," because it is better off choosing "new" no matter what Firm B does.

What is Firm B's dominant strategy? Using the same logic, if Firm A selects new, then B selects new: 10 > 0. If A chooses old, B is still better off with new: 20 > 5. In this way, the outcome of the product choice game is "new, new" shown in the upper left quadrant where each firm chooses to produce and sell the new product, no matter what the other firm does. This outcome describes the real-world incentive to adopt new technology or offer new products that consumers desire to purchase. The game is a simplistic game showing a straightforward dominant strategy for both players.

In many games, one or more players may not have a dominant strategy. In such cases there is a second method of searching for an optimal strategic decision. Named for the mathematician John Nash,[2] the "Nash Equilibrium" allows each player to do the best that s/he can, given what the other player is doing. The result is stable because no player is left with an incentive to change. Nash strategies are often the same as the dominant strategies, but need not be. In the product choice game depicted in Figure 10.1, the Nash strategies occur in the following way: focus on each quadrant and determine if each firm would like to stay or change strategies. If Firm B chooses "new," and firm A chooses "new," then Firm A does not have an incentive to change, since it would lose money (10 > 0). Similarly, B desires to stay with "new" if A selects "new" (10 > 0). So the game's "new, new" solution is a Nash Equilibrium with neither firm desiring to change. Therefore, the solution "new, new" qualifies as both a dominant strategy (each firm is doing the best that it can, no matter what the other firm chooses) and a Nash Equilibrium (each firm is doing the best that it can, given what the other firm is doing).

In each of the other three quadrants, at least one of the firms desires to change strategies. In the "new, old" quadrant, A would like to stay (20 > 5), given B's choice of "old." However, B would like to change from old to new (0 < 10), given A's selection of "new." Likewise, Firm A would not stay in quadrant "old, new." Both firms desire to leave the lower right quadrant, "old, old." In this game, there is no good reason for either firm to produce and sell the old product. The game's outcome has both firms producing and selling the new product, since the incentive is the same for both firms, given the choices of the rival firm.

Firm location decision: a game that brings firms together

The Nash Equilibrium concept is used extensively in economics, social sciences, biology, and military science. The crucial thing to remember is that a firm will only stick with a decision if it is the best that the firm can do, given the reactions of other firms. Nash's insights provide a useful solution to a problem that is pervasive in market economies and politics: firms that are apparent competitors locate near each other, and politicians, regardless of party, select policies that represent the "average voter." In most towns or cities, the fast food restaurants, the car dealerships, and the gasoline stations are located in close proximity to each other. This is often due to zoning regulations, but it is also a result of optimal strategic decision making by the business owners: game theory. Consider Firm A's choice of where to locate a business in Figure 10.2.

Firms A and B both sell coffee, and coffee drinkers (potential customers) are spread evenly across the 100 blocks of a city. Coffee drinkers purchase from the nearest coffee vendor. In this case, the Nash Equilibrium says both firms should locate as close to the middle of the city as possible. Why? Suppose that Firm B locates at block 75 (b' in Figure 10.2). In this case, Firm A could move to block 74, and receive nearly three-quarters of the coffee market, since all customers to the left of Firm A's location will purchase from it. Firm B would lose customers,

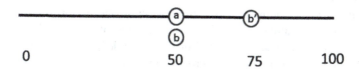

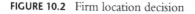

0　　　　　　　　　50　　　75　　　100

FIGURE 10.2 Firm location decision

and would desire to move closer to the middle to recover lost sales. Thus, in equilibrium, Firms A and B will both locate in the middle, at block 50, which is a stable location: a Nash Equilibrium. Obviously, but importantly, the real world is more complicated than this simple model. For example, product differentiation causes one firm to move away from the other firm. However, the simple example provides a prediction that holds in many real-world cases.

This simple game explains a great deal about market and political behavior. Firms will locate near each other, not only in physical space, but also with respect to other strategic attributes. Similarly, if the sugar content of packaged cereals is important to consumers, firms producing these products will move their products towards the sugar content desired by the average consumer. Politicians will align themselves as closely as possible to the median voter. This outcome explains why many partisan voters are frustrated at election time when candidates may appear to be advocating the same things, rather than reflecting the strong right- or strong left-leaning voters.

The outcome of this game has important implications for polarized issues in food and agriculture, since it suggests that firms starting in different places have economic (or political) incentives to move toward the same location. Economic incentives provide the catalyst to bring divergent groups together in many situations and issues. Extreme groups can provide a starting point, and can bring an important issue into the spotlight, but the policy process typically brings opposing groups together through compromise and negotiated solutions. Similarly, highly specialized niche markets can often serve a portion of a larger market, but firms often face irresistible economic incentives to provide goods and services that are acceptable to a majority of consumers.

The prisoner's dilemma

The games introduced above have straightforward solutions and outcomes that reflect relatively uncomplicated situations: new products that are superior to old products, and business decisions made to meet the needs of the average consumer. The real world is more complex, and polarized issues that remain stubbornly divisive over time often have characteristics that differ from the two games described above. Indeed, life often presents difficult choices with no easy solutions: choices that affect other players, whose reactions subsequently affect us.

The prisoner's dilemma describes a situation common in real life, where cooperation leads to the best outcome for the group, but an individual could make her/himself better off by independent action. A couple that decide to have a relationship makes both persons better off, until one person breaks from the relationship in an attempt to seek a more desirable situation. This independent action results in an unattractive (and often unintended) outcome. Similarly, two firms might agree to jointly limit production to keep prices high, but one firm might ignore the agreement to sell more units at the higher price, taking advantage of the other firm's low production. This is a common situation, much studied and debated by the architects of the US Constitution: how to maintain suitable levels of both individual freedom and democracy, without the rich and powerful passing laws that favor themselves.

The prisoner's dilemma reflects the common situation of two players with the potential to gain benefits from cooperation, but with an incentive to act independently. Such a game is depicted in Figure 10.3, where in a hypothetical case, two criminals are arrested for committing a crime and are placed in separate interrogation rooms.

The key feature of the game is that the prisoners are not allowed to communicate with each other. The police have some evidence to convict, but it is weak. Therefore, the police attempt to obtain a confession from either or both suspects. If both prisoners confess to the crime, they will both spend five years in jail, as shown in the "confess, confess" quadrant of the payoff matrix in Figure 10.3. If neither criminal confesses, the police have only enough evidence to convict each for a two-year prison sentence, as shown in the lower right quadrant. The police use this possibility of a reduced sentence as an incentive to force a confession.[3] If one prisoner confesses, and the other does not, the confessing prisoner receives a light sentence as a reward for cooperation: one year for the confessor, and ten years for the nonconfessing accomplice.

If neither prisoner confesses, each is sentenced to two years in jail. Each suspect, however, has an incentive to confess: a lighter sentence. Each individual, hoping his accomplice will confess, also has an incentive to not confess, to reduce his own sentence from five to two years.

This is a more challenging, yet more realistic situation than the two previous games, with greater applicability to the real world. The optimal strategy for each prisoner can be found by solving for the dominant strategy if one exists. The dominant strategy of prisoner A is found by first assuming that B confesses. In this case,

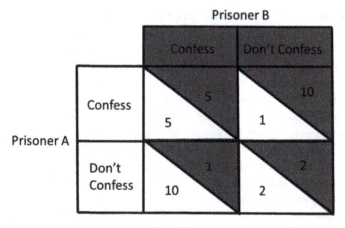

Payoffs are in number of years in jail.

FIGURE 10.3 Prisoner's dilemma

A should confess (5 < 10), recalling that smaller numbers reflect less time in jail. If B does not confess, then A should confess (1 < 2). Thus, A's dominant strategy is to confess. Since the game is symmetric (the same payoffs are possible for each player), prisoner B's dominant strategy is also to "confess," because this is the best option for B, no matter what A does. The dominant strategy of "confess, confess" is also a Nash Equilibrium for each player, since neither player could do better given the choice to confess by the other prisoner. Prisoner A would do worse given B's confession (10 > 5) and B would similarly do worse given A's confession (10 > 5).

What makes the prisoner's dilemma so interesting and widely applicable is that if the two players could agree to the cooperative solution, in this case "don't confess, don't confess," they could minimize their total sentence to four years: two for each criminal. If the two prisoners could communicate, they might well be able to agree to this outcome, which is superior to the other three outcomes for both prisoners together (4 < 10 and 4 < 11). However, if such an agreement were made, perhaps in the police squad car on the way to interrogation, there is a strong incentive for each prisoner to give up on the cooperative agreement and act independently. This would reduce the confessing prisoner's sentence to one year, as long as the partner in crime sticks to the "don't confess" strategy. If both cheat on such an agreement, they end up in the "confess, confess" outcome, which is much worse for both prisoners. To summarize, when prisoners find the cooperative solution, they are both better off ... but there is an incentive to ignore the agreement. If both cheat, there is an incentive to cooperate to achieve the superior outcome. This is the prisoner's dilemma!

BOX 10.1: FARM BILL POLITICS: FOOD SUBSIDIES AND FARM SUBSIDIES

In the US, agricultural policy is based on Congressional "Farm Bills" that are typically reviewed and updated once every four to six years. Since about 1950, the farm population in the US has diminished quite rapidly. Because of this, the political power of US farmers has diminished demonstrably. During this same period, urban populations have grown rapidly with many impoverished urban citizens having difficulty purchasing enough food. Urban voters have sought to increase the availability and value of food stamps, but have opposed government subsidies to farmers. Rural voters take opposite positions desiring increased farm subsidies, but limits on tax-supported food subsidies to urban dwellers. The opposing positions form a prisoner's dilemma, since both food stamps and farm subsidies are large budget items. In the most recent (2013) Congressional vote, neither farmers nor urbanites had enough votes to pass their favored programs through both houses of Congress. However, a cooperative solution put both policies in the same Farm Bill. The combined bill resulted in both urban and rural legislators desiring to pass initial proposals.

Senator George McGovern, a Democrat from South Dakota, and Senator Bob Dole, a Republican from Kansas, found a unique way to maintain farm subsidies in an increasingly urban population. In 1973, McGovern took the lead by proposing that the nationwide food stamp program, a subsidy for poor households, be included in the farm bill legislation. By tying food stamps, predominantly for urban people, with farm subsidies, McGovern and Dole found a legislative proposal that both rural and urban legislators would vote for. McGovern and Dole went on to propose and enact several measures that supported agriculture, including food aid to foreign nations, school lunches, and child nutrition programs in the US and abroad.

The cooperative solution supporting both food stamps and farm subsidies worked well until decades later in 2013, when the US House of Representatives voted down a farm bill proposal. Agriculture had become more consolidated, and many subsidy payment recipients were no longer living on farms. Food stamps had become a more expensive budget item due to the economic recession. In 2013, the recession and the public debt crisis caused many Republicans to become more committed to balancing the budget through greater reductions in government expenditures on food subsidies and farm subsidies. At the time, this was politically feasible because of high farm profitability in the years leading up to the vote. With high profits from markets, recipients of large farm subsidies were less opposed to reductions in government payments to farmers. In the language of the prisoner's dilemma, the cooperative solution was lost due to independent actions of independent players, who sought to better their own situation at the expense of overall welfare.

Price war game

Prisoner's dilemmas abound in a democratic, market-oriented economy. Such dilemmas always include some variation of the question, "Should I cooperate, and make us all better off, or should I go my own way, to benefit myself at the expense of the others?" This question is at the core of many disputes in the food and agriculture industries. The food industry is subject to rapid change, responding to a continuing stream of new products, new characteristics, and new policies. These changes can have large economic consequences for nearly all food firms, from a local berry grower in a farmers' market to the largest multinational food corporation. Given the universality of new food products and new production methods, agribusinesses must decide whether to enter a market, and what price to charge if they do enter.

Many new food markets are not large enough to support all entering firms. If too many firms enter, the price will often be driven down to levels below production costs. This can precipitate a "price war," where firms lower prices in the attempt to win customers away from rival firms. This relatively common situation is shown in Figure 10.4. Here, Firms A and B have entered a new food market, say locally grown apples. If both firms enter and place their apples on the market at a high price, they can each earn $5,000. This is the best of all possible payoffs, and represents the cooperative solution to the game, shown in the lower right quadrant of Figure 10.4. However, this game is a prisoner's dilemma, in which each firm is tempted to lower its price for the product. If the rival firm maintains a high price, a low price will result in increased profits, $10,000. However, in the situation where both firms charge the low price, each firm earns only $2,000.

The dominant strategy for this game can be found by looking at the optimal strategy for each firm, given the strategy of the other firm. If B chooses "low," then A will also choose "low" (2 > -5) to avoid losing sales. If B chooses "high," then A chooses "low," since 10 is greater than 5. Therefore, the dominant strategy for A is to charge a low price. The game is symmetrical, so Firm B's dominant strategy is also "low price." The two firms are locked in a prisoner's dilemma, with each earning only $2,000, instead of the cooperative solution, where they could each earn $5,000. The Nash Equilibrium is also (low, low): in the upper left quadrant, Firm A desires to stay, since charging a high price would result in a move from $2,000 to negative $5,000. Firm B also desires to stay in the low price column, so (low, low) is a stable Nash Equilibrium, with neither firm desiring to change strategies.

Is it possible to achieve the cooperative solution (high, high) in a price war game? One possibility is to think of this game as a "repeated game." This means that the two players do not make a once-and-for-all price decision, but make the price decision together with the other firm every day. Here, each player must consider not only the likely strategy of the other players, but also all future actions and reactions. Retaliation is possible in a repeated game if one player behaves in a

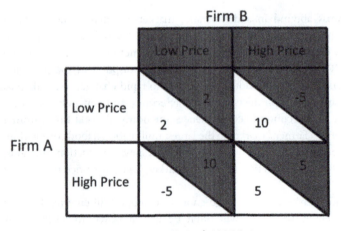

Payoffs in $ (1000s)

FIGURE 10.4 Price war game

way that yields negative consequences for the other player. However, some observations regarding the behavior of the rival firm allow informed price decisions to be made each day. Game theorists have found that players in a repeated game will often converge to the cooperative solution, since the rewards are higher for both players.[4]

The stability of the cooperative solution is likely to be tenuous in many markets. If profits are high, potential entrants are likely to enter the market with a lower price, to lure consumers away from the existing firms. In markets with many producers, the likelihood of achieving a stable outcome of high profits is less likely than in a market with only a few firms: the probability of a firm "going rogue" increases as more firms enter. Similarly, the cooperative outcome in a repeated game is more likely under stable demand and cost conditions. When demand is changing rapidly, as in many food markets, it is much more difficult to get producers/players to develop and maintain a cooperative strategy, because it is harder to detect firms who "cheat" by offering a lower price.

The repeated game story provides insights into how society works. Reciprocity provides long-term gains. Examples are numerous: being kind to strangers may not be a dominant strategy in a one-time game, but in a repeated game it may pay higher rewards. One argument for carrying concealed weapons is that people will be less likely to challenge others if concealed weapons are legal. Tipping waiters may not be optimal in a one-time visit to an up-scale restaurant. It becomes more likely in repeated visits where the waiter recalls the generous tips from earlier visits.

One major implication for polarized food issues is that polarization characterized by the absence of cooperation is more likely in volatile markets. As sales of new food products increase and become more integrated into the food production and processing system, some of the noncooperative behavior may diminish as stakeholders move towards mutually beneficial cooperative solutions. Bad behavior and noncooperative strategies quickly become obsolete in a repeated game: players with forward-looking decision processes will be much more likely to cooperate when retaliation is possible.

Sequential games: market entry

Customers, observers, and analysts were surprised when Walmart entered the organic food market in 2006 (Box 10.2).[5] They wondered why a giant chain store would enter a market previously dominated almost exclusively by small players. Game theory provides useful insights into how and why this happened. Given the rapidly increasing demand for organic, natural, healthy, and local foods, a description and analysis of how firms decide whether or not to enter a market is important and interesting. A market entry game representing organic food markets in large grocery store chains is depicted by the payoff matrix in Figure 10.5.

The players are "A-mart" and a competitor, "B-mart." The firms must determine whether to enter the organic grocery market or not. Like the price war

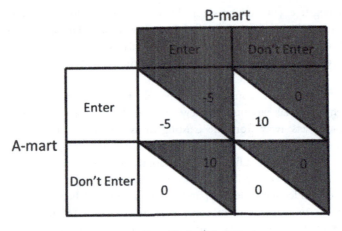

Payoffs in $ (million)

FIGURE 10.5 Market entry game

game in the previous section, the market is not large enough to accommodate both firms: if both A-mart and B-mart enter, both lose $5 million. If neither enters, then neither firm gains nor loses money, as seen in the lower right quadrant: (0, 0). The interesting feature of this game is that if one of the two firms enters, and the other does not, profits are large for the firm that enters ($10 million). Investment and entry into this new market is a risky scheme, since both large profits and losses are possible, depending on the behavior of the rival firm. This situation characterizes much of the behavior in food markets, and reveals the causes of many controversial issues.

A strategy that is optimal no matter what B-mart does is the dominant strategy for A-mart. A-mart, however, does not have a dominant strategy since it is better off not entering if B-mart enters (0 > -5), and entering if B-mart does not enter (10 > 0). This is also true of B-mart, as the game is symmetrical. There are two Nash Equilibria, in the lower left and upper right quadrants. In these two cases, one firm enters and the other does not. This makes sense. The new market can sustain a single firm, but not more. When A-mart enters and B-mart does not, A-mart earns $10 million, and B-mart earns zero. Neither firm could do better, given the strategy of the other firm: A-mart profits go to zero if it switches to "don't enter," and B-mart loses $5 million if it chooses to enter when A-mart is already in the market.

In this simplified game, either of these two Nash Equilibria represents the most desirable outcome, from a societal point of view. Total profits for all firms are highest ($10 million), and consumers can purchase the product. In a repeated game, either of these two outcomes is socially desirable, since producers and consumers are in a stable outcome that results in production and consumption of a desired good. Entry in this case causes losses to both producers and consumers. Which equilibrium occurs depends on who enters first. The rules of this game will need to change to achieve a societal goal by making this game a sequential game, instead of a game where all players make simultaneous decisions. In a sequential game, players move in turn, while responding to each other's actions and reactions. In this game, there are major economic advantages to moving first: the first mover's advantage.

If A-mart moves first, it will choose to enter the organic grocery market, with the possibility of profits equal to $10 million. This move is somewhat risky, since it could result in a loss if B-mart also enters. However, once A-mart is established as the first entrant, B-mart's decision is limited to the first row of the payoff matrix: enter and lose, or stay out with no net gains or losses. B-mart will not enter in this case, and the stable outcome has been achieved through a sequential game with a first mover's advantage. B-mart could also capture the rewards of this market by entering the organic grocery market first. If B-mart could enter first, then it could successfully induce A-mart to stay out of the organic grocery market. This simple sequential game demonstrates why Walmart quickly entered the organic grocery market, and in a big way: Walmart was demonstrating a commitment to the market, to ward off potential competitors. This strategy was not new to Walmart: it used the same strategy of entering retail markets in small towns to become the most successful retailer of all time.[6]

The outcome of this sequential game provides insights into polarized issues in food and agriculture: if first movers have an advantage of "winner take all," any business that is not a first mover is likely to be unhappy with the outcome of this type of sequential game. Once a large and powerful firm is in place, it may be extremely difficult and costly to alter the status quo. This can lead to a great deal of criticism of large, early movers in the food industry. Michael Pollan captured this line of thinking in his book, *The Omnivore's Dilemma* (2006a).

BOX 10.2: INDUSTRIAL AGRICULTURE: WALMART

Prior to World War II, all agricultural production was "organic" since few thought it important to distinguish between organic and inorganic production methods. However, since about 1950, agricultural production has increasingly relied on chemicals and synthetic fertilizers to increase crop yields. Opponents of this "industrialization" of agriculture sought to farm using organic practices; those without purchased inputs of herbicides, pesticides, and synthetic fertilizers. The movement gathered adherents during the 1970s, and the organic food movement was characterized by small, independent farmers who emphasized the environmental and health benefits of organic food. All of this changed in 2006.

With growing interest in the profits associated with organic food products, Walmart entered the organic food market. Walmart's objective was to make organic food available and affordable to everyone. Walmart's reputation was a firm that epitomized large, impersonal, and industrial capitalism, and its history of ruthless cost-cutting efficiency resulted in disappointment to many organic food proponents. To many, organic food represented a desirable counter-culture lifestyle. Michael Pollan (2001) coined the term "industrial organic" to describe the movement of agribusinesses into organic food markets. As large food corporations began to produce and sell organic products, many organic food consumers became alienated, and switched their loyalty to "local food." Oddly, "local" is not well defined, and local products can be either organic or conventional. Together with this movement towards large corporations providing organic food was an accumulation of research demonstrating that there are no discernible health benefits from consuming organic food (Brandt, 2012).

An additional concern about industrial organic is a lack of concern about strict organic standards and certification, and preservation of small organic farms. The Organic Consumers Association (OCA) claimed that Walmart's business model would drive out all competitors. And, if Walmart outsourced organic production to other nations, certification and enforcement of standards would become much more difficult with a high probability for fraud. Organic producers opposed Walmart and other large businesses in organic food markets, since the lower production costs of large enterprises would dominate the future of organic food.

Consumers typically desire the stated, USDA-sanctioned characteristics of organic food. However, if consumers desire attributes other than those used to define organic food, they will be disappointed with the organic food industry and seek alternatives. Local food has filled that void for some (Leonard, 2007).

Entry deterrence

One interesting feature of food markets is summarized by the adage, "local is the new organic." Organic food is food produced without chemicals or synthetic fertilizers. Local food is food produced within a certain distance from the market, typically 100 miles. These two types of food are quite different, and often have two significantly different production methods. Why is it that many food market participants (buyers and sellers) have substituted local for organic? One possible explanation is provided by the outcome of a sequential game. If large, politically connected agribusiness firms can enter first and stake a claim in a market, rival firms will be left out. One way to regain the opportunity to participate is to seek political intervention through zoning, regulations, or other laws that keep large firms out of a market. This type of law is commonly found in food and other retail markets: small towns and cities often ban "big box" stores, such as Walmart, Target, Home Depot and several other large commercial chains. A second possible political solution is a subsidy for local food.

The sequential game of market entry (Figure 10.5) resulted in the first mover's ability to win over the market from any potential rival firm. This outcome can be changed through straightforward policy intervention such as a subsidy to firms that produce food having characteristics considered desirable by voters or elected officials.[7] Suppose A-mart represents "Big Food" and, in general, supplies food produced by industrial agriculture. If a community desires to have food supplied to the market by small local farmers (B-mart in this example), this can be achieved using a relatively simple subsidy. Suppose local consumers see a local food market dominated by A-mart, and desire to replace it with a group of local farmers who have joined together to form a cooperative, B-mart. A subsidy of $6 million to B-mart for entering this market shifts the outcome of the sequential game from that of Figure 10.5 to the payoff matrix in Figure 10.6.

If A-mart is the first mover, and chooses to enter the market, then B-mart's optimal strategy changes to "enter" with the subsidy (1 > 0) from "don't enter" without the subsidy. The outcome in this case would be (enter, enter) in the top left quadrant, where A-mart loses $5 million, and B-mart earns positive profits equal to $1 million. If A-mart plays first and opts to not enter, then B-mart will choose to enter and earn $16 million. The subsidy has reversed A-mart's first mover advantage, and increased B-mart's profits significantly. The implications for food markets are numerous and significant. In markets characterized by a winner-take-all outcome, firms are likely to compete for the first mover advantage. If smaller firms cannot be the first mover, they may be able to reverse the outcome through government intervention.

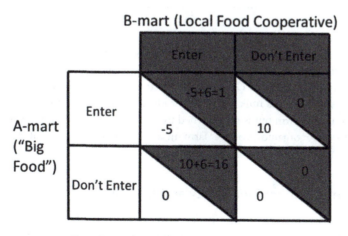

Payoffs in $ (million)
B-mart receives a $ six million subsidy if it enters

FIGURE 10.6 Subsidy to keep a rival out of the market

BOX 10.3: SAN FRANCISCO FARMERS' MARKET AND NIMAN RANCH

On a Sunday morning in September 1992, the Ferry Plaza Farmers' Market in San Francisco opened as a one-time "harvest market" for farmers and local restaurants. The event was successful, and a weekly California Certified Farmers' Market was established the following Spring. In 1994 an organizational group, the Center for Urban Education about Sustainable Agriculture (CUESA), was formed. This market had continued success, and in 2003 moved into the renovated Ferry Building, doubling the number of market stalls and serving thousands of shoppers each week.

Niman Ranch, a local California meat producer, was a vendor prior to the relocation of the farmers' market to the Ferry Building. Niman Ranch is a well-known beef company strongly committed to sustainable agriculture. Like the Ferry Plaza Farmers' Market, Niman Ranch, founded in the 1970s, grew and became successful. When CUESA selected the businesses that were allowed to participate in the new location in the Ferry Building, Niman Ranch was excluded. Tatiana Graf, CUESA spokesperson, explained: "We want things featured in the farmers' market that are small and unique. Not the same things that are at Whole Foods or at Trader Joe's."[8] Warren Weber, a market board member, clarified: "I'd say just generally speaking the purpose of the market is to serve very local small ranchers and farms as much as possible."[9]

Small food producers that become successful are controversial, as highlighted by Michael Pollan in his 2001 article, "Behind the Organic-Industrial Complex." Pollan provides several examples of large agribusinesses that staked out a first-mover advantage in organic food. His list includes Horizon Milk, which controls 70 percent of the retail organic milk market; Cascadian Farm, which started out as a local, counter-cultural farm but is now owned by General Mills; and Greenways Organic, a 2,000-acre organic produce farm near Fresno, California that also produces 24,000 acres of conventional (nonorganic) produce.

Asymmetric information: food safety and food quality

High-quality food has become a priority for many consumers in high-income nations. Food purchasers have become increasingly health-conscious, informed, and environmentally concerned. This change in food demand has resulted in food characterized by numerous food quality attributes and characteristics, including organic, local, eco-friendly, fair trade, free-range and the like. These claims by food producers typically reflect not only the quality of the food product, but how it was produced and/or processed to meet goals related to food safety, nutrition, value, packaging, and processing. These quality attributes introduce an interesting dilemma into food purchases: in many cases producers know whether they have used the claimed production methods, but consumers do not know. McCluskey (2000) points out that "many quality-differentiated food products present problems of imperfect information, which may result in inefficient market outcomes" (p. 1). Asymmetric information occurs when consumers are unable to know and verify characteristics of purchases that are important to them.

Goods can be classified into three types, based on the amount of information available to the consumer. A "search good" is one with features and characteristics easily evaluated prior to purchase: a flower might be an example, since the value of the flower is dependent on the aesthetic properties of the plant. For some goods, quality cannot be determined until the product is consumed. These goods are called "experience goods." A bottle of wine, an expensive dinner, health care, and beauty products are examples. Experience goods are typically purchased based on reputation and recommendation. A "credence good" represents the third type of good, in which quality cannot be directly observed by consumers even after consumption. Vitamin supplements and claims on how products are produced such as "organic" or "local" provide examples. The value of a credence good is often a matter of faith, or belief in the producer. Organic foods, for example, are distinguished from conventional foods by production methods rather than visible attributes. This is true of a growing number of food quality claims about how a good is produced.

Consumer demand is increasing for a variety of food quality claims, commonly resulting in price premiums for goods that are healthy, produced in sustainable ways, or environmentally-friendly. The higher potential profits associated with these products, together with the credence attribute, result in the possibility of producers or sellers making false claims about a product to capture higher prices. Game theory provides a useful way to summarize information about search, experience, and credence goods.[10] Search goods are characterized by perfect information, so by definition there is no quality issue, and no potential for fraud. Producers will produce and sell search goods based on potential profits alone, and consumers will purchase a search good based on their preferences.

The production and sale of experience goods, however, presents informational difficulties, since the consumer does not know the quality of the good until after consumption. In one-time situations, the potential for fraud is high: producers who sell experience goods to customers only once have incentives to provide the lowest-quality products available. This issue can be overcome with an enforceable warranty or repeat purchases. In a repeated game, producers have an incentive to develop a reputation for honest trade, resulting in the cooperative solution. For credence goods, the informational issue is severe: consumers have no way of knowing if the product quality claim is true or not. Monitoring by a third party provides a solution. In the US and EU, organic food is carefully defined and monitored by government agencies, a result of the credence good characteristic of food.

BOX 10.4: ORGANIC FOOD LABELS

In the US, organic products have strict production and labeling requirements. In 1990, Congress passed the Organic Foods Production Act to establish organic food standards for production and processing.[11] The purpose was to provide consistent standards for consumers. This 1990 Act established the National Organic Standards Board (NOSB). In 1998, the USDA released a controversial proposal for organic standards. The original proposal allowed bioengineered crops, sewage sludge, and food irradiation. Due to major objection, these three practices were banned, and organic products have been regulated and overseen by the USDA since 2002. Organic crops must not be produced with genetic engineering, radiation, synthetic fertilizer, prohibited pesticides, or sewage sludge.

The approved production methods are detailed and comprehensive. The approved methods are also political: a USDA committee selected production practices and methods that would become the official USDA definition of "organic." Each of the items included or banned by the committee had proponents and opponents, and the definition did not please all parties. The organic standards are provided in the "National List of Allowed and Prohibited Substances." The substance, methods, and ingredients on this list remain highly controversial, as different producers and processors have varying comparative advantages in each of the specific methods, rules, and substances. Although the national standards are controversial, they do resolve the information problem, to a degree, by insuring that certified organic producers follow the legislated guidelines of organic food production. The standards are the result of a long and contentious political process, so represent a compromise that is likely to differ from nearly every stakeholder's first choice. However, the large benefits of standardization are likely to outweigh the negative attributes.

BOX 10.5: LABELING GMOs

A genetically modified organism (GMO) is an organism whose genetic makeup has been altered using bioengineering, also called genetic engineering (GE). The basic idea of producing a GMO involves altering the genetic material through mutation, deletion, or adding genetic content. When genetic material from a different species is added, the resulting DNA, or recombinant DNA, is called a transgenic organism, first produced in 1972. In agriculture, genetically modified (GM) crops have been produced since 1996 for desirable traits such as resistance to pests, herbicides, or environmental conditions such as drought. The development and use of GM crops has been controversial for many reasons, including the ethics of producing GM crops, the safety of food produced with genetic engineering, and the environmental consequences. Public debate over the use of GE crops is intensifying in the US, driven by the possibility of adverse health effects associated with herbicide-resistant crop pesticide use, and the spread of glyphosate-resistant weeds. The US Food and Drug Administration (FDA) and the American Medical Association (AMA) consider genetically modified crops safe.

Game theory suggests that labeling GMOs would allow consumers to make informed decisions about food purchases. Currently, the use of GE crops is widespread, and no labels are required in food produced with GM crops. However, private labeling of food with no GMOs has increased rapidly. While large numbers of consumers support GMO labeling, the major biotech and food corporations oppose it, since the labels may imply that food products containing GMOs are inferior to conventional or organic food.

The first GE food to be produced was the Flavr Savr tomato produced in California by Calgene, Inc., beginning in 1994. The Flavr Savr tomato used genetic engineering to slow the ripening process to prevent softening while allowing the tomato to retain its natural color and flavor. The tomatoes were accepted by consumers, and clearly labeled, but Calgene stopped production in 1997 due to high costs and inexperience in produce production and marketing. The company was acquired by Monsanto in 1996.

BOX 10.6: TRACEABILITY IN CATTLE

The cattle industry is subject to animal health issues such as bovine spongiform encephalopathy (BSE, commonly known as Mad Cow Disease), and Hoof and Mouth Disease, highly communicable diseases that can have major negative consequences on the beef industry. One method of maintaining control of disease outbreaks is through animal traceability, sometimes called "animal identification," which would allow producers, processors, and veterinarians to trace immediately where a sick animal originated, and move quickly to slow the spread of infectious diseases. Exports are a major sector of beef profitability, and traceability systems are likely to improve US beef exports, since importing nations want to minimize the risk of imported animal diseases infecting their food supplies (Schroeder and Tonsor, 2012). The US currently faces a large number of trade restrictions related to animal age and export verification requirements, due to the discovery of BSE in the US cattle herd in 2003.

Many cattle producers object to traceability and identification systems due to the costs associated with maintaining the records and animal identification. This prisoner's dilemma has caused the US to lag behind other beef exporters such as Australia and Brazil. Individual producers see additional costs, but may not understand the potential for increased profits associated with a traceability system. Pendell *et al.* (2010) show that the gain from increased domestic demand and exports offsets these costs, making the cooperative solution to this game an optimal strategy for the beef industry. Cattle industry analysts recommend the development of a mandatory animal identification system, but producers and producer groups have opposed such policies.

Summary and conclusions

Game theory is a useful framework for understanding the origins and potential solutions to polarized issues in food and agriculture. A simple game of product choice captures the interdependence of strategic decision making of players (including farmers), food processors, and retailers. The firm location game uses the concept of Nash Equilibrium to show why food industry firms will often locate near each other, or produce nearly identical goods. The implication is that even polarized firms have economic incentives to end up in the "middle ground" between two polarized extremes. This incentive explains why some industrial firms produce organic, natural, and local goods, and why some small food producers become "industrial" in scale and production methods: profits. Business firms of all types and sizes have strong incentives to provide goods and services to the largest consumer groups, so they often target the "average" consumer.

The prisoner's dilemma adds realism and complexity to games by capturing a common situation where cooperation between players leads to the best outcome, but individuals have incentives to choose independent action instead. The price war game is an example of a prisoner's dilemma with important implications: cooperative solutions that maximize group welfare can be difficult to achieve in one-time games. In repeated games, however, incentives exist for all parties to agree to the cooperative solution. The stability of a cooperative agreement can be threatened by: (1) a large number of competing firms; (2) market instability; or (3) innovations, new products, and new ways of doing things. As markets for new food products become mature, volatility often diminishes, long-term contracts and cooperative agreements are more likely to develop and endure.

The market entry and entry deterrence games explain why many food and agricultural firms attempt to attain "first-mover advantage." In many real-world games, being an early entrant into a developing market can provide financial rewards. Large, wealthy firms may have an advantage in these cases, as small, family, or local firms may be unable to compete. Game theory is useful in showing how government intervention in the form of subsidies is used to provide rewards to favored groups: small, organic, local, or other groups with attributes considered to be favorable.

The economics of information is a useful application of game theory to food markets. Food products are often characterized by quality attributes that are unknowable to consumers: organic, natural, hormone free, or local, for example. One-time purchasers of these credence goods could be subject to fraud, but repeated purchases provide the producers with an incentive for honest trade. Monitoring and enforcement are often necessary in food markets, providing a useful role for government intervention in the food industry.

Notes

1 Game theory was developed by mathematician John von Neumann and economist Oskar Morgenstern. Their 1947 book, *Theory of Games and Economic Behavior*, is considered a classic, from which modern game theory is derived. See William (1986) and Pindyck and Rubinfeld (2013) for excellent introductions to game theory.
2 American mathematician John Nash provided some of the early seminal work in game theory, and in 1994 earned the Nobel Prize in Economics. His theories, including the Nash Equilibrium, provided insights into market economics, biology, computer science, and military theory. Nash is the subject of the Hollywood movie, *A Beautiful Mind*, which highlights Nash's brilliant contributions to mathematics and his struggle with schizophrenia. The film is based on the book with the same name by Sylvia Nasar (2001).
3 Interrogation of prisoners is common in movies and television, where police often employ "good cop/bad cop" roles and deception to elicit confessions and/or information about a case.
4 For example, see Axelrod (2006).
5 See Warner (2006) and Pollan (2006b).
6 See Lieberman and Montgomery (1988).
7 See Michael Pollan's article (2008a) "Farmer in Chief," where he describes policies that could encourage local food. Pollan's suggestions include year-round farmers' markets, agricultural enterprise zones, local meat inspection, a strategic grain reserve, and regionalized (local) food procurement.
8 See the website for the Center for Urban Education about Sustainable Agriculture (CUESA) at cuesa.org (2013). The quotes are from Severson (2003).
9 See Severson (2003).
10 See McCluskey (2000).
11 See the website for the USDA National Organic Program (2013).

11

THE FUTURE OF FOOD POLARIZATION

A party of order or stability, and a party of progress or reform, are both necessary elements of a healthy state of political life. Each of these ways of thinking derives its utility from the deficiencies of the other, but it is in a great measure the opposition of the other that keeps each within the limits of reason and sanity.

John Stuart Mill

[S]top trashing the enemy. Be much more respectful of people who you think are wrong ... They're allowed to treat you with contempt. It's a big mistake to treat them with contempt.

Peter Sandman, Risk Communication Consultant (Freakonomics, 2011)

If you want to make peace with your enemy, you have to work with your enemy. Then he becomes your partner.

Nelson Mandela

Introduction

Food is important. The way we produce food is changing rapidly as a consequence of continuous technological change. The food desired by consumers is also changing rapidly due to increased purchasing power, gains in nutritional knowledge, and innovations in food packaging, preparation, and dining. It should be no surprise, then, that food is controversial, and many issues related to the production, processing, and consumption of food are polarized. On any given day, society is moving toward agreement, compromise, and common ground in a host of polarized issues in food and agriculture. The following brief list provides examples of changes being made as a result of tensions or disagreements in food and agriculture.

- McDonald's is reducing fat and sodium content in its menu items (Spain, 2011).
- Beef processors are changing animal welfare requirements (Eller, 2013).
- Teenage consumers are eating more organic food (Montgomery, 2013).
- Genetic engineering research is resulting in major advancements in crop yields.
- China is accelerating food production through genetic engineering that will result in larger quantities of food and lower world commodity prices.
- Walmart announced in 2014 that it will carry Wild Oats organic food, with a new, affordable price position to increase access to organic food (Marks, 2014).

These tensions have been designated as "polarizations" throughout this book, as a way of describing differences that are frequently the precursors of change.

Economic progress, characterized by the adoption of new ways of doing things, is disruptive. Economist Joseph Schumpeter called this the process of creative destruction: as innovations are introduced, some individuals and groups are helped, and some are hurt.

- Farmers and ranchers feel threatened by consumer activists, and form groups of "agvocates" to advocate for agriculture.
- Beef feedlots and processors adopt environmentally friendly production practices.
- US fruit growers are ripping out orchards and replacing them with housing developments due to increased foreign competition from global fruit producers together with high housing prices.
- Large corporations pledged in 2014 to focus on increasing sustainability in agriculture, including Monsanto, Walmart, and Kellogg (Doering, 2014).

The economic principles explored in this book provide useful interpretations and explanations of some important events and issues in the food and agriculture sector by showing potential gains that arise from taking advantage of differences in people, goods, production methods, locations, and consumer preferences. Diversity in resources and consumers provide enormous potential to resolve polarized issues through specialization and trade, product bundling, negotiated solutions (bargaining), and acknowledgement and understanding of the interdependence of consumers and producers in the food industry through unique strategic interactions (game theory).

Diversity is a major driving force of a market-based economy, allowing for specialization of resources in their highest-valued use. In many cases, recognition of these differences and acting on this knowledge leads to enhanced profit opportunities for business firms, greater consumer satisfaction, and resolution of polarized issues in food and agriculture. Polarization of issues provides a strong catalyst to societal progress and economic growth by bringing consequential issues to the forefront, initiating the resolution process, and initiating new ideas and ways of doing things that polarize society in new ways.

Economics

The "economic way of thinking" is a powerful tool that leads to greater understanding of economic, political, and personal issues. It compares the benefits and the costs associated with every issue or decision. All issues have strengths and weaknesses, advantages and disadvantages. Economics promotes clear thinking by looking at both aspects of any situation, issue, event, or activity. For many, if not most issues, clear recognition, and acknowledgement of benefits and costs can lead to greater understanding of both sides of an argument. Once both sides are understood, the resolution process can begin. Many extreme positions can be tempered with this approach. As economist John Maynard Keynes replied when confronted with changing his mind, "When the facts change, I change my mind. What do you do, sir?" Extremists who are unwilling to see both sides of an issue are just that: extremists. As such, extremist groups may receive media attention, but are unlikely to have an impact on public policy or markets, where the majority of citizens hold sway.

Diversity

Polarization stems from diversity among people. Different individuals will see issues from different points of view. Interestingly, however, differences in resources are also the foundation of specialization and trade, which is a major source of prosperity and economic growth. Growing oranges and lettuce in California, apples in Washington, and corn in Iowa results in large gains in production that would not be available if each state had to produce all food products. Consumer choice is greatly extended with international trade and globalization: North Americans can enjoy coffee, avocados, inexpensive cotton clothing, and asparagus in winter months when trade between nations occurs. It is difficult to overstate the importance of international trade in agricultural goods in providing for high incomes, food security, and income growth. Individuals, regions, and nations that are identical to each other would not capture any gains from trade: differences in climate, resource bases, and skill levels are the source of all gains from trade.

A major theme of economics is that "the size of the pie is not fixed" in the sense that mutually beneficial trades, agreements, and negotiation outcomes increase the quantity of goods and services available to the trading partners and rivals. After all, any trade that did not benefit both trade participants would not occur. Careful consideration of this important principle provides a way forward for many controversial or polarized issues. Although some individuals and groups may not gain from an economic policy, the overall gain in income resulting from the policy may be large enough to compensate the losers. For example, the US imports inexpensive clothing from other nations, causing the domestic apparel industry to lose its share of the market. However, the economic benefits to consumers are large enough to totally compensate the apparel industry, and the net gains of the activity are positive.

The economic models explored in this book all suggest outcomes that make opposing parties better off by increasing "the size of the economic pie," or by increasing the level of resources available to the two parties. For example, product bundling uses consumer differences in willingness to pay to increase producer profits and consumer satisfaction. Specialization and trade allows resources to be employed in their most productive use, resulting in productivity increases. Externalities, or unintended effects of human activities, can be resolved through negotiation, or bargaining, that brings extreme positions toward a mutually acceptable position. Capturing the economies of scale that accompany increased firm size allow larger quantities of products to be produced at lower per-unit cost, leading to improved quality at lower product costs for consumers. Business firms and consumers who engage in "repeated games," or frequent business interactions, can often look forward to increased trust, stability, and consistency in purchases and sales, thus lowering costs to society.

Each of the economic models emphasizes how the desire to do better can increase the level of economic activity and make society as a whole better off. Individuals and groups who maintain polarized positions that do not recognize or respect the opportunity to do better are bound to remain locked in, and lose out on the opportunities available to firms that recognize the wants and needs of the opposition.

Consumers

Consumers are characterized by diversity in tastes, preferences, needs, and desires. Not only do the differences exist, but they are constantly changing. As incomes change, consumers make drastic changes in purchasing decisions. Economic growth and progress lead to new food desires and needs. As individuals in low-income nations become wealthier, staple foods such as rice are replaced with higher-cost products such as meat and dairy products. In high-income nations, increasing incomes bring increasing numbers of consumers who prefer local, natural, organic, and environmentally friendly food products.

Some consumers with increasing income will demand major changes in how food is produced. The activist role can be powerful in a democratic, market-based society. Over several decades, progress in food safety, food quality, animal welfare, environmental quality, worker safety, nutrition and production practices have all improved due to food and farm activists asking for and receiving improvements in the agricultural and food industries.

Consumers are the source of all profitability in a market-based economy. No farmer, food processor, or food retailer can survive in a competitive market without serving the wants and needs of the customers. Economic analysis suggests that the greatest profits are made by providing the customers with what they want. Walmart became highly profitable by placing the most desired goods on its store shelves. Zappos, a highly successful internet shoe store, has a business philosophy based on "delivering happiness" through exemplary customer service.

Starbucks revolutionized retail coffee by developing and promoting highly desirable coffee-related products (and now tea).

The firm location decision analysis from game theory suggests that successful politicians place their ideas and proposals in the middle of the political spectrum, and successful businesses align as closely as possible with the majority of consumers by producing goods geared toward the "average consumer." All of the economic models discussed in this book are predicated on taking consumer wants and needs seriously. Consumer tastes and preferences change constantly, so meeting consumer needs is a moving target. Firms that continuously evaluate, revise, and update how they can best meet consumer needs will be more successful than producers who do not take consumer positions into account.

Producers

The history of agriculture in high-income nations is one of large and continuous productivity growth. Since 1950, agricultural production practices have replaced labor with machines, chemicals, and synthetic fertilizers. This substitution of capital for labor continues today, as tractors and field equipment are steered by satellites and robots replace workers. Producers who adopt new technology early are more likely to be successful than those who wait in a competitive market-based economy. The ability to deal with market changes, or disequilibrium, is highly valued in rapidly changing food markets. Allocative ability allows producers to quickly and easily shift resources to the most profitable activities, adopt new technology, diversify into new and different products, and meet the ever-changing wants and needs of consumers.

One feature of allocative ability is the skill to identify differences between short-term food fads and long-term trends in consumer food demand. Some trends die out quickly, but others persist and become the "new normal." Producers will do best by: (1) acknowledging consumer sovereignty: in a market economy, businesses exist only to serve the needs of consumers; and (2) separate the "signal from the noise," or carefully identify the food products and production practices that best meet the needs of consumers in the future.

Many polarized issues in food and agriculture arise when consumer groups begin to question technologies or production practices that have been in common use for long periods of time. Current practices under such scrutiny include the use of antibiotics in meat production, hormone use in the meat industry, growth promoters in feedlots or CAFOs, chemical use in crop production, and modern methods of plant breeding. The economic approach to these polarized production practices yields useful ideas about how to best proceed when traditional production practices (chemicals) or new innovations (Zilmax growth promoters) come under attack. The following list identifies some aspects of agricultural and food issues that are frequently associated with the creation and existence of polarization. Recall that there are benefits and costs associated with every technology, innovation and method.

- The costs of some traditional production practices have later been found to outweigh the benefits: DDT and Zilmax are examples.
- Over time, societal values change, and some practices become unacceptable: slavery, child labor, chemical use without safety precautions.
- Productivity enhancement is a major benefit of many production practices, techniques, and innovations, but such practices must be carefully examined to determine their effects on other characteristics such as the environment, food safety, and animal welfare. The goal of increasing food output is only one goal among numerous worthy and worthwhile societal goals.
- Societal decisions about how to produce and consume food are complex, and are based on a combination of science, culture, history, and value judgments about taste, ethics, and feelings. Science is an important component of decision making that helps provide quantitative evidence regarding human health, production, and the environment. However, science ignores other important determinants of societal decision making, including emotions, ethics, and tastes.
- Rapid response with factual information, openness, and the desire to share information can go a long way toward defusing individuals and groups who have become linked to highly polarized positions. Even better is proactively avoiding heated issues, when possible.
- In the future, consumers and consumer groups are likely to desire or demand more transparency about how food is produced, processed, and delivered. The firms that best meet these consumer desires proactively are likely to gain an advantage over firms that do not.

Interdependence

Interdependence is the defining feature of the game theory used in economics. Interdependence is among the actors, who are called "players." Each player's actions affect the outcomes of the other players. Moreover, actions and their consequences are likely to cause a reaction that will affect the initial player, causing her/him to re-think her/his original actions. Recognition of this interconnectedness among business firms, their rivals, and their customers provides greater understanding of many polarized issues in food and agriculture.

One fascinating aspect of many polarized issues is the interdependence and co-dependence of opposing factions. Lobbyists, proponents, and activists are often dependent on public concern about the issue at hand. If everyone in society agreed, there would be no polarization, and no activism, no public relations, and no marketing.

An important case of interdependence is the case of a niche market served by early adopters in organic agriculture. These early adopters can often earn high rates of return by offering a small quantity of a desirable good such as organic apples, local berries, or natural grass-fed beef. If all farmers were to switch to organic apples, the increase in supply and economies of scale would result in greatly reduced prices and profitability. As a result, the early adopters rely on opponents to keep their organic apple niche market small. This helps explain the polarization of organic producers about "industrial organic" or large-scale production of organic products and the entry of Walmart into organic food retailing. For many groups, success depends on the existence of an opponent. In almost all cases, interdependence between firms and consumers is crucial to recognize and move toward strategic decision making. In game theory, most firms find themselves in a "repeated game," where in iteration after iteration, good business practices result in higher profitability.

Repeated games may also be useful in markets for credence goods: goods where quality cannot be observed until the good is consumed. Credence is a characteristic of numerous food products such as those with an attribute about how the food is produced: organic, local, hormone-free, and environmentally friendly, for example. If the costs of producing a good without the attribute are lower than the production costs of the good with the attribute, there is potential for fraud, in the form of selling a good without a quality attribute as if it possessed the characteristic. Repeated purchases, monitoring, and enforcement provide incentives to good business practices and avoidance of fraudulent activity. Credence goods often provide the motivation for a positive role for government intervention in food markets: monitoring, enforcement, regulation, and labeling of food products can enhance societal welfare in some cases.

Markets

A market-based economy provides benefits to society in the form of an enormous range of consumer choice and high income levels. However, markets are volatile. Any change in production or consumption can lead to unanticipated changes in market prices. In a global economy, volatility is expanded and has larger effects. For US food exporters, market events in China or Mexico often have larger impacts on market prices than actions among US consumers. Importantly, price movements are good for some and bad for others: a price increase helps producers but hurts consumers. Market impacts can be polarizing, since producer livelihood depends on market prices. Knowledge of how different individuals and groups are affected by price changes and market impacts is a powerful guide to understanding polarized issues and their resolution.

The defining characteristic of a market-based economy is creative destruction: new innovations bring large benefits, but they make some individuals and groups obsolete. Progress is the source of polarization. In times of rapid change, new innovations replace older technologies, production practices, and ideas. Economic growth can accelerate the process of creative destruction, and reduce the economic and emotional costs of polarization. In agriculture, new innovations and regulations affecting producer behavior have caused massive changes in how food is produced, and have resolved many polarized issues by making the issue obsolete: slavery, DDT, and the treatment of field workers are examples.

Politics

Polarization in politics plays an important role in moving society forward. Criticism and dissent often lead to improved outcomes: the US was formed with the objective of improving the political system. Many nations throughout the world are currently attempting to move forward by working through differences in beliefs, customs, and lifestyles. Openness and transparency can mitigate polarized issues by presenting factual information to both advocates and opponents of the issue. Education and knowledge can be powerful antidotes to polarized political issues: the political process requires compromise, and through negotiated settlements, effective solutions can be found. A dynamic economy requires openness, liberty, and continuous innovation. Successful economies will champion and promote social, economic, and political institutions that promote growth and innovation, often through disagreement, debate, and polarization.

The field of public choice proposes that small groups can have political power greater than the group size would suggest through the "importance of being unimportant." Special interest legislation allows farmers in high-income nations to lobby for and receive large subsidies, in spite of being a small percentage of the total population. Spreading subsidy costs across a large group of taxpayers allows program benefits to be concentrated on a small group who receive large per-person benefits. This result is increasingly important for consumer groups, as political success is attainable from small groups, even in a democracy. Consumer groups that are unsuccessful in the marketplace can turn to politics to achieve goals such as animal welfare requirements, environmental rules, and labeling laws.

Summary and conclusions

An economic approach to polarization recognizes that all issues have both benefits and costs. Agricultural and food issues are no exception. Agriculture allows humans to eat and survive, but can also pose challenges to the environment and human health. Consumer activism has threatened many agriculturalists who would prefer to maintain existing ways of doing things. Many farmers and other interested parties have become "agvocates" to promote issues and policies that benefit farmers and agriculture. Educating others about agriculture provides new information and knowledge. In a market-based economy, however, the only source of prosperity is providing consumers with what they desire. For continued success, farmers and ranchers must pay close attention to future consumer needs. Therefore, economic theory and analysis suggest that the flow of information from consumers to producers may be more important than providing consumers with knowledge about agriculture.

Polarization provides a catalyst for societal progress, economic growth, prosperity, greater knowledge, high levels of understanding, longer life expectancy, and a high quality of life. The most effective way to resolve polarized issues in food and agriculture is to develop innovations that replace polarized activities and methods with new products, technologies, and ideas that retain the benefits and shed the costs of the older activities. The history of agriculture demonstrates that constant technical change will help resolve many polarized issues by introducing new innovations and methods even though the change will likely create a new generation of polarized issues. Although human civilization will always be characterized by polarized disagreements, the process of open debate results in advancements in agriculture that have extended the length of life and greatly improved the quality of life.

REFERENCES

Adamy, J. (2007) 'Burrito chain assembles a winning combo: ignoring fast-food formula, Chipotle promotes service, costly natural ingredients', *The Wall Street Journal*, 23 November, www.wsj.com (accessed December 16, 2013).

AgChat Foundation (2013) agchat.org/agvocates (accessed December 4, 2013).

Alston, J. M. (2000) 'A meta-analysis of the rates of return to agricultural R & D: ex pede herculem?' *IFPRI Research Reports*, vol. 113.

Alston, J. M., Andersen, M. A., James, J. S., and Pardey, P. G. (2009). *Persistence Pays: US Agricultural Productivity Growth and the Benefits from Public R&D Spending* (vol. 34). New York: Springer.

American Meat Institute (2013) *The United States Meat Industry at a Glance*, www.meatami.com/ht/d/sp/i/47465/pid/47465 (accessed December 12, 2013).

Ammann, K. (2002) 'Summary note', in IFPRI, *Sustainable Food Security for All by 2020*, Proceedings of an International Conference, 46, September 2001, International Food Policy Research Institute, Washington DC, pp. 244–247.

Anderson, R. H. (1936) 'Grain drills through thirty-nine centuries', *Agricultural History*, vol. 10, no. 4, pp. 157–205.

Angelo, C. (2012) 'Growth of ethanol fuel stalls in Brazil: Shortages are a sobering lesson from a biofuels pioneer', *Nature*, vol. 491, pp. 646–647.

Axelrod, R. (2006) *The Evolution of Cooperation*, revised edition. New York: Basic Books.

Barkema, A., Drabenstott, M., and Novack, N. (2001) 'The new US meat industry', *Economic Review-Federal Reserve Bank of Kansas City*, vol. 86, no. 2, pp. 33–56.

Barkley, A. P. (1990) 'The determinants of the migration of labor out of agriculture in the United States, 1940–85', *American Journal of Agricultural Economics*, vol. 72, no. 3, pp. 567–573.

—— (1996) 'Are politicians addicted to agricultural protection? A dynamic model of political economy', in J. Antle and D. Sumner (eds), *The Economics of Agriculture, Volume 2: Papers in Honor of D. Gale Johnson*. Chicago, IL: University of Chicago Press, pp. 263–282.

Barnes, S. (2009) 'Integrity is key to Chipotle brand', *Times Union*, November 5, www.timesunion.com (accessed May 23, 2013).

Barta, P. (2007) 'Feeding billions, a grain at a time', *The Wall Street Journal*, July 28, p. A1.

Baumol, W., Panzar, J., and Willig, R. (1982) *Contestable Markets and the Theory of Market Structure*. New York: Harcourt Brace Jovanovich, Inc.

Better Cotton Initiative (2013) www.bettercotton.org (accessed June 2, 2013).

Bittman, M. (2011) 'Is junk food really cheaper?' *New York Times*, September 24.

Blair, R. (2012) *Organic Production and Food Quality: A Down to Earth Analysis*. Oxford, UK: Wiley-Blackwell.

Blatner, D. J. (2009) *The Flexitarian Diet: The Mostly Vegetarian Way to Lose Weight, Be Healthier, Prevent Disease and Add Years to Your Life*. New York: McGraw-Hill.

Bongiovanni, R. and Lowenberg-Deboer, J. (2004) 'Precision agriculture and sustainability', *Precision Agriculture*, vol. 5, no. 4, pp. 359–387.

Brandt, M. (2012) 'Little evidence of health benefits from organic foods, Stanford study finds', med.stanford.edu/ism/2012/september/organic.html#sthash.vmNZloyO.dpuf (accessed December 16, 2013).

Browne, A. (2013) 'All for one: China's New Deal', *The Wall Street Journal*, November 22.

Capehart, T. (2013) USDA, Economic Research Service. *Corn Background*, July 17, www.ers.usda.gov/topics/crops/corn/background.aspx (accessed October 15, 2013).

Caplan, B. (2008) 'Externalities', *The Concise Encyclopedia of Economics*, Library of Economics and Liberty, www.econlib.org/library/Enc/Externalities.html (accessed November 6, 2013).

Carolan, M. (2011) *The Real Cost of Cheap Food*. Abingdon, UK: Routledge.

Carson, R. (1962) *Silent Spring*. Boston, MA: Houghton Mifflin Company.

Center for Urban Education about Sustainable Agriculture (CUESA) (2013) cuesa.org (accessed December 15, 2013).

Charles, D. (2013) 'In a grain of Golden Rice, a world of controversy over GMO foods', National Public Radio broadcast, March 7, 2013. www.npr.org (accessed June 2, 2013).

Chetty, R., Hendren, N., Kline, P., Saez, E., and Turner, N. (2014) 'Is the United States still a land of opportunity? Recent trends in intergenerational mobility', Working Paper 19844 of the National Bureau of Economic Research. Cambridge, MA: NBER.

Chipotle Mexican Grill (2013) www.chipotle.com (accessed May 23, 2013).

Chung, J. (2000) *Central Control and Local Discretion in China*. Oxford, UK: Oxford University Press.

Coase, R. H. (1960) 'The problem of social cost', *Journal of Law and Economics*, vol. 3, pp. 1–44.

Crespi, J. M., Saitone, T. L., and Sexton, R. J. (2012) 'Competition in US farm product markets: Do long-run incentives trump short-run market power?', *Applied Economic Perspectives and Policy*, vol. 34, no. 4, pp. 669–695.

Curley, J. (2005) *Rural America: Historical Overview*, CSD Working Papers, Center for Social Development, George Warren Brown School of Social Work, Washington University, St. Louis, Missouri.

DeNavas-Walt, C., Proctor, B. D., and Smith, J. C. (2013) US Census Bureau, Current Population Reports, pp. 60–245, Income, poverty, and health insurance coverage in the United States: 2012, Washington, DC: US Government Printing Office.

Dibner, J. J. and Richards, J. D. (2005) 'Antibiotic growth promoters in agriculture: History and mode of action', *Poultry Science*, vol. 84, pp.634–643.

Doering, C. (2014) 'Corporate America pledges to boost sustainability in agriculture', *Des Moines Register*, April 29, Des Moines, Iowa.

Downs, A. (1957) *An Economic Theory of Democracy*. New York: Harper and Row.

Durisin, M. (2013) 'Chobani CEO: Our success is more than yogurt', *Business Insider*, May 3.

Economist, The (2013a) 'China and the environment: The East is grey', August 10.

—— (2013b) 'Free exchange. One of the giants', September 7.

Eller, D. (2013) 'Tyson adds cattle welfare requirements: Iowa producers are told that big customers are demanding changes', *Des Moines Register*, December 9, Des Moines, Iowa.

Engel, E. (1857) 'Die productions und Consumtionsverhaltnisse des Kongreichs Sachsen', reprinted as an appendix to *Die Lebenskosten belgischer Arbeiter-Familien*, Dresden, 1895.

Environmental Defense Fund (2014) www.edf.org/how-we-work (accessed April 18, 2014).

Environmental Working Group (2013a) 'Farm subsidy primer', farm.ewg.org/subsidyprimer. php (accessed December 13, 2013).

—— (2013b) 'Shoppers guide to pesticides in produce', www.ewg.org/foodnews (accessed April 18, 2014).

FAO (2002) *State of Food Security in the World 2001*. Rome, Italy: Food and Agriculture Organization (FAO).

FAOSTAT (2013) Food and Agriculture Organization of the United Nations, faostat.org (accessed September 10, 2013).

Fewsmith, J. (1994) *Dilemmas of Reform in China: Political Conflict and Economic Debate*. Armonk, New York: M. E. Sharpe.

Fogel, R. W. (2003) *The Escape from Hunger and Premature Death 1700–2100: Europe, America, and the Third World*. Cambridge, UK: Cambridge University Press.

Food Safety News (2013) foodsafetynews.com/tag/lftb/#.UjDScH8QPAl (accessed September 11, 2013).

Forman, J., Silverstein, J., Bhatia, J. J., Abrams, S. A., Corkins, M. R., de Ferranti, S. D., *et al.* (2012) 'Organic foods: health and environmental advantages and disadvantages', *Pediatrics*, vol. 130, no. 5, pp. e1406–e1415.

Franklin, B. (1848) 'The way to wealth', *Poor Richard's Almanac: 1758*. New York: Leavitt, Trow, and Co. Printers.

Freakonomics (2011) 'Risk = hazard + outrage: A conversation with risk consultant Peter Sandman', November 29, freakonomics.com (accessed December 18, 2013).

Friedman, T. (1999) *The Lexus and the Olive Tree*. New York: Picador.

Fukuyama, F. (1992) *The End of History and the Last Man*. Washington, DC: Free Press.

Gale, F. (2014) 'Biofuel impact on food prices and world hunger', *Global Issues in Context Online Collection*, Detroit (accessed March 21, 2014).

Gale, F. and Buzby, J. C. (2009) *Imports from China and Food Safety Issues*. Economic Information Bulletin Number 52, July. Economic Research Service/USDA.

Garner, D. (2009) 'The joys and pains of being an animal', *New York Times*, January 20, www.nytimes.com/2009/01/21/books/21garn.html?_r=0 (accessed October 7, 2013).

Garnett, T. and Godfray, C. J. (2012) *Sustainable Intensification in Agriculture. Navigating a Course Though Competing Food System Priorities*, Food Climate Research Network and the Oxford Martin Programme on the Future of Food. Oxford, UK: University of Oxford.

Gerrior, S., Bente, L., and Hiza, H. (2004) *Nutrient Content of the U.S. Food Supply, 1909–2000*, Home Economics Research Report No. 56, US Department of Agriculture, Center for Nutrition Policy and Promotion, Washington DC.

Goodwin, H. L. (2005) 'Location of production and consolidation in the processing industry: The case of poultry', *Journal of Agricultural and Applied Economics*, vol. 37, no. 2, pp. 339–346.

Gove, P. B. (2002) *Webster's Third New International Dictionary of the English Language*, unabridged. Springfield, MA: Webster's.

Grandin, T. (2006) *Thinking in Pictures: And Other Reports From My Life with Autism*. New York: Vintage Books.

—— (2008) *Humane Livestock Handling*. North Adams, MA: Storey Publishing.

—— (ed.) (2010) *Improving Animal Welfare: A Practical Approach*. Wallingford, UK: CABI.

Griliches, Z. (1957) 'Hybrid corn: an exploration in the economics of technological change', *Econometrica, Journal of the Econometric Society*, vol. 25, no. 4, pp. 501–522.

—— (1958) 'Research costs and social returns: Hybrid corn and related innovations', *The Journal of Political Economy*, vol. 66, no. 5, pp. 419–431.

Grossman, G. M. and Krueger, A. B. (1991) 'Environmental Impact of a North American Free Trade Agreement', Working Paper 3914. Cambridge, MA: National Bureau of Economic Research.

Grunert, K. G. (2006) 'Future trends and consumer lifestyles with regard to meat consumption', *Meat Science*, vol. 74, no. 1, pp. 149–160.

Guthrie, D. (2012) *China and Globalization: The Social, Economic and Political Transformation of Chinese Society*. New York: Routledge.

Gwartney, J. (2009) '2008 presidential address: institutions, economic freedom, and cross-country differences in performance', *Southern Economic Journal*, vol. 75, no. 4, pp. 937–956.

Gwartney, J. D., Stroup, R., and Lee, D. R. (2005) *Common Sense Economics: What Everyone Should Know about Wealth and Prosperity*. New York: St Martin's Press.

Haidt, J. (2013) *The Righteous Mind: Why Good People Are Divided by Politics and Religion*. New York: Random House Digital, Inc.

Hainmueller, J. and Hiscox, M. J. (2012) 'The socially conscious consumer? Field experimental tests of consumer support for fair labor standards', MIT Political Science Department Research Paper No. 2012-15, ssrn.com/abstract=2062435 (accessed June 6, 2013).

Harberger, A. C. (1954) 'Monopoly and resource allocation', *The American Economic Review*, vol. 44, no. 2, pp. 77–87.

Higgins, F. H. (1958) 'John M. Horner and the development of the combined harvester', *Agricultural History*, vol. 32, pp. 14–24.

Hu, H. H., Parsa, H. G., and Self, J. (2010) 'The dynamics of green restaurant patronage', *Cornell Hospitality Quarterly*, vol. 51, no. 3, pp. 344–362.

Humphrey, J. (2007) 'The supermarket revolution in developing countries: Tidal wave or tough competitive struggle?' *Journal of Economic Geography*, vol. 7, no. 4, pp. 433–450.

Johnson, D. G. (1991) *World Agriculture in Disarray*, 2nd edition, New York: Macmillan Press Ltd.

Johnson, R. and Becker, G. S. (2009) *Livestock Marketing and Competition Issues*. CRS Report for Congress, 2009.

Kaplan, M. D. G. (2010) 'Chipotle founder: Why grass-fed animals make a better burrito', *SmartPlanet*, 12 April, www.smartplanethome.com (accessed May 23, 2013).

Kaufman, P. (2000) *Consolidation in Food Retailing: Prospects for Consumers & Grocery Suppliers*, US Department of Agriculture, Economic Research Service, Agricultural Outlook, August.

Kay, S. (2013) 'Zilmax Zinger', *MeatPoultry.com. The Business Journal for Meat and Poultry Processors*, 13 September.

Kearney, J. (2010) 'Food consumption trends and drivers', *Philosophical Transactions of the Royal Society B: Biological Sciences*, vol. 365, no. 1554, pp. 2793–2807.

Key, N. and McBride, W. (2003) 'Production contracts and productivity in the US hog sector', *American Journal of Agricultural Economics*, vol. 85, no. 1, pp. 121–133.

—— (2014) 'Sub-therapeutic antibiotics and the efficiency of US hog farms', *American Journal of Agricultural Economics*, vol. 96, no. 3, pp. 831–850.

Keyzer, M. A., Merbis, M. D., Pavel, I. F. P. W., and Van Wesenbeeck, C. F. A. (2005) 'Diet shifts towards meat and the effects on cereal use: can we feed the animals in 2030?', *Ecological Economics*, vol. 55, no. 2, pp. 187–202.

Khoury, C. K., Bjorkman, A. D., Dempewolf, H., Ramirez-Villegas, J., Guarino, L., Jarvis, A., Rieseberg, L. H., and Struik, P. C. (2014) 'Increasing homogeneity in global food supplies and the implications for food security', *PNAS*, vol. 111, pp. 4001–4006.

Kiely, T., Donaldson, D., and Grube, A. (2004) 'Pesticides industry sales and usage: 2000 and 2001 market estimates', US Environmental Protection Agency, Washington, DC.

Kislev, Y. and Shchori-Bachrach, N. (1973) 'The process of an innovation cycle', *American Journal of Agricultural Economics*, vol. 55, no. 1, pp. 28–37.

Kuznets, S. (1955) 'Economic growth and income inequality', *The American Economic Review*, vol. 45, no. 1, pp. 1–28.

—— (1973) 'Modern economic growth: findings and reflections', *The American Economic Review,* vol 63, no. 3, pp. 247–258.

Laasby, G. (2013) 'FDA investigating 89 complaints of illness from recalled Chobani yogurt', *Milwaukee Wisconsin Journal Sentinel* (accessed September 9, 2013).

Lang, T. and Heasman, M. A. (eds) (2004) *Food Wars: The Global Battle for Mouths, Minds and Markets*. New York: Earthscan.

Lardy, N. R. (1983) *Agriculture in China's Modern Economic Development*. Cambridge, UK: Cambridge University Press.

Laskawy, T. (2011) 'Killing the competition: Meat industry reform takes a blow', *Grist*, November 9, grist.org/factory-farms/2011-11-09-killing-the-competition-meat-industry-reform-takes-a-blow (accessed September 16, 2013).

Lean, L. (2010) 'Fast food using slow food?: Talking with Chipotle's Steve Ells', *LA Weekly*, 2010-07-06, www.laweekly.com (accessed May 23, 2013).

Leonard, C. (2014) *The Meat Racket: The Secret Takeover of America's Food Business*. New York: Simon & Schuster.

Leonard, S. (2007) 'It's all native farmers markets', press release, 22 August.

Lichtenberg, E. (2002) 'Agriculture and the environment', *Handbook of Agricultural Economics*, vol. 2, *Agricultural and Food Policy*, edited by B. L. Gardner and G. C. Rausser, pp. 1249–1313, North-Holland, Philadelphia, Pennsylvania: Elsevier.

Lieberman, M. B. and Montgomery, D. B. (1988) 'First-mover advantages', *Strategic Management Journal*, vol. 9, no. S1, pp. 41–58.

Lowe, P. (2012) 'Temple Grandin urges meat packers to livestream operations', Harvest Public Media, Harvest Network, September 7, harvestpublicmedia.org/blog/1410/temple-grandin-urges-meat-packers-livestream-operations/5#.UlMoB38QM40 (accessed October 7, 2013).

Lusk, J. (2013) *The Food Police: A Well-Fed Manifesto about the Politics of Your Plate*. New York: Random House Digital, Inc.

Lusk, J. L. and Norwood, F. (2011) 'The locavore's dilemma: Why pineapples shouldn't be grown in North Dakota', January 3, Library of Economics and Liberty, www.econlib.org/library/Columns/y2011/LuskNorwoodlocavore.html (accessed July 28, 2013).

Lynas, M. (2013) 'Lecture to Oxford Farming Conference', January 3, 2013, www.marklynas.org/2013/01/lecture-to-oxford-farming-conference-3-january-2013 (accessed April 22, 2014).

MacDonald, J. and Korb, P. (2011) *Agricultural Contracting Update: Contracts in 2008*. Washington, DC: US Department of Agriculture.

Machiavelli, N. [1532] (1910) *The Prince*, vol. 36. New York: PF Collier & Son.

Madison, J. (1787) 'The federalist no. 10', *The Federalist Papers*, 78, 80.

Marks, T. (2014) 'Get lower-cost organic groceries with Walmart's Wild Oats Marketplace line', ConsumerReports.org, April 28, www.consumerreports.org/cro/news/2014/04/get-lower-cost-organic-groceries-with-walmart-s-wild-oats-marketplace-line/index.htm (accessed May 2, 2014).

Marx, K. [1857] (1993) *Grundrisse: Foundations of the Critique of Political Economy*. London: Penguin Classics.

—— [1863] (1969) *Theories of Surplus-Value: "Volume IV" of Capital 2*. London: Lawrence & Wishart, pp. 495–496.

Marx, K. and Engels, F. [1848] (2002, trans. 1888) *The Communist Manifesto* (trans. Samule Moore), London: Penguin.

Mazoyer, M. and Roudart, L. (2006) *A History of World Agriculture: From the Neolithic Age to the Current Crisis*. New York: Monthly Review Press.

McBratney, A., Whelan, B., Ancev, T., and Bouma, J. (2005) 'Future directions of precision agriculture', *Precision Agriculture*, vol. 6, no. 1, pp. 7–23.

McCluskey, J. (2000) 'A game theoretic approach to organic foods: An analysis of asymmetric information and policy', *Agricultural and Resource Economics Review*, vol. 29, no. 1, pp. 1–9.

McDonald's (2014). Food/nutrition choices, www.mcdonalds.com/us/en/food/food_quality/nutrition_choices.html (accessed March 23, 2014).

Montgomery, R. (2013) 'Research shows teens are turning to organic foods', *Kansas City Star*, www.kansascity.com, December 17.

Murphy, D. (2010) 'Holder calls for historic era of antitrust enforcement, rural America hopeful once again', *CivilEats*, March 16, civileats.com/2010/03/16/holder-calls-for-historic-era-of-antitrust-enforcement-rural-america-hopeful-once-again/#more-7068 (accessed September 16, 2013).

Muth, M., Brester, G., Del Roccili, J., Koontz, S., Martin, B., Piggott, N., Taylor, J., Vukina, T., and Wohlgenant, M. (2005) *Spot and Alternative Marketing Arrangements in the Livestock and Meat Industries: Interim Report*, US Department of Agriculture, Grain Inspectors, Packers and Stockyards Administration, Washington, DC.

Myers, R. J., Sexton, R. J., and Tomek, W. G. (2010) 'A century of research on agricultural markets', *American Journal of Agricultural Economics*, vol. 92, no. 2, pp. 376–403.

Nasar, S. (2001) *A Beautiful Mind*. London: Faber & Faber.

National Cattlemen's Beef Association (2006) *FACT SHEET: Feedlot Finishing Cattle*, www.beefusa.org/uDocs/Feedlot%20finishing%20fact%20sheet%20FINAL_4%2026%2006.pdf (accessed October 12, 2013).

—— (2013) www.beefusa.org/beefindustrystatistics.aspx (accessed September 4, 2013).

—— (2014) *2014 Policy Book*, cqrcengage.com/beefusa (accessed April 17, 2014).

National Research Council (2010) *Toward Sustainable Agricultural Systems in the 21st Century*, Committee on Twenty-First Century Systems Agriculture, Board on Agriculture and Natural Resources, Division on Earth and Life Studies.

Neuman, W. (2010) 'Justice dept. tells farmers it will press agriculture industry on antitrust', *New York Times*, March 12, www.nytimes.com/2010/03/13/business/13seed.html?_r=0 (accessed September 16, 2013).

Nicholls, W. H. (1940) 'Market-sharing in the packing industry', *Journal of Farm Economics*, vol. 22, pp. 225–240.

Nike (2012) 'FY10-11 sustainable business performance summary', www.nikeinc.com/cr-report (accessed June 1, 2013).

Oliver, M., Bishop, T., and Marchant, B. (eds) (2013) *Precision Agriculture for Sustainability and Environmental Protection*. Abingdon, UK: Routledge.

Olson, M. (1965) *The Logic of Collective Action: Public Goods and the Theory of Groups*, vol. 124. Cambridge, MA: Harvard University Press.

Onel, G. and Goodwin, B. K. (2014) 'Real options approach to inter-sectoral migration of U.S. farm labor', *American Journal of Agricultural Economics*, 96. First published online February 26, 2014; doi:10.1093/ajae/aau004.

Osteen, C. (2003) 'Agricultural resources and environmental indicators: pest management practices'. In R. Heimlich (Ed.), *Agricultural Resources and Environmental Indicators, 2003*, Agriculture Handbook No. AH722 (Chapter 4.3). Washington, DC: USDA.

Ottoson, H. W. (Ed.) (1963) *Land Use Policy in the United States*. Lincoln, NE: University of Nebraska Press.

Paarlberg, R. (2009) *Starved for Science: How Biotechnology is Being Kept Out of Africa*. Cambridge, MA: Harvard University Press.

—— (2010) *Food Politics: What Everyone Needs to Know*. Oxford, UK: Oxford University Press.

Palumbi, S. R. (2001) 'Humans as the world's greatest evolutionary force', *Science*, vol. 293, no. 5536, pp. 1786–1790.

Parker, M. L. and Unrath, C. R. (1998) 'High-density apple orchard management techniques', www.ces.ncsu.edu/hil/hil-360.html (accessed September 10, 2013).

Paulsen, G. (1998) *Hard White Wheat for Kansas*. Kansas State University Agricultural Experiment Station SRL 120.

Peek, G. N. and Johnson, H. H. (1922) *Equality for Agriculture*. Moline, IL: Harrington Co.

Pendell, D. L., Brester, G. W., Schroeder, T. C., Dhuyvetter, K. C., and Tonsor, G. T. (2010) 'Animal identification and tracing in the United States', *American Journal of Agricultural Economics*, vol. 92, no. 4, pp. 927–940.

Peterson, E., Grant, J., Roberts, D., and Karov, V. (2013) 'Evaluating the trade restrictiveness of phytosanitary measures on US fresh fruit and vegetable imports', *American Journal of Agricultural Economics*, vol. 95, no. 4, pp. 842–858.

Peterson, H. H., Barkley, A., Chacon-Cascante, A., Kastens, T. L., Marchant, M. A., and Bosch, D. J. (2012) 'The motivation for organic grain farming in the United States: profits, lifestyle, or the environment?' *Journal of Agricultural and Applied Economics*, vol. 4, no. 2, pp. 137–155.

Pigou, A. (1932) *The Economics of Welfare*, fourth edition. London: McMillan & Co.

Piketty, T. and Goldhammer, A. (2014) *Capital in the 21st Century*. Cambridge, MA: Belknap Press.

Pindyck, R. and Rubinfeld, D. (2013) *Microeconomics*, eighth edition. Upper Saddle River, NJ: Prentice Hall.

Pitcher, P. (1997) *Swine Production*, University of Pennsylvania School of Veterinary Medicine, cal.vet.upenn.edu/projects/swine/index.html (accessed October 7, 2013).

Polansek, T. and Huffstutter, P. J. (2013) 'Halt in Zilmax sales fuels demand for rival cattle feed product', *Reuters*, August 23.

Pollan, M. (2001) 'Behind the organic-industrial complex', *The New York Times*, May 13 (accessed December 15, 2013).

—— (2006a) *The Omnivore's Dilemma: A Natural History of Four Meals*. New York: Penguin (USA) Books.

—— (2006b) 'Wal-Mart goes organic: and now for the bad news', *The New York Times*, May 15.

—— (2007) 'You are what you grow', *The New York Times*, April 22.

—— (2008a) 'Farmer in chief', *New York Times Magazine*, October 12.

—— (2008b) *In Defense of Food: An Eater's Manifesto*. New York: Penguin Books.

Popkin, B. M. (2006) 'Technology, transport, globalization and the nutrition transition food policy', *Food Policy*, vol. 31, no. 6, pp. 554–569.

—— (2009) *The World is Fat: The Fads, Trends, Policies, and Products that are Fattening the Human Race*. New York: Penguin Books.

Pretty, J. (2008) 'Agricultural sustainability: concepts, principles and evidence', *Philosophical Transactions of the Royal Society B: Biological Sciences*, vol. 363, no. 1491, pp. 447–465.

Pretty, J., Toulmin, C., and Williams, S. (2011) 'Sustainable intensification in African agriculture', *International Journal of Agricultural Sustainability*, vol. 9, no. 1, pp. 5–24.

Pringle, P. (2003) *Food, Inc.: Mendel to Monsanto – The Promises and Perils of the Biotech Harvest*. New York: Simon and Schuster.

Putnam, J. J. and Allshouse, J. E. (1999) *Food Consumption, Prices, and Expenditures, 1970–97*. Food and Rural Economics Division, Economic Research Service, U.S. Department of Agriculture, Statistical Bulletin No. 965, Washington DC.

Ragas, M. W. and Roberts, M. S. (2009) 'Agenda setting and agenda melding in an age of horizontal and vertical media: a new theoretical lens for virtual brand communities', *Journalism & Mass Communication Quarterly*, vol. 86, no. 1, pp. 45–64.

Reardon, T., Timmer, C. P., Barrett, C. B., and Berdegué, J. (2003) 'The rise of supermarkets in Africa, Asia, and Latin America', *American Journal of Agricultural Economics*, vol. 85, no. 5, pp. 1140–1146.

Reed, M. R. (2001) *International Trade in Agricultural Products*. Upper Saddle River, NJ: Prentice Hall.

Ricardo, D. (1971) *On the Principles of Political Economy and Taxation*, vol. 165 (edited by R. M. Hartwell). Harmondsworth, UK: Penguin Books.

Rickard, B. J., Okrent, A. M., and Alston, J. M. (2013) 'How have agricultural policies influenced caloric consumption in the United States?' *Health Economics*, vol. 22, no. 3, pp. 316–339.

Rogers, E. M. (2003) *Diffusion of Innovations*. New York: Free Press.

Rogers, R. T. (2001) 'Structural change in U.S. food manufacturing, 1958–1997', *Agribusiness,* vol. 17, pp. 3–32.

Ronald, P. C. and Adamchak, R. W. (2008) *Tomorrow's Table: Organic Farming, Genetics, and the Future of Food*. Oxford, UK: Oxford University Press.

Russell, E. J. (1926) *Plant Nutrition and Crop Production*. Berkeley, CA: University of California Press.

Ruttan, V. W. (1984) 'Social science knowledge and institutional change', *American Journal of Agricultural Economics,* vol. 66, no. 5, pp. 549–559.

Ryan, B. and Gross, N. C. (1943) 'The diffusion of hybrid seed corn in two Iowa communities', *Rural Sociology,* vol. 8, no. 1, pp. 15–24.

—— (1950) *Acceptance and Diffusion of Hybrid Corn Seed in Two Iowa Communities*, vol. 372, Agricultural Experiment Station, Iowa State College of Agriculture and Mechanic Arts, Ames, Iowa.

Schlosser, E. (2004) *Fast Food Nation: The Dark Side of the All-American Meal*. New York: HarperCollins.

Schlosser, G. (2012) 'Animal welfare expert: Ag producers have to show everything', *West Central Tribune*, Willmar, Minnesota, September 6, www.wctrib.com/content/animal-welfare-expert-ag-producers-have-show-everything#sthash.dds2kAbf.dpuf (accessed October 14, 2013).

Schnepf, R. (2013) *US Farm Income*. Washington, DC: Congressional Research Service.

Schroeder, T. C. and Tonsor, G. T. (2012) 'International cattle ID and traceability: Competitive implications for the US', *Food Policy*, vol. 37, no. 1, pp. 31–40.

Schroeder, T. C., Barkley, A. P., and Schroeder, K. C. (1996) 'Income growth and international meat consumption', *Journal of International Food & Agribusiness Marketing,* vol. 7, no. 3, pp. 15–30.

Schultz, T. W. (1975) 'The value of the ability to deal with disequilibria', *Journal of Economic Literature*, vol. 13, no. 3, pp. 827–846.

Schumacher, E. F. (1973) *Small is Beautiful: Economics as if People Mattered*. New York: Harper and Row.

Schumpeter, J. A. (1962) *Capitalism, Socialism, and Democracy*. New York: Harper & Row.

Segal, R. (1995) *The Black Diaspora: Five Centuries of the Black Experience Outside Africa*. New York: Farrar, Straus and Giroux.

Severson, K. (2003) 'Food fight boils over at Ferry Building/Beef Company, bikers get all steamed up', *San Francisco Chronicle*, April 26.

Sexton, R. J. (2013) 'Market power, misconceptions, and modern agricultural markets', *American Journal of Agricultural Economics*, vol. 95, no. 2, pp. 209–219.

Shields, D. and Tuan, F. (2001) 'China's fruit & vegetable sector in a changing market environment', *Agricultural Outlook*, USDA, ERS, June–July, pp. 10–13.

Shughart, W. F. II (2008) 'Public choice', *The Concise Encyclopedia of Economics*, Library of Economics and Liberty, www.econlib.org/library/Enc/PublicChoice.html (accessed November 6, 2013).

Sinclair, U. (1935) *I, Candidate for Governor: and How I got Licked*. Berkeley, CA: University of California Press.

Sjaastad, L. A. (1962) 'The costs and returns of human migration', *The Journal of Political Economy*, vol. 70, no. 5, pp. 80–93.

Smith, A. (1776) *An Inquiry into the Nature and Causes of the Wealth of Nations*, first edition. London: W. Strahan.

Smith, K. (2013) 'The greatest food in human history', *New York Post*, July 28 (accessed September 9, 2013).

Soane, B. D., Ball, B. C., Arvidsson, J., Basch, G., Moreno, F., and Roger-Estrade, J. (2012) 'No-till in northern, western and south-western Europe: a review of problems and opportunities for crop production and the environment', *Soil and Tillage Research*, vol. 118, pp. 66–87.

Spain, W. (2011) 'McDonalds to cut fats, sugars, sodium,' MarketWatch, Market Pulse Archives, www.marketwatch.com, July 26 (accessed May 8, 2014).

Spurlock, M. (2004) *Super Size Me*. Documentary film. Kathbur Pictures.

Stigler, G. J. (1954) 'The early history of empirical studies of consumer behavior', *The Journal of Political Economy*, vol. 62, no. 2, pp. 95–113.

Sumner, D. A., Thomas Rosen-Molina, J., Matthews, W. A., Mench, J. A., and Richter, K. R. (2008) 'Economic effects of proposed restrictions on egg-laying hen housing in California', University of California Agricultural Issues Center, July, aic.ucdavis.edu/publications/eggs/egg_initiative.htm (accessed October 12, 2013).

Swift, J. (1726) *Gulliver's Travels*. London: Benjamin Motte.

Swinnen, J. F. M. (2007) 'The dynamics of vertical coordination in agri-food supply chains in transition countries', *Global Supply Chains, Standards and the Poor*. Oxon, UK: CABI.

Tillotson, J. E. (2004) 'America's obesity: Conflicting public policies, industrial economic development, and unintended human consequences', *Annual Review of Nutrition*, vol. 24, pp. 617–643.

Timmer, C. P. (1986) *Getting Prices Right: The Scope and Limits of Agricultural Price Policy*. Ithaca, NY: Cornell University Press.

Triplett, G. B. and Dick, W. A. (2008) 'No-tillage crop production: a revolution in agriculture!', *Agronomy Journal*, vol. 100, Supplement 3, p. S153.

Tulip, K. and Michaels, L. (2004) *A Rough Guide to the UK Farming Crisis*, www.corporatewatch.org (accessed April 17, 2014).

Tyson (2013) Grow with Tyson. A Resource for Independent Growers for Tyson Foods, Inc. Chicken Production Process, www.growwithtyson.com/chicken-production-process (accessed October 7, 2013).

United Nations Food and Agriculture Organization (2013) FAOStat, faostat.fao.org (accessed December 12, 2013).

US Bureau of the Census (1914) *Statistical Atlas of the United States*. Washington, DC: US Government Printing Office.

—— (1975) *Historical Statistics of the United States, Colonial Times to 1970*. Washington, DC: Government Printing Office.

—— (2013a) *Current Population Survey, Annual Social and Economic Supplements*, www.census.gov/apsd/techdoc/cps/cpsmar12.pdf (accessed May 7, 2014).

—— (2013b) *Poverty Statistics*, www.census.gov/hhes/www/poverty (accessed August 7, 2013).

US Congress, House Committee on Interstate and Foreign Commerce (1919) Government Control of Meat-packing Industry: Hearings Before the Committee on Interstate and Foreign Commerce of the House of Representatives, 65th Congress, 3d Session, on H.R. 13324, Volumes 2–3. U.S. Government Printing Office, 1919 – Meat industry and trade.

US Department of Agriculture, Agricultural Marketing Service/National Organic Program (USDA/AMS/NOP) (2013) www.ams.usda.gov/AMSv1.0/nop (accessed December 15, 2013).

US Department of Agriculture, Economic Research Service (2007) Structure and Finances of U.S. Farms: Family Farm Report, 2007 Edition/EIB-24. Washington DC: Government Printing Office.

—— (USDA/ERS) (2013) www.fas.usda.gov/gats (accessed December 15, 2013).

—— (2014) *Fertilizer Use and Price*, www.ers.usda.gov/data-products/fertilizer-use-and-price. aspx (accessed May 5, 2014).

US Department of Agriculture, Grain Inspection, Packers and Stockyards Administration, Packers and Stockyards Program (USDA/GIPSA/P&SP) (2013) Stockyards Administration (GIPSA) 2012 Annual report of the packers & stockyards program. www.gipsa.usda.gov, (accessed September 16, 2013).

US Department of Agriculture, World Agricultural Outlook Board (2012) *World Agricultural Supply and Demand Estimates*, usda.mannlib.cornell.edu (accessed December 12, 2013).

US Department of Labor, Bureau of Labor Statistics (2013) *Occupational Employment Statistics, Occupational Employment and Wages*, www.bls.gov/oes/current/oes513023.htm#ind (accessed December 12, 2013).

US Department of Transportation (2013) 'Research and Innovative Technology Administration. Bureau of Transportation statistics', www.rita.dot.gov/bts/ (accessed November 30, 2013).

US Environmental Protection Agency (2013) 'Cap and trade', www.epa.gov/captrade (accessed December 13, 2013).

US Food and Drug Administration (2012) 'Guidance for industry: The judicious use of medically important antimicrobial drugs in food-producing animals', CVM GIF#209, April 13.

US Government Accountability Office (1999) 'Food Safety: The Agricultural Use of Antibiotics and Its Implications for Human Health', RCED-99-74, April, www.gao. gov/products/GAO/RCED-99-74, (accessed April 17, 2014).

—— (2009) *Agricultural Concentration and Agricultural Commodity and Retail Food Prices.* GAO-09-746R, June 30, www.gao.gov/new.items/d09746r.pdf (accessed September 24, 2013).

Von Neumann, J. and Morgenstern, O. (1947) *Theory of Games and Economic Behavior*, Princeton, NJ: Princeton University Press.

Wacziarg, R. and Welch, K. H. (2008) 'Trade liberalization and growth: New evidence', *The World Bank Economic Review*, vol. 22, no. 2, pp. 187–231.

Wade, M. A. and Barkley, A. P. (1992) 'The economic impacts of a ban on subtherapeutic antibiotics in swine production', *Agribusiness*, vol. 8, no. 2, pp. 93–107.

Walmart Corporate (2014) corporate.walmart.com/our-story (accessed April 17, 2014).

Ward, C. E. (2002) 'A review of causes for and consequences of economic concentration in the US meatpacking industry', *Current Agriculture, Food and Resource Issues*, vol. 3, pp. 1–28.

—— (2010) 'Assessing competition in the US beef packing industry', *Choices*, vol. 25, no. 2, pp. 1–14.

Warner, M. (2006) 'Wal-Mart eyes organic foods', *The New York Times*, May 12.

Waterfield, G. and Zilberman, D. (2012) 'Pest management in food systems: An economic perspective', *Annual Review of Environment and Resources*, vol. 37, pp. 223–245.

Welshans, K. (2014) 'Grandin warns: Don't let bad become normal', *Feedstuffs*, vol. 86, no. 11, March 13, 2014, feedstuffsfoodlink.com/story-grandin-warns-dont-let-bad-become-normal-0-109991 (accessed April 17, 2014).

Whoriskey, P. (2009) 'Monsanto's dominance draws antitrust inquiry', *The Washington Post*, 29 November, www.washingtonpost.com/wp-dyn/content/article/2009/11/28/AR2009112802471_pf.html (accessed September 16, 2013).

Wilde, P. (2013) *Food Policy in the United States: An Introduction*. New York: Routledge/Earthscan.

William, J. D. (1986) *The Compleat Strategyst: Being a Primer on the Theory of Games of Strategy* (No. RAND/CB-113-1). Santa Monica, CA: Rand Corporation.

Wolff, R. D. (2013) 'A Socialism for the 21st Century', posted on Truthout, June 11, 2013 (accessed August 12, 2013).

World Bank (2007) *World Development Report 2008: Agriculture for Development*. Washington, DC: World Bank.

—— (2013) *World Development Indicators*, data.worldbank.org (accessed August 7, 2013).

—— (2014) *World Bank Data*, data.worldbank.org (accessed February 22, 2014).

World Business Council for Sustainable Development (WBCSD) (2014) Eco-efficiency learning module, www.wbcsd.org/Pages/EDocument/EDocumentDetails.aspx?ID=13593&NoSearchContextKey=true (accessed April 29, 2014).

World Trade Organization (2014) *Statistical Database*, stat.wto.org (accessed February 23, 2014).

Wunderlich, G. (2011) *Seven Creations: Agriculture to God*. Annandale, VA: Self-published.

Zilberman, D. (2012) 'Lessons from Prop 37 and the future of genetic engineering in agriculture', Energy and the Environment blog, December 20.

Zilberman, D. and Marra, M. (1993) 'Agricultural externalities', in G. Carlson, D. Zilberman, and J. A. Miranowski (eds), *Agricultural and Resource Economics*. New York: Oxford University Press.

Zilberman, D., Schmitz, A., Casterline, G., Lichtenberg, E., and Siebert, J. B. (1991) 'The economics of pesticide use and regulation', *Science*, vol. 253, no. 5019, pp. 518–522.

Zwerdling, D. (2009) 'Green Revolution trapping India's farmers in debt', National Public Radio, 14 April, www.npr.org/templates/story/story.php?storyId=102944731 (accessed July 25, 2012).

INDEX